The
Union
That
Shaped
the
Confederacy

The Union That Shaped the Confederacy

Robert Toombs & Alexander H. Stephens

William C. Davis

 UNIVERSITY PRESS OF KANSAS

© 2001 by the
University Press of Kansas
All rights reserved

Published by the
University Press of Kansas
(Lawrence, Kansas 66049),
which was organized by the
Kansas Board of Regents and
is operated and funded by
Emporia State University,
Fort Hays State University,
Kansas State University,
Pittsburg State University,
the University of Kansas,
and Wichita State University

Library of Congress
Cataloging-in-Publication Data
Davis, William C., 1946–
   The union that shaped the Confederacy :
Robert Toombs and Alexander H. Stephens /
William C. Davis.
      p.   cm.
Includes bibliographical references and index.
   ISBN 0-7006-1088-x (alk. paper)
   1. Stephens, Alexander Hamilton, 1812–
1883—Friends and associates.   2. Toombs,
Robert Augustus, 1810–1885—Friends and
associates.   3. Confederate States of America—
Politics and government.   4. Friendship—
Confederate States of America—Case studies.
5. Vice-Presidents—Confederate States of
America—Biography.   6. Statesmen—Confed-
erate States of America—Biography.   7. Legis-
lators—United States—Biography.   8. United
States. Congress—Biography.   9. Governors—
Georgia—Biography.   I. Title.
E467 .D3 2001
973'7'13'092—DC21   00-011725

British Library Cataloguing in
Publication Data is available.

Printed in the United States of America

10   9   8   7   6   5   4   3   2   1

The paper used in this publication meets
the minimum requirements of the American
National Standard for Permanence of Paper
for Printed Library Materials z39.48-1984.

Green be the turf above thee,

Friend of my better days;

None knew thee but to love thee,

Nor named thee but to praise

Fitz-Greene Halleck

CONTENTS

PREFACE

History has been governed by friendships, both those that lasted and those that did not. Through myth and reality their names echo on, emblematic of the ties of affection and fraternity that can make or break nations. Damon and Pythias, Caesar and Brutus, Henry II and Becket. Friendship is inseparable from the great events of state simply because men and women, in positions of power or times of crisis, turn naturally for support to those whom they most trust. Their opposition inevitably regards it as cronyism and corruption, yet just as sure as any ruling faction is turned out, that which replaces it will judge the talents of those it entrusts with power and responsibility by the same measure. So it was with the brief life of the Confederacy. Placed in the highest office, Jefferson Davis turned at once to those whom he knew and trusted most for his most intimate counsel and bestowed command wherever possible among men who enjoyed his goodwill. His closest friends stayed in power the longest, despite the growing chorus of critics who decried his favoritism.

Yet there were other friendships that exerted dynamic influence upon the course of the brief Southern nationhood and none more so, indeed none so much, as the peculiar and, to many, mystifying pair of Georgians who for half a century were the Damon and Pythias of Southern politics. Two years, social class and wealth, personality, character, and physical makeup, all should have kept the two apart by any rational measure. Yet almost from their first meet-

ing they became fast friends, and in their rise in Georgian and national politics, they became arguably the most potent pair in the
South, if not in the nation. And when it came to the breakup of the
Union and the formation of a new nation, no two men together exerted so much influence on the creation and framing of the new
government. Ironically, when each suffered the same disillusion-
ment and disappointed ambition, no two friends did more to snipe
at and erode the sustainability of their own creation. Alike not only
in their strengths and elements of greatness, they were united in
their weaknesses, the failings perhaps of all who would be great, ambition, intolerance, and vengeance. Robert A. Toombs and Alexander H. Stephens did not create the Confederacy alone, nor did they
destroy it by themselves, yet in the story of their friendship is to be
read a virtual metaphor for the full range of the Confederate experience and for much of what America endured in the days of their
generation.

This book is not intended as a conventional biography of either
or both of these Georgia giants. Fuller accounts of their lives individually are elsewhere available. This, rather, at least so much as is
possible, is a "biography" of their friendship. As a result, though
dealing generally with their pre- and postwar lives, it concentrates
on their Confederate years, the days when that fraternity between
them had its greatest impact on their times. But for their individual
acts, and perhaps fate, either might have been president in Davis's
stead, with results that none can chart from hindsight, though the
evidence of their Confederate careers should be sufficient to
demonstrate what might have been expected, and that no better
than what Davis achieved and most likely not as good. Of course,
the same can be said of most founding fathers.

Moreover, most revolutions rapidly distance themselves from the
extremists who bring them about and race toward the center for
strength and the greatest chance of survival. Yet Toombs and
Stephens began in the center and still saw their movement leave
them behind, for as it gained life, it was they who drifted toward
radicalism. In the midst of their revolt, they rebelled against their
own revolution, not because they rejected its ends but because they
could not stomach the means necessary to achieve that goal. To-

gether they absolutely embody the fate almost always suffered by those more dedicated to principle than to survival, those who would rather be "right" than succeed. Theirs is the tragedy of a generation of statesmen too mired in the pride of their opinions to countenance the changing of the times around them. In not one country but two, they were out of step with all but a few and occasionally with all but each other. Theirs were times when friends most needed one another. Through five decades of personal, sectional, and national crisis, for all that they may have failed the Union and the Confederacy, they never failed each other. Out of a lifetime of defeat and vicissitudes unimagined in most generations, the fact that their bond lasted only to become the stronger was their final victory.

Many friends and colleagues kindly assisted in the writing of this book, especially Robert K. Krick and T. Michael Parrish, who brought to light numerous sources, especially for Toombs, that might otherwise have been overlooked. Michael Musick, friend to all Civil War historians, graciously passed along obscure items from the National Archives; and J. Tracy Power at the South Carolina Department of Archives and History at Columbia and the several staff of the Georgia Department of Archives and History in Atlanta were all most cordial. George Rable, a distinguished historian of the Confederacy and its politicians, offered a careful reading of the finished work and made many useful corrections and observations. Finally, thanks are due to Fred Woodward, director of the University Press of Kansas, for the vision to undertake a somewhat unconventional approach to these two men and the patience to wait for a manuscript that is more than a year late.

1

Disunion and Reunion

In lives heavy laden with irony, the greatest one was that it took the destruction of their Union to bring them back together. Out of ruin came reunion. United as they were in their opposition to the election of the Republican candidate Abraham Lincoln in 1860, the two still veered further and further apart in their opinions as to how the slave states should react to that inevitable event. Alexander H. Stephens always felt a stronger tug of loyalty to the idea of the Union and a greater confidence in the ability or willingness of the peoples of North and South to make some accommodation short of eternal separation. His closest friend during his adult life, Robert Toombs, was at once more impulsive and more erratic, more prone to be swept along by the tide of his own arguments. Like so many others of his time, his own eloquence in advocacy could seemingly take the lead of his judgment. More than once Toombs had talked himself into a near-duel, and his style of rhetoric and impatience with compromise naturally aligned him with compatriots in their native Georgia who crossed the line to support secession after Lincoln's victory.

As late as October 1860 the two men were still close in spite of the strains of the campaign. They had started their political lives as Southern Whigs, which united them until the sectional controversy went on the boil. Even then they both supported Democratic opponents to Lincoln, but the difference was crucial. Toombs backed the candidate of the avowed secessionists, John C. Breckinridge, a Kentuckian and himself no secessionist at all, while Stephens supported Stephen A. Douglas. The latter was a Democrat to be sure, but an apostate in most of the South, thanks to his popular sovereignty doctrine. It would allow the settlers in new lands to decide the issue of slavery for themselves prior to applying for status as a territory, instead of recognizing the constitutional right of slaveholders to go with their property where they pleased in the commonly held territories and thereby have a chance themselves to influence a new state's position on slavery right up to the moment of admission. In that issue lurked the crucial balance of power between North and South, free and slave. Yield or be beaten in that contest, and the slaveholding states would be doomed to perpetual minority, and eventually, to the anticipated inevitable attack on slavery where it existed. Political, economic, and social vassalage seemed to many Southerners the inescapable result. The only alternative—secession.

When Douglas actually braved threats and came to Georgia to make a few campaign speeches, Stephens stood by him on the dais to show his support, coming out ever stronger himself against the extremists who would lead the state and the South to secession and, he felt certain, disaster. Stephens won himself few friends in so doing. At the very same time, Toombs took the stump for Breckinridge, though with little expectation of success. Rather, soon after the Democratic Party split and fielded two candidates, thus all but ensuring Lincoln's victory, Toombs addressed himself to what Georgia and the South should do after the inevitable defeat, and he put himself in the camp of the disunionists, to which his impulsive and sometimes hot-tempered nature led him.

Political differences strained their friendship in those fevered days, but the two Georgians remained cordial, though their separate involvements in the campaigns necessarily meant that they saw

little of each other that summer and fall and had scarce time or opportunity even to correspond. They did appear together once at a
political barbecue west of Atlanta, but that may have been their only
time on the same stump.[1] Perhaps sensing their drift apart, or fearing it, Toombs invited Stephens to spend a week or two with him at
his plantation late in October.[2] Toombs also may have had an ulte-
rior motive in the invitation, for had Stephens accepted he would
have missed accompanying Douglas on his brief Georgia tour, presumably thus weakening him even more. Beyond that, Stephens
would have been with Toombs on election day itself. It would be an
opportunity for them to bury their differences, or just as well it
might have allowed Toombs a few minutes of gloating, for theirs was
a friendship in which Stephens's gift of political forecast had been
far more often right than Toombs's. In the event, Stephens did not
accept, but accompanied Douglas and later delivered a speech on
his own in which he denounced those who would break up the
Union. By election day he was back home at Liberty Hall in Crawfordville, to receive the inevitable result. "We are going to destruction," he confided to his brother Linton after learning the poll results. "Nothing can arrest our course." Just a day later his
melancholy, with him even at the best of times, plunged him further
into the gloom. "So we go," he moaned. "I really apprehend that no
power can prevent it. Our destiny seems to be fixed."[3]

Toombs agreed, but instead of destruction coming out of dissolution, he foresaw a bright future for a new Southern slaveholding
nation. Still, his friend's attacks on secessionists in general—among
whom he now numbered himself—stung at least enough that
Toombs was in the mood for a cold dish of revenge when the legislature asked the two of them as well as other prominent leaders to
come to the capital to present their views on what the state should
do. The addresses opened on election day November 6, but the real
fire came six days later with an earnest appeal for secession from the
smug, self-important, generally intolerable Thomas R. R. Cobb, who
already foresaw himself as an influential man in any new confederation of seceding states. Despite their growing differences, Toombs
and Stephens remained united in their mutual loathing of Cobb
and felt little less distrust for his much more affable brother How-

ell. Nevertheless, Toombs followed the next night with a secessionist harangue of his own. Tracing the indignities and injustices suffered at the hands of the Northern majority, he reminded the legislators of the incendiary raid by John Brown just a year before, and
how it betokened a Yankee intent to foment servile insurrection
with rape, destruction, and ruin. How could they not love such fellow countrymen, he shouted in envenomed sarcasm. "Oh, what a
glorious Union," he sneered, once more pronouncing the adjective
"gullorious" in derision as he had throughout the recent campaign.[4]

Stephens listened silently as the one friend he had loved more
than any other assailed the Union he had himself revered since
youth. Toombs did as he often did and went beyond rationality as
his passion rose, accusing the North of incendiarism and even of attempting to poison Southerners. When Lincoln took office in
March he would have all the might of the federal government, its
army and its navy, to use for his fell purpose. "Will you let him have
it?" he shouted amid the uproar produced by his words. "Then
strike while it is yet today," he demanded. They must secede, take
their sons from Yankee regiments and ships, buy their own arma-
ments, and "throw the bloody spear into this den of incendiaries
and assassins, and let God defend the right." He went far beyond
just a call for secession. Consumed by his own rhetoric, he seemed
to be asking for an offensive war. "Strike," he cried. "Strike while it
is yet time," and should the North resist, then Southerners must
emulate their forebears and "make another war of independence."[5]
He said even more, imploring the legislature to put the sword into
his hand, "for if you do not give it to me, as God lives, I will take it
myself."[6]

Stephens's turn came the next night, November 14. As Toombs
glowered down from his own seat on the dais, his diminutive friend
rose to speak for patience, forbearance, and moderation. Unlike his
friend, he refrained from sarcasm or the play of wit. A moderate editor in Georgia responded to Toombs's boast of taking the sword by
suggesting, "Let him take it, and, by way of doing his country a great
service, let him run about six inches of it into his left breast," but
there would be none of that for Stephens.[7] Still, in a pointed reference to Toombs's overblown emotionalism, Stephens warned that

"good governments can never be built up or sustained by the impulse of passion." He came to speak to their intellect, not to their emotions. The Union was like a ship, tempest-tossed and perhaps leaking badly, but built still of sound timber and worth saving for the rich cargo of democracy that she bore. "Don't give up the ship," he urged, "don't abandon her yet." Lincoln might have won the White House, but the Republicans would not control Congress, and by staying in the Union the slave states, with the help of only a few Northern Democrats, could hamstring virtually all Lincoln's legislation, prevent him even from getting senatorial consent on his cabinet choices. They had but to stay in the Union to save it, and themselves. However much they deplored the recent election, it had been in every way legal and was after all the result of their own folly when slave states bolted from the Democratic convention and split the party. It thus ill became them—and he meant Toombs—to cry foul and threaten secession or worse when they had themselves authored this latest misfortune.

Stephens was no more than five or six minutes into his address when Toombs began to interrupt him, and though Stephens calmly asked any who differed with him to remain quiet and "on some other occasion give your views," Toombs thereafter broke in repeatedly, often for nothing more than gainsaying, his points invariably overcome by a logic in Stephens that was considerably superior to Toombs's mere banter. In all, he interrupted Stephens ten times, increasingly toward the end of the address, severely taxing the speaker's patience. Before the close, it became almost a joke, the audience anticipating Toombs's next interruption and his friend's riposte. In the process Stephens made something of a fool of Toombs, who seemed not to realize it at the moment, when the former used his own words to suggest that the latter did not trust the will of the people of Georgia, and further suggested that some of their present difficulty arose not from matters of political consequence but from disappointed personal ambitions. Everyone, Stephens better than any, knew that Toombs had ambitions that in the present confederation could never take him beyond his current seat in the U.S. Senate. In a new Southern nation, however, he might well come to stand even taller.

Once more Toombs revealed his excessive zeal and new-found militancy, when Stephens reminded the legislature of his friend's declaration the night before that if the state would not put a sword in his hand, he would take it himself, and in yet another interruption Toombs shouted out, "I will" to great applause. The whole tone of Stephens's address was to draw the line between the disunionists on the one hand, and the calm patriots on the other, and he allowed Toombs by his own words and behavior to paint himself as not just a secessionist but a hothead and an extremist. In a seriously divided state like Georgia, where Breckinridge gained less than half the recent vote, the more the disunionists could be depicted as irresponsible, and perhaps self-serving, the better the chance that the moderates could gain control and repudiate secession. Stephens knew that passion could not remain high indefinitely, for he had seen this sort of fire before in South Carolina and even in Georgia, and it had never shown enough heat to sustain itself. "This will pass off with the excitement of the hour," he counseled, referring to Toombs's expressions as nothing but "excessive ardor."[8] And yet he later confessed that the great shout from the crowd at Toombs's defiant cry, "I will," gave him his first real fright that Georgians and the South might really be heading for a collision of arms.[9]

Toombs could not resist the compulsion to have both the last word and one more jab at his friend, for as Stephens sat down, he rose to his feet and called for three cheers for "one of the brightest intellects and purest patriots that lives." It was no compliment, however, for when another on the dais congratulated Toombs on the generous motion, he replied by quipping, "I always try to behave myself at a funeral."[10] Yet beneath the apparent good humor, Toombs soon may have come to realize that Stephens had bested him and made him look unstatesmanlike, if not foolish. Worse, Stephens actually said nothing critical of his own but let Toombs convict himself with his own words. Georgia's decision on secession was likely to be close, and if it failed it would be even more bitter if Toombs had unwittingly been himself made an agent of its demise, and with it any ambitions he may have had for his own advancement.

Beyond this disagreement something else may have rankled. Although Stephens worshiped Toombs as his friend and ideal, in his admiration frequently overestimating the larger man's intellect, the fact was and always had been that despite his physical strength and power of personality, Toombs almost invariably came around to Stephens's side of an argument. Though he may never have admitted it, Toombs stood in silent awe of what he had to recognize as the superior mind of his small friend. Certainly others saw it. "I have always understood that Aleck governed Toombs much more than Toombs did Stephens," declared one who knew them both. Just days after the speeches before the legislature, in which he gave the clear victory to Stephens, A. W. Redding commented, "I never had any difficulty in awarding very superior ability in Stephens over Toombs."[11] Privately, Toombs no doubt recognized it, too, and no matter how close friends become, when one is too repeatedly revealed to dominate the other, whether in contests of the body or the mind, resentment almost inevitably erodes even the strongest bonds of brotherhood. The North had too often and for too long outdone the South in strength and unity, and resentful slave states were about to abandon the Union. So often in the public shadow of his almost shadowless little friend, Toombs had perhaps had enough. With a new cause that suited his temperament, and associated with men of equal emotion and recklessness, he was ready to emerge to stand alone in the light. Within days of their speeches to the legislature, Toombs and Stephens were known throughout Georgia virtually to have severed relations.

Ironically, partisans in both camps were pleased. "I am glad that Aleck is separated from Toombs," a moderate declared on December 1. "I have more confidence in his ability and his intentions to do right when I know he is freed from the influence (if any) of Robert Toombs."[12] At the same time, the ardent secessionists like Thomas Cobb welcomed the rift, for however much some may not have liked Toombs, they still recognized his power, and an estrangement from Stephens meant freeing him from the restraining influence of one too closely attached to the Union.[13] Just the past spring Toombs had still been side by side with Stephens in trying to heal the national Democratic Party in order to defeat Lincoln and keep the Union together. His popularity with Georgians was such that his addition to the ranks of secessionists might well help make

the difference, and a break with Stephens and removal from his influence was all to the good.

Yet Stephens, too, came away from the capital harboring resent-
ments. Superficially he no doubt felt chagrined at Toombs's behavior during his address, though that sort of irritation should have
been transitory. Far more distressing was the realization that his closest friend sat solidly in the enemy's camp. They had disagreed before, but never on an issue approaching this importance, and
Toombs's action well may have seemed disloyal, on top of a much
more subtle betrayal. Standing in awe as he always had of Toombs
physically in the drawing room and the legislative chamber,
Stephens at least had felt the compensation of leading his friend in-
tellectually and politically. It was what had equalized them, and with
that now seemingly gone, the always insecure little Georgian became even smaller in his own eyes, even more a "malformed ill-
shaped half finished thing," as he called himself sometimes in the
depths of self-loathing.[14]

No wonder, then, that within a few weeks Stephens was thinking
the worst of Toombs, even when the latter acted just as the former
had predicted and in mid-December apparently began to moderate
his bellicose tone by addressing a letter to constituents in which he
suggested that secession could be averted by a constitutional amendment guaranteeing slaveholders' rights in the territories. If Congress would pass such a measure, then Toombs would support post-
poning secession until there was time to see if the Northern states
would join the Southern ones in ratifying such an amendment. If
Congress should not enact guarantees, however, then he counseled
seceding before Lincoln took office on March 4, 1861.[15]

On the surface it seemed that Toombs was holding out one last
hope for peace and the Union, and Georgia's secessionists felt betrayed for a few days, but Stephens saw in it nothing but dissembling
and craft. This sudden show of conciliation, he suspected, was only
to lure undecided and moderate men to Toombs's notion of an
amendment, which all would in fact welcome. Yet Toombs well
knew, thought Stephens, that no such amendment would ever pass
this Congress, and especially not in less than three months. In short,
Toombs was setting up Georgians who longed for a peaceful settle-

ment for a disappointment he knew would come, assuming that in their shattered hopes they would see there was no alternative left but secession and resistance. "I look upon it as a masterstroke to effect his object," Stephens wrote cynically on December 22. Despite their estrangement, still Stephens acknowledged that Toombs "has more sense than any man in this movement." He fully expected Toombs to try to erect, and presumably lead, a new Southern government after secession, yet marveled that his friend could not see in the fickle reaction of secessionists to his proposed amendment the basic instability of his new associates. The moment anyone disagreed with them, on the slightest grounds, they would turn on him for straying from the new orthodoxy. Such doctrinaire attitudes would cripple any new movement if these men were in charge. "If the violent cannot now see his motive, how shall they appreciate his efforts hereafter?" he wondered.[16]

If Stephens's imputation of Toombs's motive was tinted by resentment, still he was not far off the mark. Even before writing his conciliatory letter, Toombs privately suggested that South Carolina, then hurtling toward secession, ought to hold off until Georgia, Alabama, and Mississippi could hold their state conventions, and then the four states could secede as a bloc on February 1, 1861, which would have far greater impact. Some observers thought he suggested this only so that they would impress the North even more with the need to make concessions; others thought it was designed to embolden the other, more wavering, slave states to make common cause for a new confederacy.[17]

Georgia's legislature had already issued a call for election of delegates to a state convention to meet in January to decide the issue of secession. Just ten days after writing his much criticized conciliatory letter, Toombs sent another open telegram to the people of Georgia from Washington, where Congress had convened. Having been appointed by his own request to a Senate committee of thirteen charged with finding a solution to the sectional crisis, he had introduced six constitutional amendments, knowing full well that by the nature of the procedural rules of the committee, the Republican minority could and would vote them down, as they promptly did, along with other similar proposals. He all but gave away his intent—just as perceived by Stephens—when he opened by saying, "I came here to secure your constitutional rights or to demonstrate to you that you can get no guarantees for these rights from your Northern confederates." What he got, of course, was that demonstration, which he expected. Having erected his own false hope for guarantees just to see them to their grave, he once more— and with rather unseemly haste—turned bellicose again. The Republicans were "your enemies, who only seek to amuse you with delusive hope until your [convention] election, in order that you may defeat the friends of secession," he declared. "I tell you upon the faith of a true man that all further looking to the North for security for your constitutional rights in the Union ought to be instantly abandoned." When they voted for convention delegates on January 2, "secession by the fourth of March next should be thundered from the ballot-box by the unanimous voice of Georgia."[18] It was all a bit obvious, revealing what many observers long knew, that for subtlety and finesse Toombs could never match Stephens.

Perhaps the behavior of his seemingly alienated friend helped to account for Stephens's strange lassitude in the weeks after his speech to the legislature. Betrayed by Toombs, and seeing the Union about to crumble, he gave way to the despondency and depression that overcame him occasionally. He simply stayed at home in Crawfordville, read his mail, wrote gloomy letters to his friends, and did nothing to try to stem the steady tide of public opinion toward secession. For the first time in their association, he stepped completely out of the contest and left the field entirely to Toombs and the energized secessionists like Cobb who canvassed the state widely in support of secession candidates for the convention. The secession of South Carolina on December 20 gave them added impetus. Viewing the events around him, Stephens gave way utterly. "All is now dark and gloomy," he told a friend on the last day of the year. "I see no ray of hope." He took a prosecession result in the convention balloting for granted. "The times are distempered. The people are misled, and will see their course I fear when it is too late." For himself he would do nothing, not even pray. "It is past praying for I fear."[19]

Stephens's lethargy contrasted dramatically with the activity of his estranged friend Toombs in Washington. He continued to sit on the committee of thirteen through its brief futile life, then ushered in the New Year by sending a warning to Georgia that the abolitionists in Washington were bellicose and defiant. The message was clear. With South Carolina seceded, with Southern members of President James Buchanan's cabinet resigning, and with the so-called Black Republicans—whom Toombs like everyone else equated with abolitionists—in triumphant mood, Georgia needed to look to itself. As if his meaning were not evident enough, he warned that the empty federal Fort Pulaski off the Savannah River was in danger of being reinforced, a heavy hint that Georgians should act at once to take it before it became for them what Fort Sumter had become for South Carolina, an armed Yankee garrison in Charleston Harbor. Toombs sent his message to a newspaper in Augusta, but it was obviously meant for Georgians at large, and Governor Joseph Brown heard him well enough.[20] Two days later Georgia state forces occupied the fort, outraging the authorities in Washington. Toombs, a sitting U.S. senator from a state that had not seceded, had encouraged an act of unlawful seizure at best, and at worst one of open hostility. If he had not decided already that his remaining days there were few, his action made staying in the capital unwise, to say the least.

In fact, the very day that he sent his telegram, his wife Julia started packing the family's furniture and belongings in their rented house in the capital. When Stephens retired from Congress in 1859, he had left with the Toombses the furniture that he kept in his rented lodgings. Now they needed to know what to do with it. Perhaps significantly, Toombs himself did not write to his old friend; indeed he had not written to him for some time, confirming the estrangement, and when Julia wrote even she addressed him stiffly as "Dear Sir."[21] Six days later her husband made an inflammatory farewell speech in the Senate, in which he issued his own ultimatum to the North. Guarantee Southern rights to share equally in the states to be formed from the new territories, honor the Fugitive Slave Law, and the Union could remain whole. Fail to do that and the slave states would leave in peace. Deny that, he warned, and there would be war. "We accept it; and inscribing upon our banners the glorious words, 'liberty and equality,' we will trust to the blood of the brave and the God of battles for security and tranquility."[22] Rarely subtle, always larger than life in public and private, Toombs chose to say his farewell to the Senate and to the Union in a manner perfectly true to character, with boast, bluster, and threat.

True also to his new surge of bellicosity, Toombs did not leave Washington before coming to harsh words with General Winfield Scott, commanding the U.S. Army. Three days after Toombs's farewell address they both attended a party, and inevitably conversation turned to Charleston and Fort Sumter, where just the day before a supply vessel sent to the federal garrison had been fired upon by South Carolina batteries and forced to withdraw. With characteristic bluster, Toombs declared that both the ship and those who had sent her—meaning President Buchanan and Scott himself—should have been sent to the bottom. Apparently only the intercession of others, plus Scott's seventy-four years, prevented a scuffle from ensuing. Three days later the Georgian left Washington.[23] Henry Cleveland, who had read law as a young man in Toombs's office, knew him well and observed that he was an "honest hater but steadfast friend."[24] Both Stephens and the United States, it seemed, had seen the end of that steadfast friendship. It remained to be seen if he would feel with the Union the brunt of Toombs's enmity as well.

Certainly had they wished to stay apart, circumstances beyond their control were not about to cooperate; in the election on January 2 for delegates to the state convention, voters selected both Toombs and Stephens, despite the latter's disinclination to serve. Disappointed though he may have been at the result, Stephens had to see a reality even more disheartening in the balloting. The heavens poured sheets of wind-chilled rain all across the state. Even then the voter turnout was heavy, with the final result being so close that of over 84,000 votes cast, secession candidates received a majority of just 1,000, less than 1 percent. Indeed, so close was it that in the days ahead the secessionists who finally controlled the convention refused to publish the actual result, and more than a year later Governor Brown simply lied about the vote rather than admit just how equivocal Georgia had been about leaving the Union.[25]

Stephens soon came to believe that the weather, which was especially bad in the hill and mountain country in north Georgia where Union sentiment was strongest, had kept 10,000 from coming to the polls, giving secessionists as many as twenty seats in the convention that would otherwise have gone to the moderates like himself. Stephens chose to assign the result to God, but that may have been only his effort to relieve himself of responsibility.[26] Given as he was to reflection, he could hardly fail to realize how costly had been his weeks of sulking and lethargy. Had he gone out on the stump to rally conservatives, might he not have made those who stayed home sufficiently aware of the true danger ahead, to impel them to brave the elements and cast their votes? If his estimate of twenty seats lost to the secessionists was correct, then by the narrowest margin of just two seats, they decided the majority in the convention to come. How many of those might he have turned around had he roused himself? Granted that he admitted publicly that, all else failing, he would support forming a new Southern confederacy based on the U.S. Constitution, still he much preferred finding an accommodation that would keep the Union intact. Who could say but that if the Georgia convention stopped short of secession, then the groundswell started by South Carolina might not flatten, as it had more than once in the past when the rest of the slave states shied from following extremist Carolinians? Even if Georgians might eventually vote for secession, still the respite gained, and the blow to secession struck by the most populous and important of the cotton states rejecting disunion even temporarily, could have purchased enough time to calm passions elsewhere in the South and to put the North in a mood to offer some kind of conciliation. By January 10, six days before the convention was to convene, he told his brother Linton confidently that "the State will secede."[27] Though he never went so far as to express the sentiment, still Stephens's canny mind must at least have considered the possibility that had he acted differently, he alone might have saved the Union, however unlikely that might have been, giving him even more reason to shift any responsibility from his own stooped figure to those infinitely broad shoulders of the Almighty.

Toombs and Stephens saw each other for the first time in two months when the delegates gathered in Milledgeville on January 16.

Toombs was firmly intent on securing secession and was already in correspondence with South Carolina's governor Francis Pickens, sending information and warnings from Washington; Stephens was just as determined to do nothing, to take no lead or responsibility, seemingly paralyzed by his fatalistic conviction that it was in God's hands and by his own despair that nothing could be done.[28] Given the chance to exert some force in the convention when he was offered the gavel as president, he turned it down. Asked to write resolutions on behalf of the moderates, he declined. On January 18 a resolution asserting the right to secede and calling for the drafting of a secession ordinance was introduced, and in opposition came another set of resolutions calling for delay and more consideration before taking action. When finally he rose to speak, Stephens gave a pallid effort in which he frankly admitted there was no point in resisting secession, a performance that contrasted dramatically with Toombs's advocacy of the secession resolutions. When the vote came, the latter carried 166 to 130, punctuating for Stephens the difference those twenty lost seats had made.

A cruel irony put both Stephens and Toombs on the committee of seventeen created to draft the secession ordinance. They may not have been speaking, or if so only formally, but in any event Stephens spoke little if at all on the committee. As his brief speech made clear, he had given up, and nothing suggests that he exerted any effort to influence the resulting document during the brief time the committee consulted. Toombs, too, probably exerted scant energy on affecting the ordinance, since the committee seemed to leave that chiefly to the author of the original secession resolutions, Eugenius Nisbet. Instead, and in keeping with his recent bellicosity, Toombs was working on a resolution of his own to approve Brown's taking of Fort Pulaski. The next day the committee reported the ordinance, and to no one's surprise it passed 208 to 89, Toombs voting in favor and Stephens in a final, futile gesture, voting "nay."

Then came a motion for signing the approved ordinance, and only then did Stephens stir from his lethargy. His brother Linton, a fellow delegate, prepared resolutions declaring that in view of the lack of unanimity in the vote on the ordinance, all members should sign regardless of how they had voted, as a pledge to support and sustain the state. When Linton presented this to Stephens, the elder brother approved entirely but suggested that it would have the best chance of adoption if it came from Nisbet of the majority. Linton gave it to Nisbet, and it carried. As a result, Stephens joined his brother, Toombs, and all but six others in affixing their signatures to the ordinance. According to Thomas Cobb, not always a reliable source, the one hope that Stephens felt was that "we can make better terms out of the Union than in it." Having failed to get their guarantees in Congress, perhaps a united stand of slave states withdrawing from the federal compact would force the North to awaken to the danger and make the concessions needed to bring the slave states back into the Union. He believed that many delegates who voted for the ordinance felt the same. Just where he stood himself he never explicitly said, though for several years to come fellow Southerners suspected that whatever he said or did, he secretly hoped for reunion, too.[29]

The afternoon of the vote the boom of cannon outside the state-house announced the result, and two days later the delegates actually signed. It seemed almost as if the ink that flowed from his pen when he signed the ordinance drained with it Stephens's store of hurt and resentment both at what had happened and at Toombs as well. In accepting the inevitable, there remained no purpose in clinging to pointless animosity and resentment. Toombs, too, could afford to let go his anger. He had what he wanted, Georgia out of the Union and soon no doubt to confederate with South Carolina and any other states that seceded, with all that might promise for his ambitions. Moreover, in signing the secession ordinance, Stephens had finally, and for the first time, openly accepted Toombs's lead on a public issue, even if out of little more than resignation. Their signatures now united them on a common course for Georgia, eliminating except as bad memories all the causes that broke them apart. Sometime during the remaining week of convention debates, they began to speak to one another once more, and in tones increasingly less formal and strained.

Indeed, now they were once more on the same path, and typically, Stephens began to assert his influence once again, not just on Toombs but on the convention as a whole. South Carolina had issued a call for delegates from the seceded and seceding states to meet in Montgomery, Alabama, in February to determine their future course, and if possible to frame a new Southern nationality. On January 23 the convention acted on Toombs's resolution to send ten delegates to the Montgomery convention, and then selected not only Toombs himself but also Stephens, who felt both surprised and reluctant to accept. Since he had opposed the movement from the start, it is no wonder that his being chosen startled him somewhat. Even though resigned to the inevitable when it came to secession, that did not mean he felt any enthusiasm for the cause or a desire to be an active participant in what he feared was a ride to ruin. But others in the convention began pressuring him to accept, perhaps even Toombs, knowing how important it would be to have the most eloquent spokesman for the moderates involved in order to ensure full representation of Georgia's interests. Besides, everyone recognized that little Stephens was the most able and cogent parliamentarian among them. Though he later claimed that his election was unanimous, in fact one delegate from the district he was to represent voted against his election. But it was clear to all, even his former opponents, that if a new government were to be framed properly, he must be there.[30]

Stephens actually may have been dissembling at least a little in his diffidence. He always affected reluctance when pressed to take up a public duty; that was simply a conceit of the times and of the man himself. But by so doing he may also have been holding out for a concession from the others, including the secessionists like Toombs. As he said before the convention met, if there must be a Southern nation, he wanted it modeled on the U.S. Constitution. On January 28 he offered a resolution that the delegates to Montgomery be empowered to consult in framing a provisional or permanent government and to put it into immediate operation, so long as it was modeled on the Constitution and government of the United States. "It was my duty to do all I could to preserve and perpetuate the principles of our model Federal system," he said later. The convention passed his resolution, and that done he announced that he would go to Montgomery.[31]

One reason the convention could comfortably assume that it had the power to appoint delegates and enrobe them with the authority to commit Georgia to such dramatic action was that before Stephens introduced his resolution they had already debated at length the sovereign powers of the state. Toombs dominated the discussion, asserting that the people held unlimited authority, and that therefore their representatives held the same power through them. "We are only limited by God and Right," he said with characteristic boldness. "We are the People, owing no allegiance to any Prince, Potentate, Power, or anything under Heaven, but ourselves and our society." The debate continued for some time, but few doubted that ultimately, at least so far as sending a delegation to Montgomery was concerned, they acted within their mandate.[32]

As his last act at the convention, Toombs submitted a report he wrote that defended the state's decision to secede. The direction of the North and the rapidly growing Republican Party, especially the election of its candidate Lincoln to the presidency, posed an undeniable threat to slavery, he declared. The Black Republicans would "subvert our society, and subject us, not only to the loss of our property but the destruction of ourselves, our wives, and our children and the desolation of our homes, our altars, and our firesides."[33] In a sentence redolent of irresponsible hyperbole, he used the election of a minority president with no majority in Congress to raise the specter of social disruption and economic ruin, and with it to hint at racial amalgamation, blacks raping whites' wives and daughters and disinheriting their children, the loss of religious freedom, and armies of freed slaves wantonly burning and looting their way across the South. The flair for exaggeration and caricature that made Toombs so entertaining in drawing room conversation could make his political declarations models of demagoguery, but this time they suited the tastes of the time.

When the convention adjourned on January 29 Toombs and Stephens returned to their homes with only a few days to prepare for the trip to Montgomery. They left with dramatically differing expectations. Stephens still felt cast down and depressed, despite his resignation. He feared that little good would come of this movement, and from what he saw of some of its leaders, he apprehended even worse. There was a lack of integrity in too many of them, he believed, not enough loyalty to principle, not enough of that "pure disinterested patriotism" that ought to activate public men. In short, there was too much personal ambition and demagoguery at the root of this, he told a friend the day before he left for Montgomery. He did not name particular offenders, though most likely he had in mind the archsecessionists like Robert Barnwell Rhett of South Carolina, who had been singing the secession song for a generation and had come to Milledgeville to try to influence the Georgia convention as well. "They are selfish, ambitious, and unscrupulous," he charged.

Yet he may have thought of Toombs, too, for he recognized in his friend the signs of ambition for high office in the coming new confederation. "My word for it," he lamented, "this country is in a great deal worse condition than the people are at all aware of."[34] At home in Washington, Georgia, Toombs felt entirely the opposite. He was full of optimism, convinced as so many were that the North would never really fight in the end and that the new Southern nation to come would enjoy a peaceful and auspicious birth. Moreover, as Alabama, Florida, Louisiana, and Mississippi had also seceded and were sending delegations to Montgomery, he and everyone else knew that Georgia's delegation would be the largest and most influential. All across the slave states, other delegates readying for the trip assumed that Georgia would thus be entitled to the presidency in any new government framed, and Toombs had no difficulty in thinking himself a likely candidate. Indeed, his friend John Reed was convinced that Toombs expected the office, and Stephens frequently hinted the same.[35]

That would be decided in Montgomery, and with the die cast, both men could do no more than pack for an absence whose duration might be a few days or many weeks. Yet they could plan definitely on one aspect that brought relief to both. Their estrangement was over. Shortly after the secession vote, they joined with their signatures in recommending men to Governor Brown for state military appointment.[36] Probably before the close of the convention they agreed to make the journey together and decided with no apparent sense of irony to meet at the Georgia Railroad Station at Union Point. On the evening of February 2 the two stood on the platform, along with the despised Thomas Cobb, and boarded for the first leg of their trip, to Atlanta. In the car they found James Chesnut of South Carolina, an old friend from days in Congress, and his wife Mary. No doubt to leaven the less felicitous company of Cobb, with whom they had no choice but to be civil, they took seats by the Chesnuts. But even more important, Toombs and Stephens sat side by side as the train rumbled westward in the night. They were friends again.

The Making of a Friendship

Birth, geography, and circumstances destined them to meet, though hardly to be friends. They first saw each other in the Wilkes County Court in Georgia's north circuit late in July 1835. For Alexander Hamilton Stephens, who had passed his bar examination only days before, this was his first trip as a fledgling lawyer in search of business. It was a twenty-mile journey from his home in Crawfordville, and being poor he had no horse. As he recalled years later, perhaps with a bit of nostalgic hyperbole, he walked the whole way, carrying saddlebags on his frail back. It took him two hot, dusty days; and when just outside the county seat in Washington, he disappeared from the road into the woods and changed into a clean white suit. He stood five feet, seven inches tall and weighed a mere ninety-six pounds, which accounted for older men often thinking him just a fresh-faced teenager instead of a man aged twenty-two who had already made his first political speech.[1]

When he walked into the courthouse, Stephens saw in the crowd a familiar face that had been in his home county courthouse a few days before when he was admitted to practice. No one had introduced them then, but this time someone presented him to twenty-four-year-old Robert A. Toombs of Washington.[2] Something instantly attracted them to one another, though it can hardly have been any similarity in physique, temperament, or personality, for they were and always remained dramatic opposites. Toombs stood six feet tall or more and was robustly built, with a large, handsome head above his broad shoulders and thick, glistening dark hair that hung in long locks so that when he swung his head from side to side, as he often did in debate, his hair flew like a lion's mane. He smiled easily and a lot but was always ready to adopt a serious or scowling cast when his quick temper flared. His gleaming white teeth were extraordinary and arresting, and people, especially women, found his dark eyes positively impertinent.

Toombs looked much more than just two years older than his new acquaintance, but that soon reversed as the years ensued and Stephens's ailments and almost perpetual melancholy aged him prematurely. He had been what people called "sickly" from the day of his birth, heir to a host of illnesses and conditions that would nearly but never quite kill him, consigning him instead to a lifetime of nearly constant physical discomfort and occasional outright torment. Despite being of average height for a man in his time, he looked almost emaciated. Much of his life he weighed under eighty pounds, and never did he top one hundred. His shoulders sloped, and his back was already somewhat stooped as a result of a host of complaints, including rheumatoid arthritis, pinched nerves in his neck, and degenerating disks in his back. His head was too small, his hair already thinning into wisps and clumps, and his ears too large, sticking out to make him look like an elf. As handsome as was Toombs, so was Stephens almost featureless, his complexion forever pale and his mouth perpetually set in the downturned cast of one too long familiar with pain and disappointment. Always cold, obsessed with his health, he was a hypochondriac with good cause. His own jape about his being a "half finished thing" betokened more bitterness than wit.[3]

By background and upbringing the two young lawyers differed dramatically as well. Stephens was born to near poverty, forever sensitive about his humble origins. His father, Andrew, was a simple farmer and teacher in Wilkes County, and his mother died within months of his birth on February 11, 1812. She had been weak and unhealthy most of her life and bequeathed her poor constitution to her son. It was left to his father and his second wife to raise young Alexander, and it is apparent that he grew up in a home without much warmth and precious little affection. In later years he said nothing of his stepmother except that she was quick to wield the cane, and even his father, whom he came to idealize, was also a stern disciplinarian, typical of the rude country schoolteacher. No one really understood the small, sensitive, sickly boy, except one favorite aunt. Everyone else, he felt, "*seemed* to me to think I was a bad boy." His father taught him at home until he was eight; then young Alexander attended Andrew Stephens's school intermittently for four years. When he was just fourteen his father died and a week later so did his stepmother, leaving the boy with a preoccupation with death that lasted all his life and contributing mightily to a melancholy nature almost homeric in its breadth and impact on him.

Combining that nature with his sensitivity about his size and looks and his recurring bouts of pain and illness left him with an outlook on life and the human condition that was gloomy at best and that did not improve when he underwent a religious awakening that made him a lifelong Calvinist in the mold of his Scots Presbyterian ancestors. Being an orphan only made it worse, the more so since the five Stephens children by his father's two wives were separated and placed in different foster homes, removing Alexander from his closest sibling and friend, his half-brother Linton. For the next several years, however, he lived with a lenient and understanding uncle, and then in 1827 he entered the Washington Academy just three years after young Robert Toombs left the school to go to college. After a year Stephens moved on to Franklin College in Athens, later the University of Georgia, for a time thinking of entering the ministry, and graduating in 1832 at the top of his class, penniless and with no clear idea of what he wanted to do in a life that at times had already become a burden. He taught school for a few months and hated it, and worse, fell in love with one of his students. Too self-conscious about his unnatural physique to risk professing his affection, too fearful that his health condemned him to an early death like his parents, and too poor to support a wife in any event, he kept his love a secret, speaking of it to no one except perhaps Linton for some forty years or more. If he ever succumbed again to such feelings, he kept them locked in his tortured heart to the grave. Painfully, resignedly, he decided that love and marriage and children and the domestic happiness he saw all around him were never to be his. It was one more reason to be almost ceaselessly unhappy.[4]

At the time that Stephens stopped his teaching and submerged his wounded heart in studying the law instead, Robert Toombs had already been a practicing lawyer for four years, if not very successfully, and was already overcoming a few setbacks of his own. At least his birth had been no handicap. The spread of cotton to Georgia had left small subsistence farmers like the Stephenses behind, but Major Robert Toombs, originally from Virginia, prospered in cotton planting and eventually came to own more than 2,000 acres in Wilkes County and some forty-five slaves. Though he died when Robert Augustus, born July 2, 1810, was just five, still the elder Robert left an estate valued at over $34,000. It was hardly a fortune, but still a handsome patrimony even when divided among his several children from three marriages.[5]

His will provided for the education of all his children, and young Robert appeared that he would need it. "He was not precocious," wrote a later friend, nor did Robert give early promise of the robust man he would become. Rather, he grew slowly, acquiring from schoolmates the nickname "Runt" that followed him through college. His slenderness in youth was the only trait he had physically in common with the young Stephens, however, for this boy enjoyed positively wonderful health. Never ill it seemed, he stayed constantly active and was often into mischief. Especially when he was on horseback did his friends and family note his audacity. They often saw him galloping through Washington when he was still a lad, sometimes with his younger brother precariously clinging on to him from behind as they rode to school. Riding gave him strength and agility that helped compensate for his slow physical growth. From youth, almost into middle age he never required a doctor or a drop of medicine, and his mother later quipped that he caused her so few concerns that he grew up almost without her noticing.

He started his education at one of the local "old field" schools, so called because they were built on donated land so farmed out and exhausted that no cash or subsistence crop would grow—literally an "old field." At the age of twelve he went to the Washington Academy and came under the tutelage of Alexander Hamilton Webster, who in a few years made such a mark on young Stephens that the boy adopted the teacher's middle name as his own in reverence. Toombs stayed at the academy for two years and while there his mind finally caught fire for learning, especially literature and history. By the time he left he was already impressing adults with his command of the events of the past and with a winning, outgoing, even vivacious personality, punctuated by those electric dark eyes. He was fourteen, his hair already changing from auburn to a darker hue, when he left for Athens to enter Franklin College. Perhaps thinking it time that she notice him, his mother went with him.[6]

It was at college that Toombs's personality as well as his interests truly developed, and where he first showed on a public stage the best and the worst in his character. He did not excel as a scholar, lacking the discipline to apply himself and being too gregarious and fun-loving to let studies distract him too much from the freedoms of college life, even with his mother in town. His romance with literature continued, and he became attached especially to Shakespeare's Falstaff and to Cervantes' Don Quixote though most likely because he already saw in them something of himself.

His first year passed uneventfully, and with no distinction either, but by the time he was a sophomore Toombs was fully a part of the extracurricular subterranean life of a boys' college. He drank and chewed, smoked and gambled, and he got caught. He also displayed the impudence bordering on arrogance that in later years so enflamed and enraged friends and foes. Found gambling by a proctor, Toombs got to the president of the college first and requested a formal discharge from the school for a few days. Only after it was granted, and with Toombs on leave and out of his official reach, did the president find out what had happened. He met Toombs on the campus a few hours later and started to upbraid him for the gambling offense, but the youth impudently reminded the president that at that moment he was not addressing a student under his authority but "a free-born American citizen" under official discharge. What the president did when Toombs inevitably returned to classes and was once more under his authority is not known, but such stories about Toombs eventually became a part of the lore of the school, evidence enough that he saw quite a bit of the president and proctors, and probably of the rod as well.[7]

Inevitably there were more serious offenses. As a sophomore he got into a schoolboy feud with two brothers, employing some of his growing store of profane and obscene vocabulary at the expense of one. The brothers waylaid him one night and gave him a good beating, but when he recovered, and though only fifteen, he armed himself, went to the room they shared, and burst in. He threw a handy bowl at one of the boys and then pulled out and pointed the pistol at the other. Fellow students rushed to the room and took the gun from Toombs before he could do any harm, and that seemed to end the matter, at least to all but Toombs. Once calm had settled, he drew a knife from his pocket and renewed the assault, adding a hatchet to his arsenal probably grabbed from the fireplace in the boys' room. Once more others stopped him, and he finally left, only to waylay the brothers the next morning with his pistol and a club. Happily, no serious injury was done, his attacks probably being as much bluster and intimidation as malicious in intent. This time Toombs could not escape through sleight of hand. The president dismissed the brothers and ordered Toombs, too, to be expelled. Only a contrite letter from him, endorsed by the school literary societies, persuaded the president and faculty to allow him to remain.

He passed the next year uneventfully, or at least with no infractions that hazarded his tenure as a student. His senior year, however, the one in which seventeen-year-old boys like Toombs are most wont to rebel when an end is in sight, scarcely commenced before he was reprimanded for his swearing, and after that came fines for being too loud in his college room and, typically, for becoming even more boisterous after being told to stop. In January 1828, just months short of graduation, the authorities decided they had endured enough. Without citing the immediate cause, they expelled him and this time ignored his appeal in another letter of contrition. With no alternative but to finish school elsewhere, Toombs went to Union College in Schenectady, New York, and there he behaved himself, did well in law and the classics though barely passing in botany, and received his degree. That fall he attended the fledgling University of Virginia to start the two-year course of law, but both his application and his deportment began to revert to his Athens days. Students were to wear the school uniform at all university functions, and yet Toombs repeatedly broke the rule and came in his own clothes, a further example if any were needed of his deep-seated rebellion against regulations and authoritarian control of his behavior. His loudness and boisterousness got him into trouble again, too, especially when returning to campus from Charlottesville, and no doubt its taverns. Meanwhile, at the end of that first year, he stood at the very bottom of his small class, scoring less than 25 percent on his examination. Seemingly that was enough. When school let out, he went home and never returned. Typically, rather than seeing the message implied by the reprimands and his abysmal class standing, he chose to turn his back on the university.[8]

Just as typically, when he got home he decided that if he and the rules did not suit each other, then the rules ought to change. State law required a man to be past twenty-one to go before the bar to become a practicing attorney. Toombs was just nineteen. Rather than wait, and somehow confidant that in spite of his poor performance at Virginia he could pass an exam, he or his family presented a special bill before the state assembly in December 1829 allowing him, though a minor, to take the bar examination and enter practice if he passed. Three months later, no doubt after serious and careful application, of which he was quite capable when so moved, he passed the bar in Elbert County and became the state's first nineteen-year-old lawyer.[9]

If that were not sufficient evidence of his impatience, before the end of the year, at twenty, he married Julia DuBose, a girl almost as much his opposite as Stephens. Yet all his life Toombs was as devoted to her as to his closest friend, suggesting that there was something within him naturally attracted to quiet, introspection, and frailty in others. His law practice did not commence auspiciously, and even his examiners, watching the progress of this upstart youngster with more than usual interest, observed that he did not immediately appear destined for success. He was never a man for paperwork, and he paid less than careful attention to day-to-day business of the office, too easily lured away by interesting friends, a convivial glass, a horse race or a game of cards. When he did take cases to the county courts, he too often went overboard in argumentation. He had been a member of more than one literary and debating society in college, which only furthered his natural bent for the limelight and hyperbolic speech, and the courts offered a stage on which his oratory frequently became too excited and strident and the logic of his arguments too weak.

He had much to learn, and it took him years gradually to acquire the discipline to attend carefully to business and to prepare properly for his appearances in court. Part of the problem lay in his being a remarkably quick study. "He can acquire more in less time than any one I ever saw," Stephens discovered. "Self-control and mental discipline he lacks more than anything else." Mastery of the larger points in a considerable body of case law or evidence came to him easily, with the result that he all too often neglected the more careful and methodical—not to say plodding—study and preparation required for someone less gifted, someone like Stephens at this age. Yet it came to him in time, and with maturity.[10]

As with his friend-to-be, Toombs's was a country practice, but that suited him well, for he loved to spend hours and even days on horseback and rarely if ever took a carriage to county courts. He could ride sixty miles in a day and arrive so little fatigued from the trip that he might go to a dance that same evening, energized by the flow of wit and the opportunity to shine before an audience. The cases themselves usually turned on disputes over land boundaries and slave sales, which occupied the bulk of the rural attorneys in the South. Almost beyond doubt, cases such as this took him to the Wilkes court that day in July 1835 where he met Stephens for the first time.[11]

Why they should take to each other, and how quickly they did, is unknown, but it is apparent that each found something beyond his previous experience in the other. Toombs's friends had been the roisters and fun-loving crowd at college and on the circuit. Nothing suggests that he had ever associated with someone like the man already dubbed Little Aleck. For his part, Stephens seemed to have had few if any friends, and his melancholy nature and sickly body hardly encouraged the sort of outdoor play and frolic that built most boyhood associations. Rather, he had a history of fixing his admiration on older men, father figures. He was pious where Toombs was all but heathen, serious in the face of Toombs's buoyant wit, fastidiously rule-bound while to his friend rules were inconveniences to be ignored. The larger Georgian rejoiced in revelry and overt pleasure; Little Aleck sometimes confessed that the only happiness he could take was in watching that of others, and even then his envy of their joy sometimes took over and turned him cynical. Everything that so set them apart in outward appearance was reflected within and should have conspired to make them incompatible. Yet never did two greater opposites attract.[12]

The friendship grew as rapidly as impediments of time and distance allowed, but Stephens recalled that "our acquaintance soon grew to intimacy." Within the year they worked together on a few cases. By 1836 they were fast friends, and thereafter whenever they were to attend the several different court days in the counties they worked, they always shared a room on the circuit.[13] They also learned from one another at their trade. Stephens applied cold logic before the juries that invariably heard all county cases, but his nature seemed to have precluded the emotionalism and dynamic oratory of his friend. Yet he learned to be passionate in time, and juries always loved that, as he could see clearly whenever Toombs argued. Despite his high, girlish voice, Stephens could shift tone and volume to emphasize his points and heighten drama. Equally important, he had sufficient intuition and sensitivity to read the tenor of a jury and suit his approach accordingly. It was a skill that any poor-born "cracker" needed to have to succeed in business or politics. Though his practice did not flourish—he had turned down the certainty of $1,500 a year by entering a partnership in Columbus, preferring to practice at home—he received his first fee of $25 within a few weeks, though it was the last salary he would see for four months. Not until 1836 did his business start to accelerate, and even then, in keeping with their contrasts, never to the level that Toombs attained.

For his part, only after becoming friends with Stephens and observing his careful study and preparation did Toombs start really to develop as a mature and diligent lawyer. In 1837, from a very meager beginning, his practice burgeoned, especially with all the litigation set in train by the financial depression of that year. Few attorneys in the area, including Stephens, enjoyed the rapid rise in business that Toombs attracted in the next six years, his fees at a single court session amounting to $5,000 or more. One who knew him well ascribed this success to the sudden change in Toombs's attitude toward his craft. He remained always and foremost a dynamic pleader and showman before a jury, "a robust, handsome, outspoken fellow with a high-pitched voice and large, dark, piercing eyes," wrote one observer, but after becoming close to Little Aleck he grounded his arguments by devoting himself "diligently and systematically to the practice of his profession."[14]

The two men found they had something else in common as well. Stephens had been raised a Jeffersonian Democrat from birth, a believer in the limitation of the power of the government in Washington and the reservation of principal sovereignty in the states. When the Democrats split over the issue of Nullification and secession in opposition to federal authority in 1832–1833, he cast his first vote for the new and less radical states' rights wing that acknowledged the right of secession, but he opposed Nullification. He did so in spite of his home county running heavily in favor of the Nullifiers, not the last time that Stephens arrayed himself against a majority. Indeed, as a lawyer he frequently started with most of a jury against him and then won them over. The next summer he made his maiden political speech on July 4 in Crawfordville, again in support of the states' rights platform, showing that he, like others, was breaking with Andrew Jackson and tending toward the newly forming Whig Party then attracting many anti-Nullifiers. He fully believed in the institution of slavery, and though unlike Toombs, he never became a large slaveholder, he never doubted the propriety of slavery or its salutary effects both upon the Southern society and economy and upon the blacks themselves. As slavery and federal relations and states' rights became more and more the topic of sidewalk and courtroom conversation, Stephens found himself drawn increasingly into the discussion, his views meeting friendly ears in Crawfordville and Taliaferro County. Not surprisingly, when a vacancy appeared in the state assembly for the county, Little Aleck was encouraged to seek the seat, especially after an unlikely victory in a difficult and much publicized domestic case won him considerable notoriety in the area. It looked like a hopeless uphill battle, the county having been 19 to 1 in favor of Nullification candidates in the previous two elections, but meanwhile that party was badly fragmented, disintegrating there as elsewhere in the South and coalescing in new allegiances. Moreover, the soon-to-be Whig ticket carried the state that year in the presidential election, providing a broad coattail for Stephens in his race. He protested afterward that friends put his name forward against his wishes, but that was always the accepted ethic of the public man in his time, the office seeking the man and not the other way around. There is little doubt that Little Aleck wanted the legislative seat. He enjoyed the contest, he found that politics was one of the few pleasures he could allow himself, and the idea of the approbation of victory at the polls went a long way toward assuaging the perpetual pain of the look in people's eyes when they first saw him and wondered if he were a freak. He threw himself into the campaign, and despite being accused of being an abolitionist and a supporter of Jackson because of his opposition to Nullification, he earned the reward of a 2 to 1 victory.[15]

For once, Stephens actually beat Toombs to a finish line. Not until the next year did his friend commence his own political career, and then perhaps with the example and urging of Little Aleck before him.[16] Toombs's political awareness began in the opposite camp from Stephens, as he grew up a Jacksonian Democrat and voted for Old Hickory's reelection in 1832 when he cast his first ballot. But then came South Carolina's nullification of the tariff and Jackson's Force bill threatening to use the army to enforce federal law in a sovereign state, and that immediately drove Toombs across the line to the states' rights element, just as any attempt at arbitrary or authoritarian power invariably raised his antagonism. Toombs left no record of what impelled him to seek elective office, but it was a natural outlet for a man of his personality and temperament, and statehouse politics in the South had ever been the playground of county lawyers. Wilkes County was no friendlier to an anti-Jacksonian than Taliaferro, however, and when he made his run for the legislature in October 1837 he faced stiff competition. Of the three delegates chosen, two were Democrats and only Toombs represented the states' rights element, and that by little more than 100 votes. His election may have owed as much to his recent and blood-less service in the militia to put down a Creek insurrection as to his arguments on the hustings. Military rank always won votes at the polls in the South, and being Captain Toombs did not hurt him, even if the "war" was over before he and his company from Washington could get to it. When he went to Milledgeville, there he found Stephens awaiting him, if in fact they did not make the journey together, as henceforward they often did.[17]

Toombs sat in the lower house for five of the next six years, not seeking reelection in 1841, and Little Aleck for four, leaving in 1840 to attend to his business but returning in 1842 when he won a single term in the state senate. These were busy apprenticeship years for both men, whose affection and intimacy had a chance to grow and develop considerably as they spent several weeks together during the sitting of the assembly and had ample leisure time with each other. Not surprisingly, Toombs soon outstripped Little Aleck through force of personality, though when it came to intellect and thoughtful legislation, Stephens was generally in the lead. Indeed, Stephens enjoyed his only real moment in the limelight during his first term, before Toombs won his seat, when he spoke dynamically in favor of an appropriation to finance a railroad from Atlanta to Chattanooga. The bill carried and many observers gave him the credit, but thereafter he attracted almost no public attention for the remainder of his legislative career. He drew the less significant committee assignments as well, engrossing, public schools, finance, with only the judiciary committee of real importance. The rest of the time he was a workmanlike legislator, introducing no bills of moment and speaking seldom if at all.[18]

Toombs, on the other hand, made his mark less quickly but more deeply when he came to Milledgeville. No follower of the Southern demigod John C. Calhoun, Toombs favored the controversial National Bank and a protective tariff. Yet he also rebelled against imperious Jacksonianism, and by 1837 this stance placed him squarely in the ranks of the burgeoning Southern Whig Party, advocating strong states' rights on the one hand but a conservative fiscal policy on the other, an issue made the more pressing because of the outbreak of the panic of 1837, which Toombs blamed on Jackson's destruction of the National Bank and his successor Martin Van Buren's meddling. Before long he, too, found himself on the judiciary committee, only he rose to chair the group, meanwhile gaining appointments to the internal improvements and the even more important banking committees as well as becoming chair of the state of the republic committee. By 1842, while Stephens entered the state senate, there was even a brief movement to elect Toombs speaker; though it failed, he rose to chair the banking committee instead, a position reflecting his lifelong interest in financial affairs and safe fiscal policy.[19]

It was while Toombs helped oversee banking affairs that he and Stephens had the chance to work on their first legislation together, and Toombs found the one field in politics in which Little Aleck would take his lead consistently. A supporter of the state bank, Toombs opposed a measure to allow the bank to borrow money to make private loans to distressed citizens. The affairs of individuals being beyond the control of the state government, it seemed ridiculous for that government to indebt itself to protect people from default, especially in the current depression when many people were going bankrupt and the rare loans were those repaid. Little Aleck joined with him in opposing the measure, and though they lost, it set the stage for many a partnership to come.[20]

Thereafter Toombs authored more banking legislation, always with an eye toward conservative policy and learning well from the current economy shattered by speculation and risky investment. Being now Whigs, he and Stephens alike were accustomed to sitting in a minority and could successfully influence little legislation and generate less. The best they could do was to oppose governmental interference in private business matters and to uphold the responsibility of individuals for their own actions without seeking remedy from the state. They still saw a national bank as the surest method of making sense of the chaos of American state, local, and private banking and of preventing the sort of financial calamity then upon them, but they never saw its return. Despite their uphill battle, they and their colleagues came to be regarded in the state as reformers. Toombs, for a change, joined Stephens in the effort to support state internal improvements with the Western & Atlantic Railroad to connect their major city with Chattanooga, and on this measure at last they were successful, putting the state in the railroad business.[21]

Fellow Whigs saw the makings of genius in Toombs, a man of bravery and ability. "Often eloquent, always sensible and convincing, he is a formidable adversary in debate." But they noticed, too, his sarcasm and his occasional carelessness. He could dominate a debate, holding the floor for half an hour extemporaneously, just as on the stump he could speak for up to two hours. Some thought he rolled over his debating opponents "like a steam car under full pressure," and more than a few noticed that he paid scant attention to nicety or politeness. His speech, said one, was "not very remarkable for its balminess or conciliation."[22] By contrast, Stephens made his best impression in his home county. His verbal eloquence and dramatic—if high-pitched—delivery made him a popular speaker on public market days and the Fourth of July, and he showed an interest in and an awareness of politics beyond Georgia somewhat in advance of his friend. The Whig Party was gradually forming, initially a coalition of disparate forces united chiefly by dislike of Jackson and his successor Van Buren. They included antislavery men from New England, expansionists like Henry Clay of Kentucky, and arch–states' rights advocates like Calhoun for a time, and in spirit at least even some extremists like Robert Barnwell Rhett. Stephens faced squarely the problems with the national party that he and Toombs were gravitating toward. The Whigs were too acquisitive both of money and power. Born a Jeffersonian, Stephens feared a resurgence of the old Federalist spirit with its instinct to centralize power in Washington. Though he sympathized with the tariff so long as it was imposed solely to raise revenue to run the government, he feared that protectionism was too one-sided, favoring the

North. He felt even more uncomfortable with the internal improvements schemes of Clay and others, who would spend everyone's tax money to promote or even subsidize the encouragement of industry that lay chiefly in the North or of public works projects whose benefit was limited largely to the border states. Still, Little Aleck had nowhere else to go, and in 1840 he, like Toombs, supported the campaign of the Whig William Henry Harrison for the presidency. Yet he resisted the growing trend toward Southern regionalism and discouraged those who began to speak of "Southern politics" in opposition to those of the North. His adherence to the idea of the Union was strong and deep.[23] The two men together typified the contradictions that made the Whig Party in the South always a shaky coalition merely waiting for an explosive issue to rend it apart, desperate for some issue besides slavery to hold them together.[24]

Toombs and Stephens performed their last act together as state legislators and budding Georgia Whigs in 1842 when the Democratic majority in the legislature voted a censure of the state's Whig senator John Berrien in Congress. Though not a member of the state of the republic committee, Stephens wrote its minority report supporting Berrien, and in it took much the same ground as Toombs. When the censure resolution came to a vote in the house, the Whigs refused to vote and then claimed that the remainder did not constitute a quorum. The parliamentary tactic failed, but not before Toombs stamped in outrage to the speaker in a final demonstration of defiance.[25]

By 1843 both young Georgians were ready for something more. Toombs's flourishing practice had made him a wealthy man, giving him the security to look beyond his home state for a forum. Little Aleck's law work had certainly progressed, but nowhere near the extent of his friend's, though now he was buying small parcels of land and had acquired his first slaves. Still, each continued to attract attention among constituents for his performance in court as well as in the capitol. Their styles before juries contrasted markedly, Little Aleck starting calmly and in measured pace, gradually gaining pitch and volume and becoming more eloquent as he went. Toombs, predictably, began with fire and wit and sustained the mood throughout. A friend found him "vehement and overpowering," and everyone noted—and some deplored—his ready resort to sarcasm and overstatement.[26] Audiences warmed to them both, and as the Whigs gained strength in Georgia, Toombs and Stephens came quickly to be regarded as two of the most promising of the new party's leaders. Inevitably there was talk of higher office.

Both men had already stepped on the national stage, Stephens as a delegate to a Southern commercial convention, and Toombs as a state delegate to the 1840 Whig convention that nominated Harrison. When it came time to pursue an office, Stephens, though apparently the least likely, moved first. For four years people had been suggesting that he try for a seat in Congress, but he declined in 1840 and again in 1842. The next year, however, when a seat suddenly became vacant, he felt ready to try, and he conducted an able campaign that, in fact, invigorated him and actually improved his health for a time, suggesting the degree to which psychosomatic effects added to his admittedly miserable constitution. The general trend throughout the state toward the Whigs helped him enormously; while on the stump he performed with unexpected vigor and aggression. In the election the whole state, the governorship and both houses in the legislature, went to the Whigs, and that sweep only enhanced his own efforts, winning him a still close race by just over 1,500 votes. In January 1844 he took his seat in the House of Representatives for the first time, a seat that would be his home for years to come.

Toombs also left the legislature in 1843 and again attended the party convention in 1844 that nominated Henry Clay. On his return he prepared to seek his own congressional seat. Very likely he did not seek a seat the year before because at that time Wilkes County had been included with Taliaferro in the same district, meaning he would have had to contest Stephens's nomination. Meanwhile, the districts had been changed and Wilkes moved, which left him entirely free. His campaign was spirited, the more so because of Democratic attacks on a Southerner supporting the tariff and protection and a revival of the National Bank. Toombs also opposed the annexation of Texas. It would add a much needed slave state to redress the balance of power in Congress, but he feared that gain would be

outweighed by the prospect of annexation precipitating a war with
Mexico. Some critics even accused him—a substantial slaveholder—
of being an abolitionist for standing against admission. His response
was typical. He felt only "scorn and contempt" for his accusers, he
declared, and refused to make any other answer to "these common
sewers of filth and falsehood."[27]

Toombs joined Stephens in the campaign that year, stumping the
state for Clay and the Whig ticket, both of them hammering on the
Texas danger, though Stephens saw more likely issues. He believed
that the president lacked the power to acquire territory like Texas
by treaty but denied that such power lay with joint action by Congress either, which was how President John Tyler wished to handle
this annexation. Stephens preferred that, properly acquired, Texas
bypass the territorial stage and gain immediate statehood and then
later that it should be divided into several states. "The acquisition
would add to our political strength," he observed trenchantly, for
by the terms of the Missouri Compromise, these states would have
to be admitted as slave states; thus instead of gaining one in the contest for balance of power with the free states, the South might gain
four or five. Unfortunately, there was little fear of a war in the South
and an increasing paranoia over slavery, and the Southern Whigs
could never overcome the argument that opposing the admission
of another slave state would be a betrayal to their region, their institutions, and their domestic and economic security. Meanwhile,
the stern opposition of Northern Whigs to admission of another
slave state—Stephens found the Pennsylvanians especially "a curious people," likening them to Mandarins "as *soft headed* as they are
iron hearted"—threatened to split the party.[28] Clay lost all the cotton
belt states in the fall, and with them the election, but Toombs managed to take his district by a sizable majority, and Stephens won reelection in his newly configured constituency by a comfortable margin as well. They would go to Washington together.

With a year before the opening of the next Congress, Toombs attended to business while Stephens served out the balance of his incumbent term. In February 1845 Congress finally voted to annex
Texas, and seeing that the majority could not be overcome, Little
Aleck voted in favor as well. As he did sixteen years later when

Georgia made an even greater decision, he knew when to bow to the inevitable. Throughout the debate on the issue, he received counsel from Toombs, who wrote to him frequently, also advising that he yield on annexation since apparently there was no choice, so long as the perpetuation of slavery in the new states, and any future states to be subdivided from it, remained unthreatened.[29] Moreover, Mexico seemed to be suffering inner political turmoil at the moment, possibly making any international conflict less likely. In January Stephens made his first major speech on the House floor. He advocated annexation with protection of slavery in the hope that it would put an end to the controversy and possibly avert the split of the Union. On the other pressing matter, the assumption of Texas's substantial debt, he very likely reflected Toombs's advice when he called for the government not to assume it but to leave it to Texas.

He did not say in the House what he also felt about balance of power. The South needed Texas to strengthen its voice in Washington. In the end, Congress did exactly as Stephens suggested, though he may have exaggerated his own influence on the outcome. Of most importance, however, for the first time he had stepped across party boundaries to vote with the Southern Democrats on sectional grounds. In spite of himself, he was being drawn into the realm of regional politics rather than national.[30] Even Toombs, for all his bombast, saw the danger inherent in Texas. The more politicians agitated over the slavery aspect of annexation, the more it encouraged abolitionists and their Southern Democrat opponents, embittering feelings on both sides. Outcry and agitation served the ends of both, toward no good to the Union. Better halt the debate by giving in rather than to stand on a principle and lose a greater end. "I see nothing but evil to our party and the country that can come out of this question in future," he wrote Stephens in February.

After passage of the Texas bill, and its signing by incoming president James K. Polk, the session ended and Little Aleck came home, having invited Toombs to come for a long visit at Crawfordville, where he that spring bought the home in which he had been boarding for several years and which he called Bachelor's Hall, later changing it to Liberty Hall. But he found Toombs quite ill for a change, suffering severe rheumatism, and hoping that Stephens could come to see him.[31] In April and May the two and Julia went together in a buggy to Tallahassee, Florida, for Toombs's recuperation, their first vacation together and a sign of the continuing evolution of the closeness of their friendship. By then they had gained sufficient notoriety in Georgia that it spread south across the border, and their leisure in Florida was interrupted by press accusations that these two prominent Whigs had come to the state to make trouble for Democrats.[32]

Toombs recovered, and very likely they also traveled in company to Washington several months later to take their seats for the opening of the Twenty-ninth Congress on December 1, 1845. Important future associations were then made for both the Georgians. Howell Cobb was there, too, though as a Democrat. Stephen Douglas was there, soon to formulate his volcanic popular sovereignty policy. Among the most ardent Southern extremists were William L. Yancey of Alabama and the even more intemperate Rhett of South Carolina, sometime henchman of Calhoun but frequently out of favor even with the great Carolinian over his intransigence and radicalism. From Massachusetts Daniel Webster sat in the Senate, much admired by Stephens, and former president John Quincy Adams held a seat in the House. From Mississippi came Jefferson Davis, there for his first and only term and destined soon to resign for other fields. James Buchanan sat in the Senate for Pennsylvania, and the great Calhoun for South Carolina. Within a few weeks Sam Houston came on behalf of newly admitted Texas, and Toombs's friend and one-time college classmate Robert M. T. Hunter of Virginia sat in the House. There were many others soon to be famous, and even more destined never to acquire acclaim, though all of them were about to embark on the most fitful years in the history of the Republic. Toombs and Stephens could hardly know just how prominent they would themselves become in this august company.

Typically, where Little Aleck was wont to wait and acclimate himself to a new environment and then make careful and measured steps to put himself forward, Toombs waited scarcely more than a month before he took the floor to make a major speech, ignoring the convention that freshman congressmen were seen and not heard. He threw himself into the debate over the Oregon Territory, opposing Polk's bellicose declaration that the United States was entitled to all of the area and threatening war with Britain if its claims were refused. Ironically for a man later so bellicose himself, Toombs twice at the opening of his national career used the prospect of war as justification for opposing measures, arguing over Texas and Oregon. But there was a more subtle motivation. In fact, he preferred that the Union not acquire any of Oregon at all. "I don't want a foot of Oregon or an acre of any other country, especially without 'niggers,' " he told a friend three weeks after his speech. He, too, was coming into the camp with Stephens, and not so gradually. Indeed, he dissembled in public by keeping his motivation confidential among a few friends and not declaring it in his speech. No Oregon meant that no new states from that territory, by terms of the Missouri Compromise, which he thought an abomination, would become free states and thus shift the balance of power in Washington in favor of the North.[33]

Thereafter Toombs spoke frequently in opposition to the Polk administration's measures. He supported the tariff and disdained the cry of "free trade" that came from men like Rhett. When Polk sent troops into Mexico on an equivocal provocation, Toombs condemned him for reckless adventuring and warmongering, and Stephens stood—literally—right beside him. Little Aleck said nothing during the Oregon debate, but when it came to a vote on authorizing Polk to notify Britain that the United States was unilaterally ending joint occupancy—what some feared the first step to war—he voted with Toombs in opposition. The diminutive Georgian also opposed the war with Mexico. He refused to vote on the declaration of war itself, and this time he spoke out, repeatedly, opposing one after another of the administration's war measures. Like most other Whigs he would vote in favor of appropriations bills to supply their armies in Mexico, unwilling that the soldiers suffer because of their leaders' squabbles, but all the while condemning the campaign as one of conquest, despite the fact that any new territory could well furnish future slave states. That such was the hope of the leading hawks was made manifest when Yancey attacked Little Aleck in debate, calling him an abolitionist and asserting that he was all but a traitor to the South. In so doing, he only confirmed Stephens's accusations as to the real purpose of the Democratic-backed war, but he also so angered the Georgian that within forty-eight hours Stephens handed Toombs a note to deliver to Yancey containing a challenge to a duel over the insults. Only negotiations by Toombs and Yancey's friends averted a meeting, though it was not the last time that Little Aleck turned to the *code duello* to redress a slight to his sensitive pride. And a pistol in his hand would be a great equalizer. "Half finished" or not, his bullet was just as deadly as any opponent's.[34]

Almost all Whig efforts to thwart Polk's administration proved futile, and Stephens's and Toombs's opposition did them neither good nor harm in Georgia. Little Aleck did issue another challenge to an insulting editorial writer, though nothing came of it. When he and Toombs went home at the end of the session they found the Democrats making strenuous efforts to defeat them for reelection in the fall, but each still carried his district handsomely, and Toombs scarcely campaigned at all. The two of them actually had time to qualify together to plead before the new state supreme court and to argue a case together just before returning to Washington for the next session.[35] They lost, however, and perhaps in part because Little Aleck, at least, was seriously distracted by what was coming when Congress convened.

At the end of the previous session legislation dubbed the Wilmot Proviso had been introduced, its object being to prohibit slavery from any territory acquired as a result of the war with Mexico. On a strictly sectional vote, Northern Whigs and Democrats joining together in favor, it passed the House but died when adjournment prevented the Senate from considering the measure. Clearly it struck at the very heart of Southern Democrats' motivation for the war in the first place and created an immediate uproar, once more thrusting slavery and abolition to the fore in debate, the discussion that Stephens and Toombs both wanted to halt lest it lead to disunion. As soon as he reached Washington in December—Toombs did not arrive for another three weeks—Stephens prepared for the inevitable reintroduction of the proviso. Against the advice of most

of the Whig leaders in House and Senate, he rose to offer a resolution declaring that the war should be ended as quickly as possible
and that it was not being waged for territorial gain, essentially an assertion that however the conflict ended, the United States should
annex no Mexican land. Parliamentary tactics, this time conducted
on party lines, forestalled him, but among the Whig public at large,
even in the South, Little Aleck's proposal made him an instant hero
and an acknowledged party leader in the House.[36] If no territory
were taken, than neither slave nor free states would be added and
neither section could gain advantage. Even Henry Clay adopted
Stephens's position, but it mattered little since Polk was having the
war his own way and there was no question that Mexico was going
to lose a lot of ground, extending all the way to the Pacific. Stephens
could only continue to rise and attack Polk himself, his misman-
agement, his perfidy, his partisan meanness and want of statesmanship.[37]

The proviso eventually failed to pass at the end of the brief session, and Stephens himself returned home to attend to his practice
without waiting for the final gavel. So did Toombs, who was uncharacteristically quiet during those few weeks except to speak once
in opposition to increasing the size of the standing professional
army. His opposition was of little importance in itself but for what
it said of his attitude toward the nation at war. Americans should defend themselves as volunteer citizen-soldiers, he argued. Influenced
by the Minute Man mythology of the Revolution, he thought the
regular army rather suspect. Volunteers would always be beholden
primarily to the Constitution and to the Republic, he argued, unlike professionals who were liable to hold primary allegiance to authorities in Washington who were literally their employers. Moreover, in the best spirit of democracy, volunteers raised within the
several states chose their own officers, but commissions in the professional army came from the president, giving him undue influence. Stephens applauded his friend's address, thinking it his best
yet in the House. "The effort has added full fifteen cubits to his
stature as a statesman and a man of talents," Little Aleck exulted.
"He is destined to make a very high position here." It was the pride
not just of a friend and supporter but of genuine brotherly love.

Toombs's voice went unheeded when it came to a vote, but in years to come he would be heard again.[38]

The new Congress opened on December 6, 1847, with most of the same faces in evidence but also a few new ones, including a first-term Whig from Illinois named Lincoln with whom Stephens especially formed a close friendship. The major issue for Toombs and Stephens was dealing with the victory in Mexico that came in February 1848. Toombs tried a resolution of his own repudiating any territorial acquisition, but failed, and when Congress approved taking one-half million square miles from Mexico, the focus shifted inevitably to the fight over the new territories and eventual states to come. For a change, the two friends split over the Clayton Compromise, the first attempt to organize territorial governments for Oregon, New Mexico, and California, leaving the issue of slavery to be decided by the Supreme Court. Since Mexico had abolished slavery some years before, Stephens maintained that even conquest did not give the Court the right by international law to introduce it now. Thus he voted against the compromise, fearing the Court would have no choice but to find against slavery, settling the matter forever and thus ensuring at least three new free states. Disagreeing, Toombs declared that the plan would be conciliatory by taking the slavery decision out of the heated chambers of Congress and leaving it to the Court, or at least that is what he said for public consumption. Privately he said that the South should never surrender the new territory to become free states. It would be degrading to the slave states and leave them too weak to resist future free state expansion. Better that the Union perish in the fury over the territories than that Southern rights and honor should die in its place. "To this complexion must it come at last," he predicted. Thus, despite their differing votes on the territorial bill, he and Stephens stood essentially in accord, Toombs even more ardently dedicated to a militant stance for Southern rights.[39]

By this time, those who knew them virtually took it for granted that the friends would stand on the same side on every issue. The two Georgians usually shared lodgings when in Washington, but this term Julia was in the capital with Toombs so Stephens took his own room. Still, they generally dined every evening at the United States

Hotel with several other congressmen, making up a "mess." The group included Jefferson Davis, who had resigned his House seat to lead a regiment in Mexico and become a war hero and who now sat in the Senate. They were a convivial group, though Davis himself seemed often stern and aloof and was always rather formal, at least with Toombs, whose emotionalism and flamboyance he would have found undignified. Davis's vivacious wife Varina entered much more into the social spirit of the mess, however, and especially enjoyed the hearty, bluff Georgian and his wife. In casual conversation Toombs often adopted a studied ignorance, with much slang and country dialect, which could be useful when campaigning among the "crackers" at home. However, it was ever evident that he had perfect grammar and diction at his command when he wanted or needed such. Varina especially noted the feminine beauty of his hands, and those eyes that had "a certain lawless way of ranging about that was indicative of his character." She also could not help but observe in their months together at the same table that Toombs genuinely loved Stephens "with a tenderness that was almost pathetic, and was as much beloved by him." Varina Davis was also perceptive enough to see in Little Aleck "a virile mind sustained by an inflexible will." Despite his diminutive size, and the beardless, prematurely wrinkled face that already had begun to make him look more like a wizened old widow than a thirty-six-year-old man, she also saw the intellectual influence he could exert on his best friend. "In all matters of importance," she concluded, "Mr. Toombs came up, in the end, on Mr. Stephens's side."[40] Soon afterward, when the Toombses rented a house and moved, the inseparable Stephens went with them.[41]

The Clayton Compromise was defeated in the House, but Stephens's opposition raised an uproar among the Democrats in his district—another reason that Toombs publicly, at least, supported the popular measure. As a result, Little Aleck faced at first a serious resistance when he went home and ran for reelection, but he soon turned it around and looked confidently toward victory. Toombs faced no serious opposition at all. Both of them worked that fall for the election of Whig nominee Zachary Taylor. Indeed, Stephens had organized a club among House members backing

Taylor's candidacy almost two years earlier, with Toombs one of its members and Lincoln another. Then after Stephens moved with Toombs to their new house, the two men provided the content for a letter written by fellow lodger John J. Crittenden, which soon appeared in the press along with one by Taylor, and that really launched his candidacy. In later years Little Aleck liked to believe that it was this club and his action that started the movement that eventually led to Taylor's victory in 1848.[42]

It nearly cost him his life. A friend and associate on the local circuit, the Democrat judge Francis Cone, along with his party in the state, had decried Stephens's opposition to the Clayton Compromise, and rumor held that in terms customary to the time, he suggested that Little Aleck had betrayed the South. When the two met at a Whig political dinner that fall, Stephens confronted him during the meal, and Cone denied the charges, which satisfied Stephens, though not before he added that had they been true he would have slapped Cone's face, an invitation to a duel. Word soon spread, and the idea of Little Aleck smacking Cone, who was virtually twice his size, left Cone the butt of many a joke and comment, the implication being that he had quailed before the diminutive congressman, which everyone but Cone thought highly amusing. Angered and embarrassed, Cone demanded that Stephens take back his threat. Stephens wrote a response in which he declined, stating that as Cone had denied the rumors, there was no cause for discord between them. Before the judge received it, however, the two encountered each other in an Atlanta hotel, and Cone demanded again a retraction. Little Aleck told him that he had sent a letter already and that was the only reply he intended to make. In a fury, Cone did call him a traitor, or worse, a "puppy," which meant both figuratively and literally a son of a bitch, and in reflex reaction Stephens struck him in the face with a hand that happened to be holding a cane, adding pain to provocation. Cone pulled a dirk from his pocket and began stabbing at Little Aleck's chest. Only by grabbing Cone's umbrella and using it to deflect the blows did Stephens save his life, but still he took eighteen stab wounds ranging from superficial to nearly fatal. Finally Cone threw all his weight against his target, and the two fell back to the floor, the umbrella breaking and Cone putting the knife to Stephens's throat. "Retract, or I will cut your ——— throat!" shouted the judge. "Never!" Little Aleck shot back. "Cut!" When Cone thrust with the blade, Stephens grabbed it with his hand and held as tightly as he could, his hand enduring severe slicing as Cone tried to yank it free. They were back on their feet somehow, still fighting for control of the knife, when bystanders finally pulled them apart.

Stephens was perilously close to death from wounds and loss of blood. Taken into the hotel, he feebly looked on as they examined and bandaged his injuries. A physician determined that one of the thrusts had come within one-sixteenth of an inch of his heart, and another had cut an artery from which he might have bled to death had it not been sutured in time. Flesh hung in ribbons from his savaged right hand, and many observers doubted that he would live. He remained in Atlanta for several days before being well enough to take the train home to Crawfordville, and when he arrived a crowd of friends and constituents met him, still fearful for his life. Stephens's ire cooled as his health gradually returned, and though a court indicted Cone for assault, Little Aleck declined to prosecute. In the end the judge was convicted of a lesser charge and simply fined. In later years the two even became friends again.[43]

If there was ever a question that Stephens was a politician above all, his ensuing actions settled the matter. The affair had been entirely personal in nature, but at once the Whigs, especially Toombs and Stephens himself, made campaign capital of the fact that Cone was a Democrat. "Stephens was cut down by a cowardly assassin," Toombs declared, setting the tone, and the Democrats soon complained that "they are trying to make a martyr of Stephens." Worse was the fact that Cone was a large man with a knife, suggesting premeditation, and Stephens small and unarmed. Even though his chest was still healing, and his right hand so badly cut that his thumb was nearly severed and doctors feared they would have to amputate the hand if tetanus set in, Little Aleck returned to Atlanta just eleven days after the incident to attend a grand Whig rally.[44] They did all but wave his bloody shirt. Young Whigs refused to have horses pull him through the streets in their evening torchlight parade, for fear the animals might give him too rough a ride. Instead, several men pulled the open barouche in which Stephens, frail and pale, his right hand heavily bandaged, was virtually put on display. Even though this was a Taylor rally, the banners and illuminations focused on Cone's attack, showing Stephens defending himself manfully in a metaphor for the supposed underdog Whigs trying to regain the White House from their entrenched opponents. The crowd repeatedly shouted Little Aleck's name, and when the other speakers had finished, he actually managed to hobble to the platform, though pleading—whether in truth or for effect—that he was too weak to say more than to tell a brief anecdote and urge them to vote for Taylor. That done, he returned home to convalesce for a full month before he could go out again and make a few appearances in the final two weeks of the campaign. He did not use his right hand to write again for a year, and his handwriting—never handsome—remained a messy scrawl for the rest of his life, leading to more than one amusing miscommunication, as when he wrote an order for two Dagon plows and was sent two dozen, and again when he received fifty pounds of ice when he had actually ordered rice.[45]

Julia Toombs showed considerable solicitude while he recuperated, and Stephens, now the most popular Whig in the state, had no choice but to leave the principal management of Taylor to his friend, who not only stumped his own district but also Little Aleck's, essentially campaigning for Stephens's reelection while also promoting Taylor. Toombs even went as far afield as New York to speak before Taylor rallies. "He has done gallant service," Little Aleck repeatedly said of his friend's efforts, feeling restless until he could get back on the stump himself. "I think Mr. Toombs has had the weight of the canvass long enough," he told Julia in October, and during the last three weeks of the campaign he managed to get out to address a few crowds in his district.[46] On election day, when Taylor took the state, Toombs himself boasted, "I have worked hard and feel amply rewarded."[47] The two friends were rewarded, too, by their own comfortable reelection for another term in Congress.

When the friends returned to Washington in December for the opening of the next session, they were enthusiastic over the victory of Taylor, a Southern Whig elected largely by Southern Whig voters, with the cooperation of Northern party members disappointed that their preferred candidate Clay had lost the nomination. Within weeks antislave Yankee Whigs tried to revive the Wilmot Proviso or to accomplish its aims by other means, and they renewed direct attacks on slavery in the District. Calhoun began to organize Southerners against the threat, calling for a caucus of Southern members on December 22, but Toombs and Stephens both distrusted his motives. Little Aleck characteristically called for calm deliberation and patience, and Toombs denounced the meeting but determined to attend and attempt to undermine it from within. When Stephens declined an invitation to chair a subcommittee to which he was appointed to prepare resolutions and an address to the public stating their concerns, Calhoun chaired it instead and reported to the caucus his Southern Address, heavily influenced by Rhett, and calling for the Southern states to brook no more assaults on their institutions but to organize to resist. The address was redolent with the scent of secession. Toombs set about deliberately to kill it on its presentation on January 15, 1849, arguing that it was neither desirable nor possible to unite the South "until we were ready to dissolve the Union," and that secession should never be considered until the government itself committed some overt act of aggression on Southern rights. Stephens led a movement to have the address tabled and effectively killed, and when that failed he and three others resigned from the committee. Then Toombs took over and was largely responsible for having the address recommitted for reconsideration. Though that did not kill it, it bought time for the reflection that Little Aleck wanted, and by the time the caucus met again on January 22, few Whigs were willing to go with Calhoun any longer. Stephens, Toombs, and many others either did not bother to attend or declined to vote when Calhoun's report came up finally for a vote. Only 48 of 121 Southern members signed on to the address, fatally weakening the effort in Congress. Though they did not act alone, never had Toombs and Stephens worked so ably together to achieve a common aim, and Toombs himself could not resist boasting that "we completely foiled Calhoun in his miserable attempt."[48]

Nevertheless, Calhoun's address and the Wilmot controversy stirred Southern fears anew, and for the next several years the question of organizing territories and states from the Mexican conquests kept Congress and the country in turmoil and the Georgians in the thick of it. Toombs and Stephens favored a plan to organize all of it into a single megaterritory, though Toombs granted that it would almost inevitably wind up repudiating slavery. Still, that would result in only one additional free state instead of three or more under other plans, thus presumably greatly reducing the danger to the balance of power and to the future of slavery itself. This would "rescue the country from all danger of agitation," he believed. Indeed, he had come to this session firmly committed to putting an end to the slavery controversy and thought that he had the goal in sight.[49] He reckoned without the radicals North and South who, each for their reasons, did not want agitation to cease, and the plan was soon killed.

Stephens took up once more his effort to stymie acquisition of any of the territory by opposing the appropriations contingent to the peace treaty and land cession, but to no avail. There would be no easy solutions to the territorial question after all. He and Toombs could only hope that when Taylor took office in March, his new administration would find a way to ease the situation. Taylor himself consulted with Little Aleck in the formation of his cabinet, and the Georgian approved almost entirely of his appointments. Yet the appointees were generally weak and inexperienced, and very soon after Taylor's inauguration it became evident that he was going to allow the Northern antislave Whigs to begin eclipsing the Southerners in power and influence, one more indication that the party was starting to shift away from the Georgians and to form along purely sectional lines.[50]

The session ended the day of Taylor's inauguration, and Stephens and Toombs went home to look on anxiously from afar to see how the administration developed. By June Toombs was expressing his concern at Taylor's inexperience and the influence of men he did not trust, but he was still confident in the president himself.[51] Then Taylor made ill-advised remarks indicating that he regarded slavery as a great evil, further dividing Whig ranks, and in the off-season elections that fall, the party lost its majority in Congress to the Democrats, with neither Toombs nor Stephens making their usual efforts to support party candidates. Little Aleck was ill most of the summer, and both of them seem to have devoted most of their time to looking after their practices, yet their lethargy may at least in part have reflected their growing disenchantment with a party whose direction suddenly seemed to suggest it had no place for them or other proponents of Southern rights. If they could not countenance the Democrats either, then they faced being outcasts, and some critics in the state, even among ardent Southern rights Whigs, thought it about time. Speaking of Toombs and Stephens in particular, the Georgia Whig Iverson Harris complained after the elections that "there must be an end to the unhealthy and selfish domination of these gentlemen."[52]

Events accelerated as Mississippi's governor John Quitman—dancing on strings pulled by Rhett of South Carolina—summoned a state convention that in turn called for a convention of all the slave states in June 1850 to determine on united action in resistance to encroachments on slavery. Stephens opposed the idea but did not come out publicly, and Toombs kept his own counsel. Even worse, California petitioned for admission to statehood as a free state, by-passing the territorial stage entirely, and the discovery of gold and the flood of immigrants heading there argued strongly in favor of speedy admission. Capping it all, the first months of Taylor's administration gave every evidence that it was to be dominated by the Free-Soilers, with all but one of the president's cabinet ministers under the thumb of New York's William H. Seward.

When the Georgians returned for the opening session of the Thirty-first Congress in December 1849, they faced a crisis. Toombs called on Taylor and learned that he would actually sign the Wilmot Proviso if adopted by Congress. It was an act of apostasy so far as Toombs was concerned. "My course became instantly fixed," he declared. He intended to make repudiation of the proviso a test of loyalty to Southern rights, and if the Northerners refused to go along, then he would abandon the party for good, even if it meant "a dissolution of the Union."[53] Stephens may have been with Toombs during the visit and definitely called on Taylor a few days later. He left less disillusioned, presumably because he misunderstood what the president said of his intentions, but soon he realized his mistake.

Certainly he would stand with Toombs in the fight ahead, and before long there were press rumors that the two had formally broken with Taylor.[54]

In Stephens's lodgings, he and Toombs and others drafted resolutions repudiating the passage of any law prohibiting slavery in California and New Mexico or abolishing it in the District. This was their test, but when some others said it was premature and might foment a major split in the party, Toombs refused to back down. They presented the resolutions to the party caucus the night before the House was to organize and elect a Speaker, but the caucus, dominated by Northern Whigs, refused to act on it immediately. At that the two Georgians walked out, along with a few others, but not before Little Aleck echoed Toombs's threat to break with them when he told the caucus that he would have nothing to do with a party that adhered to those two noxious measures. "My Southern blood and feelings are up," he said the next day. Now they were bolters. For the first time in their political careers they began to think of themselves as men without a party.[55]

3

The Breaking of a Friendship

They had more maneuvers in store. When the House convened on December 3, the breakdown of members was such that clever management could disrupt the election for Speaker by producing a deadlock, a position from which Stephens and Toombs could hope to broker a concession on the Wilmot Proviso in return for delivering a majority. The strategy worked, and they held up the election for three weeks, Toombs meanwhile taking the floor and refusing to yield it in the confusion over rules and procedures prior to formal organization. He also showed just how deeply he felt the betrayal of the Northern Whigs, when he declared that if Congress succeeded in banishing slavery from New Mexico, California, and the District, then "I am for disunion." Given guarantees that the Northern majority would not injure his constituents, he would stay in the fold. Deny them, he warned, "and, as far as I am concerned, let discord reign forever."[1]

Stephens spoke, too, though with less vehemence, but confessed that it had been the most exciting day he had ever seen in Congress. He maintained that the

Speaker's chair should never be filled until the Northern wing of the party, the new Free-Soilers, and the Northern antislave Democrats as well, came to terms with Southern demands on slavery. "This is my kind of resistance," he said during the turmoil, "at least for the present."[2] Within a few weeks he was sounding increasingly like Toombs. "What is to be the result of the slavery question I cannot tell," he wrote in February 1850. He expected some accommodation, but feared that it would allay the furor only temporarily. The root disease had gone too deep into the nation's political soul for any partial remedy to work. "When I look to the future and consider the causes of the existing sectional discontent, their extent and nature I must confess that I see very little prospect of future peace and quiet." He did not hazard to predict that secession and the formation of a Southern slave state confederation would solve all their problems, though he believed that it would if there were "unity, virtue, intelligence and patriotism in all our councils." Unfortunately, even among some of his Southern friends, he saw too little of those qualities and too much of demagoguery and ambition, not mentioning or perhaps recognizing some quotient of them in himself as well.[3]

"The general signs of the times augur no good," Little Aleck told Linton in January 1850. "Men's minds are unsettled. The temper of the country is fretful." In his view, Washington was spinning, and the centrifugal force threatened to send states flying off at any time. He fully expected that even if Taylor declined to sign the Wilmot Proviso, it no longer mattered. The Union was on its way to destruction over the issue of slavery in the territories, and nothing was likely to stop that trend. "There will never again be harmony between the two great sections of the Union." Secession was unavoidable, he concluded. "I shall do nothing to favor it or hasten," he told Linton, "but I now consider it inevitable."[4]

That inevitability was hastened, thought many observers, by what became known as the Compromise of 1850. Introduced by Henry Clay exactly two weeks after Stephens's dire prediction, the bill provided for the admission of California immediately as a free state, organization of the balance of the Mexican conquests into territories without provision for or prohibition of slavery, deferring the decision to a later time, and the maintenance of slavery in the District of Columbia but the abolition of buying and selling within its limits. Other provisions, including the Fugitive Slave Law, provided further sops to the South in return for the loss of California and the potential loss in the rest of the new territory, most of which under the terms of the Missouri Compromise should otherwise have been slave states when admitted. The slave states would lose more than they would gain in the long run, but at least it put an end to discussion of the dreaded Wilmot Proviso, and for the time being it did at least pour oil on the most immediately troubled waters.

Stephens sat on the floor in the Senate chamber as part of the audience to hear Clay introduce his resolutions, and in spite of his years of distrust of Clay personally and politically, found himself won over and even warmed to the Great Pacificator. Little Aleck seldom harbored extreme or emotional views for long, and having given vent to his exasperation after breaking with his party, he felt immediately attracted to a compromise that could settle the slavery issue short of disunion. Toombs, too, liked the compromise, and by March thought he saw in it what he called "a tolerable prospect for a proper settlement of the slavery question."[5] Thereafter he and Stephens, perhaps thanks in part to their being all but free agents, were able to take an active and positive role in the ensuing months of debate, trying to bring together elements of both sides. The Georgians wanted to bring together Whigs, Free-Soilers, and Democrats to agree to accept Congress's opting out of deciding the slavery question for the territories, instead allowing their inhabitants to decide it for themselves when they became formal territories, essentially the same doctrine that later became controversial when championed by Stephen Douglas of Illinois. In return for that agreement, abandonment of the proviso, and no interference with slavery in the District, they proposed to withdraw objection to the admission of California. Stephens drafted a letter setting forth basically these principles as worked out between the two of them, and it served as the subject of a meeting late in February when he and Toombs met with members from Kentucky, Ohio, and Illinois at the home of Howell Cobb, by then Speaker of the House. There they reached an agreement that all could support, an agreement that was the foundation of the eventual vote that passed the compromise measures in August and also of the political affiliation of Stephens and Douglas.[6]

They were often tense days of debate, the enemy frequently not the Yankees, but the ultra-Calhoun and Rhett Democrats who were unwilling to yield anything, and Rhett at least anxious to bring about secession. Little Aleck used his command of parliamentary procedure to gain time when needed or to postpone votes he feared they might lose. He also showed that he could compromise, for though he had hitherto condemned the popular sovereignty idea he now saw it as the salvation of the Union, at least for the moment. He and Toombs called together on President Taylor, trying to press their solution on him and seeking from him a promise not to sign the proviso if it were adopted in the meantime, but Taylor balked and then became threatening himself when they raised the possibility of secession as an alternative.[7]

At the same time, the sudden death of Calhoun and the fizzle of his Southern convention in June, which six slave states did not bother to attend and which produced no conclusive plan of action, deflated the Southern extremist faction clamoring for secession. The almost perceptible exhaustion on all sides opened the way for renewed movement on the compromise. In April the Senate addressed the impasse by referring the compromise to a committee that a month later produced the Omnibus bill. Both Toombs and Stephens spoke frequently in the debates that followed, Toombs more formally and at greater length, and each occasionally became frustrated and angered and reverted momentarily to a more extreme position. Toombs especially lost his patience and regressed to bluster and threat, when in June he became so exasperated that he flared out and declared that if the North did not recognize the Southerners' right to participate in settling the territories with their slaves, "It is then your government, not mine," and "then I am its enemy." He would swear himself and his children and his constituents to eternal hostility to Washington. "I will strike for *Independence*."[8] Indeed, Toombs's vehemence may have been a bit studied, overstating the case as Little Aleck often did, to get the attention of the House and deflect it from a course certain to lead to confrontation. If so, it worked, for Northern members thereafter became more conciliatory and less immovable.

In the long days of often impassioned debate, Toombs relaxed in the mornings before the gavel by studying French with his daughters and was often to be seen in the House during the speeches, correcting proofs of his latest address with one hand while holding a copy of a French play or burlesque in the other. Varina Davis asked him how he could find enjoyment in such lowbrow works. "Whatever the Lord Almighty lets his geniuses create, He makes someone to enjoy," he replied, then added more seriously, "These plays take all the soreness out of me."[9] In fact, the labors and tension of the session were telling on him. He missed his family increasingly, for meanwhile Julia and their two daughters had returned to Georgia. Julia was sick of Washington, and although he thrived upon it, Toombs himself was wearying of the constant strife. He wanted a more peaceful and genteel life. He wanted to take his family on a tour of Europe and have time to enjoy his prosperity. By late April he was telling friends that at the end of his current term he intended to "bring my public life to a speedy termination."[10]

In fact, by late April Toombs believed they were over their major hurdles and even on their way to a fair settlement of the slavery question that could satisfy all sections, though perhaps not completely. "It has been an enormously difficult question here," he confided on April 20, "& no man not behind the scenes can understand the extent of the dangers & difficulties." What he called "the secret struggle here" had been intense, and he and Stephens and their confederates acknowledged that they had taken on and defeated Whig Party organization in the House and maintained for themselves what he called "an armed neutrality towards the administration." To use his own word, they had "extorted" concessions from the party and the White House. There were still some breakers ahead, but at least he believed the proviso was dead at last and had no qualms about giving himself chief credit for its demise by his recent impassioned speech, of which he sent several hundred copies out for public consumption. "I brought the North to see clearly that they cannot work the government without doing us justice in this matter," he boasted. Indeed, he felt he—and presumably

Stephens—had done more than any other to bring them to this stage, but he recognized the importance of keeping their role quiet for the moment, so as not to make themselves even bigger targets for some of their former Northern Whig compatriots than they were already. "The time will come," he told a friend, "*but it is not now.*" Yet he was already receiving suggestions that he should seek the next vacant Senate seat from Georgia.[11]

The problem meanwhile seemed to be the president, for Taylor still apparently preferred the proviso to the Omnibus bill. Toombs and Stephens called on him repeatedly through May and June, but each time they left disappointed; by July 3 Little Aleck, once more out of temper, threatened afterward in front of Toombs and others that he would start impeachment proceedings. But then they made one more call on July 9 to try again, only to be told that the president had died that afternoon of a sudden and severe attack of gastroenteritis. Within a few days opponents of the compromise had heard of the impeachment remark and manufactured from it a scenario in their press that had Toombs and Stephens calling on Taylor when he was actually on his death bed and threatening him with House censure if he did not give them what they wanted, suggesting that by this action they hastened his death. Rhett's organ, the *Charleston Mercury,* made an especially harsh attack, typical of his virulent and irresponsible verbal assaults on opponents; with Toombs and Stephens being party bolters and apparently the more vulnerable, he could hope to weaken them further. Stephens took pains to deny the reports, though they persisted in some quarters, but that was soon overshadowed by good news, for a change.[12] Millard Fillmore of New York became president, and suddenly the prospect brightened, for he favored the Omnibus.

At the end of the month, however, the Senate voted down the Omnibus, and a disgusted Stephens declared, "The world is made up of fools"; deciding that nothing was going to happen for some time, he went home. But then Clay and Douglas divided the Omnibus into five separate bills, reintroduced them, and saw them all to passage within two weeks. The legislation went to the House, and for the next three weeks it debated, with Toombs in the thick of the maneuvering as he had been from the first. He chaired a commit-

tee dedicated to Southern rights, which issued resolutions providing benchmarks, and took the floor to defend not only the passage
of the separate bills but also himself from attacks by the radicals that
he was a traitor to the South. He would ever be ready to resist any
encroachment on Southern rights, he declared. The concessions
made were only such as were reasonable to achieve "the peace and
tranquility of the Republic." Even then, while the several bills
passed, one after another, Toombs could not bring himself to vote
when the final one abolishing the slave trade in the District came
before the House. It passed anyhow, and ironically, it was the only
one on which Stephens was able to vote at all, having just returned
from Georgia to find that events, for once, had moved much faster
than he had. Little Aleck voted against the bill, no doubt knowing
that it was going to pass in any event. His "nay" and Toombs's ab-
stention were most likely genuine opposition in part, and more so
a realization that they needed to reinforce their standing as pro-
tectors of Southern rights.[13]

Indeed, those last votes were probably aimed at their Georgia
constituents, for the state was in a turmoil over the split in the Whig
and Democratic Parties on sectional lines and the polarization of
voters on slavery. When they returned home, Stephens and Toombs
found the secessionists trying once more to assert themselves, egged
on by men like Rhett and Yancey who, unable to effect a crisis in
their own states, attended extremist rallies in Macon and elsewhere
hoping to foment resistance and revive the intent of the failed
Nashville convention. They succeeded to the extent of ruining the
state Democratic Party and giving rise to a new Southern rights
group. That left moderate Democrats nowhere to go, just as the
moderate Whigs still in that party were seemingly homeless in their
own state.

Into that void stepped Toombs and Little Aleck and Howell
Cobb. As soon as they got home they saw the problem and went to
work forming a coalition to oppose the Southern Rights Party. At
the instance of the assembly, the governor had called for a state convention to meet in order to consider the recent controversies and
what the state should do.[14] The Southern rights men hoped to dominate, and in order to counter them Stephens, Toombs, and Cobb

went to work feverishly in the campaign for the November election of delegates. Toombs stated the issue succinctly: "We must either repudiate this policy, or arm."[15] Under the banner of their new Union Party, they spoke all across the state, Little Aleck reckoning that he alone traveled 3,000 miles, and were in turn harshly attacked as traitors to their section by their opponents. Both men, Stephens especially, trimmed a bit on some of their earlier positions in order to blur their records, but in the main they and their supporters never backed away from a commitment to the Union so long as the rights of the slave states were protected, which they argued the recently passed compromise measures accomplished.

The two men usually traveled together, and especially when they went to Columbus, the heartland of their opposition. On November 2, late in the canvass, they arrived for a stump meeting only to find a hostile audience and no one to debate them. Instead, they saw effigies of Toombs hanging from the trees. Undaunted, Toombs went on the stand and began to harangue the crowd. Being Democrats, he said, they had probably never seen a man in a white shirt before, and that was why they did not know how to behave properly. Warming as he always did, he asked them how they could hope to overthrow the Union, when from what he could see of them and their kind, they had neither the wit nor strength among them to turn over an outhouse. Not surprisingly, tempers flared and knives and pistols were drawn, but fortunately, as fights broke out between Southern rights men and the small number of Unionists in the crowd, no one suffered serious injury. When Toombs and Stephens left to speak elsewhere, the editor of the local paper observed that the two had "operated like sparks on a tinderbox in this community."[16]

Secession fever was never strong in Georgia, and Stephens could see it fading as the election approached. On election day the candidates backed by what they called the Constitutional Union Party simply swamped their opposition in a popular vote of almost 2 to 1, electing convention delegates that were 10 to 1 opposed to resistance—meaning secession. It was a triumph noted all over the nation, and one that took the steam out of efforts in South Carolina and Mississippi. Toombs, Stephens, and Georgia had halted the march to disunion and bought precious time for tempers to cool and compromise to go to work, if it could.[17]

The two friends were both themselves chosen as delegates to the convention that convened in December and played a large role in the chief result, the drafting of the so-called Georgia Platform. On the one hand, it asserted the state's adherence to the Union and to general, but conditional, endorsement of the recent compromise. On the other, however, it declared that if Congress abolished slavery in the District or prevented the admission of a future slave state, tampered with the new Fugitive Slave Law, or interfered with the slave trade between the states or tried to prevent Southern settlers from taking their slaves into the other territory taken from Mexico then such action or actions would be justification for secession.

Toombs and Stephens did not help frame the document, though they suggested later changes that appeared in the finished version, and each recognized that it had something not only to suit the majority of men in their own new Union Party but also to meet the concerns of all but the extremists among the Southern rights crowd. It was conciliatory and assertive at one and the same time. Toombs tried to get the platform adopted as a whole, but the convention chose to consider and debate each of its five resolutions separately, in an echo of the handling of the Omnibus bill. The opponents tried delaying tactics to disrupt consideration, and when someone accused them of being obstructionists they pointedly reminded the convention that Toombs and Stephens had delayed the election of a Speaker of the House for weeks. Nevertheless, the platform passed virtually intact.[18]

While the convention met, Stephens, Toombs, and Cobb led the way in the formal organization of the new Constitutional Union Party, and Stephens made it clear that he hoped their state organization would grow to be a national Union Party to come. He failed to recognize that in the North the old party alignments continued intact, though the Free-Soilers had somewhat fragmented the Whigs. Even in most of the South the old parties still held together, at least enough to present coherent platforms and to offer voters a clear choice. Only in Georgia, Mississippi, and Alabama had the internal disorganization produced by the compromise debate and the work of the extremists succeeded in polarizing sentiments along new lines that trampled the old parties. But as Little Aleck and his friend would find, three states were not enough to launch a major national movement, not without a continuation of crisis and provocation. The Compromise of 1850 forestalled that, at least for a while, and thus the measures they had supported to save the Union ironically worked against their hope for a political party that would do the same.

The new party lasted scarcely three years, in fact, though it managed to elect Howell Cobb to the governorship, keep Stephens in the House, and in 1851 elect Toombs to that vacated Senate seat. When the two returned to the capital for the last session of the sitting Congress, they found themselves somewhat lionized by Washington society for their Union-saving efforts. It was just as well for Toombs, for his weariness with the day-to-day business of the House showed. He spoke seldom, stayed away from the Whig caucuses, and declined almost all invitations to political meetings and rallies. Little Aleck was tired, too, just as the tension of the last few years had left the nation exhausted, anxious for a rest. He could find the young ladies at soirees charming, even diverting, though he would descry their wanton flirtatiousness. "Sometimes I have thought that of all men I was most miserable," he wrote that winter, "that I was especially doomed to misfortune, to melancholy, to grief." He accepted his almost constant physical pain, but the mental anguish he suffered so often truly plagued him in his hours alone.

"An evil genius was my inseparable companion, following at my side, forever mocking and grinning, and making those places which in the lives of others are most pleasant, to me almost miserable." A simple look from someone could churn his insides, for in those looks he could see pity, mockery, even contempt for that "half finished thing" that constituted his diminutive shadow. He could only try to turn those wounds to his advantage. "The secret of my life has been—*revenge reversed*," he told Linton. By rising above the contempt of others, by meeting and overcoming the obstacles that normal men would find if trapped in his body, he could have his victory. It was no wonder his temper was so hot, even uncontrollable, or that he so frequently found himself in arguments leading to challenges. More than anything, he wanted to see a second look on those faces that underestimated or condescended to him. He wanted to see the surprise and chagrin they would register when Little Aleck beat them, proved himself smarter, more enduring, or simply braver. No wonder he was spending his life going from one battle to another, and most often against opposition, for it was in winning against the odds that he would get his greatest reward, that look of surprise and amazement and chagrin as a big man saw himself bested by a little one.[19] His was not just the ambition of one who wanted to get ahead, but of one who needed to prove to himself and to others that he belonged ahead.

The two friends spent the rest of 1851 in Georgia, trying to perfect their new party organization and helping elect Cobb to the governor's mansion, Toombs doing most of the work when Stephens fell ill again that spring and summer. Little Aleck could only write letters of advice from Crawfordville, but still his advice was sound. Their opponents soon dubbed the three the "triumvirate," suggesting that Toombs, Stephens, and Cobb were in league to run the state to suit themselves, which was not far from the mark. Nevertheless, Cobb won handily, and Constitutional Union candidates took huge majorities in both houses of the legislature while Stephens and Toombs were reelected to their congressional seats by their biggest majorities ever. The accusations of unseemly ambition soon came home again when the state senate no sooner had met than it elected Toombs to the Senate for the term commencing in March 1853. Everyone knew the current incumbent, who had opposed the compromise, stood no chance of reelection, but by rights the election of his successor should not have taken place for another year. It looked a bit too hasty, although within the law. "Mr. Toombs made Mr. Cobb Governor, Mr. Cobb made Mr. Toombs Senator, and Mr. Stephens is to have what he calls for at all hours," complained an opposition editor, calling the three a "Mutual Insurance Company."[20]

Yet there were individuals, too, who would have preferred Stephens for the higher office, and some even sounded him out on the matter, suggesting that since he had entered the House before

Toombs, it was only fitting that he be considered first for this elevation. Little Aleck did not act, however, most likely because he knew how much Toombs wanted the Senate seat and was reluctant ever to find himself pitted against his friend. He felt no rancor toward Toombs, of course. Still, when the state senate did not even include him along with Toombs among the several nominees, the omission constituted another of those "looks" that he could not forget.[21]

The friends found themselves outsiders when they returned to Washington in December, but the ensuing session lacked the excitement of what had gone before. Toombs was less active and went home ill before the adjournment, but Little Aleck struggled to advance the new party, soon finding that Cobb actually hoped to bring it into coalition with the Northern Democrats as a base for high ambitions of his own. Word came that the Constitutional Unionists were having trouble staying together even in Georgia, and at home and in Washington Stephens and Toombs alike could see that with the compromise an accomplished fact, the old parties were settling down again and on lines much more defined by sectional issues, with bolters from each going into the other, but still strong, with relatively few defections to the Georgians' party. Though Little Aleck refused to see the inevitable for months, the fact was that they were dead in the water as a movement, and for a change Toombs was little succor, given his bad health.

In fact, Toombs was starting to drift himself. Separated permanently from the Whigs, and distrusting Cobb's motives in trying to bring their new party and the Democrats together, still he recognized that in 1852, when they elected the next president, only the two major parties would have nominees. That meant that if they were to be heard at all, they would have to back one or the other, or else futilely stand on the margins as gadflies. By spring 1852 the ever-practical Toombs decided that if the Democrats presented a good nominee, sound on the compromise and also on Southern rights, then he could support him. But in the end, as usual, he finally chose to stand beside Little Aleck, who resisted to the last minute, and even when the Democrats nominated Franklin Pierce on a platform amenable to Southern interests, he still held out for a separate nominee from his new party, clinging to the hope of ushering the Constitutional Unionists onto the national scene.

If they needed any final evidence of the futility of that dream, it came when their party in Georgia held its own state convention, and promptly Cobb engineered its endorsement of Pierce. It was the beginning of a break with Cobb for Toombs and Stephens, and though they took no part personally in the convention themselves, their supporters staged a boycott after Cobb's action, but to no purpose. Even if they recognized the logic of the act, Cobb's instinct for self-serving shifts in advancing his own career left them irritated and feeling somewhat betrayed. It also signaled the end of the party, which was formally disbanded in August, though its die-hard adherents continued to make noise for some time to come. In the campaign that followed, Stephens supported the pointless candidacy of Daniel Webster, nominated by the bolters from the Union Party's state convention, and Toombs did the same, but neither had his heart in the obviously parochial movement. Then, to punctuate the movement's futility, Webster died before the election. Still, when the day came, the counties of middle Georgia where Toombs and Stephens lived and held sway actually returned majorities for Webster, the vote of a dead party for a dead candidate.[22] If there was any consolation for the two men, it was that the election virtually saw the end of the Whig Party that had betrayed them; and with Pierce, even though he was a Democrat, they could hope to have peace and security for the South.

Certainly public affairs remained quiet for the balance of that Congress, and when Toombs and Stephens returned home for the long break in 1853 the only real excitement was the campaign for governor. Even though Toombs especially dominated their now unnamed faction's convention and selection of a nominee, it was useless, and he and Little Aleck in the end supported the hopeless candidacy of a fellow Constitutional Unionist whose defeat in the fall was the last gasp of the party in the state. In fact, after the defeat Georgia's Democratic press smelled blood, and sensing the evaporation of Toombs's power base, actually called for him to resign his seat in the Senate before he had even taken it. It did not help that Toombs had attacked some of Pierce's appointments, including Jefferson Davis, the new secretary of war, for being opponents of the compromise that the president himself had pledged to support. Soon Toombs was rumored to have charged Davis with being a disunionist. The charge reached Davis, who replied in a published letter that, knowing his views as Toombs surely did from their time together in Washington, only a man who was "radically false and corrupt" could accuse him of being a secessionist. He regarded secession as a right, but only as a final resort. Of course Toombs and Davis had not been "congenial" as Varina Davis put it, when they had shared lodgings several years before. Still, knowing it was all a misunderstanding, Toombs had no need to respond in kind, but he would not have been Toombs if he had not. In his own open letter he observed that when a man like Davis felt himself insulted, it was customary first to write privately to the presumed offender to seek an explanation or denial, and not to go to the press with insults founded on rumors. But Davis had taken the path of "swaggering braggarts and cunning poltroons," he said. It could have resulted in a duel, but did not, though it would be nearly four years before the two resumed cordial, if formal, relations.[23]

The uneasy truce in the country after the Compromise of 1850 rather matched that which ensued between Toombs and Davis, and it lasted until the very day that the new senator first took his seat on January 23, 1854. That same day the Senate received a Pierce-endorsed bill to organize the territories of Kansas and Nebraska. Included in its language was an abrogation of the Missouri Compromise, which the Compromise of 1850, providing for no congressional interference in the matter of slavery in the territories, seemed to have superseded. At once a storm blew up that threatened to eclipse all that had gone before. The Missouri Compromise had stipulated that no slave states could be formed from Louisiana Purchase territory above the mandated line of 36°30′. Remove that bar, however, and any territory, including Kansas or Nebraska, could become a slave state, casting the whole issue of slavery and the balance of power immediately into the headlines. Southerners like Toombs and Stephens, regardless of party affiliation, leaped to support the bill; Northerners, Whig and Democrat alike, reacted equally.

Stephens had followed the progress of the bill from its first introduction on January 3 but had shown little interest until the Missouri Compromise repeal became a part of it, and an administration measure as well. Now he supported it, and so did Toombs immediately upon his arrival, even though there was a vagueness about just when the issue of slavery was to be decided, whether opponents were right in charging that inhabitants of a territory could decide on slavery before framing a state constitution—which they called "squatter sovereignty"—or only at the time of applying for statehood with a constitution already framed that settled the matter. The point was vital to Southern interests. If a territory had to wait on the decision until it drew up its constitution, then slaveholders and their property would be free to immigrate to said territory, and thus by their numbers and vote influence delegates to the framing convention. But if slavery could be excluded prior to that time, then no slaveholder would be likely to move when he had to leave his biggest investment and his labor force behind, virtually ensuring that only free state proponents would make up the population, guaranteeing slavery's exclusion in the eventual constitution. It was a point that could decide the ever-present balance of power, which was the only security Southerners felt for the protection of slavery's continuation where it already existed.

The bill passed the Senate without real danger of failure, helped along by Toombs immediately chairing a caucus of Southern senators who agreed to call on slave state Whigs in the Senate to side with the Democrats in support of the interests of their section. When the debate commenced, he spoke eloquently in favor of the popular sovereignty principle and won kudos for his first Senate address. But when the bill went to the House, where there were far more antislave elements, it faced a severe battle, and then Little Aleck came into play. As he had when he and Toombs held up the speakership election and helped in securing passage of the Compromise of 1850, he skillfully managed much of the debate personally, even though he was ill. Thereafter, as the debate became heated, he feared defeat for a time, then stalemate, but in May when it finally came to a head, he was in the fight, helping save the bill from near death by parliamentary manipulation, even though he

actually did so in opposition to the wishes of the bill's principal managers. Going it on his own, as he had when leaving the Whig Party,
he stunned friends and foes alike with an obscure rule that ended
all delaying tactics and brought the bill to a victorious vote that same
day. Little Aleck, his ego ever in inverse proportion to his size, had
stood up to the "big bugs," as he called them, and had seen that
"look" that he so craved. "I took the reins in my hand, applied whip
and spur, and brought the 'wagon' out," he boasted to Linton.
"Glory enough for one day."[24]

Stephens soon referred to his role in the passage of the Kansas-
Nebraska legislation as the greatest event of his life, standing it beside his role in the 1850 compromise and his authorship of the
Georgia Platform. What is more, the bill signaled the final and
abrupt death of the Whigs, now completely disintegrated over the
issue of slavery expansion as Southern members flocked to the
Democrats and Northern figures fumbled with the Free-Soilers and
other fringe groups before coalescing in the newly formed Republican Party. Stephens himself still held aloof from the Democrats,
though clearly that was the only possible home for him, with his
Constitutional Union group too small and disorganized even to
merit being called marginal. Toombs faced the issue more realisti-
cally, having been cooperating with the Democrats for some time.
Party commitment had been fragile for Southern men since the
1820s, and now it was collapsing under the weight of sectionalism.

Toombs meanwhile faced something far more dire and personal,
the death of one of his daughters in March 1855. The Senate had
been relatively calm during the year since it passed the Kansas-
Nebraska Act, which allowed Toombs to spend much time at home
with his failing child, but he could do nothing for her. It was a loss
that struck Stephens almost as hard as her father, for he had known
her since her childhood. He was going through personal turmoil of
his own, seeing his old hold on his district starting to erode in the
face of the new party realignments. By May 1855 he announced that
he would not seek reelection but serve out his term and then retire from Congress. He published an open letter giving his reasons,
especially his detestation of the rising new American Party, a nativist,
anti-Catholic, anti-Irish, anti-almost everything group colloquially

called the Know Nothings. But then he changed his mind, and the widespread support from Democrats for his Know Nothing attack went some way in shortening the distance between them and himself. As the campaign ensued, Democrats increasingly came out in support of him, and by the time of his reelection they had won him over in all but outright declaration. A few days after his election he finally announced his new allegiance. By the end of the year he and Toombs were allied with the organization that had once represented their greatest enemies. Slavery and sectional controversy had finally taken precedence over support for the Union in defining their political allegiance, especially for Toombs, ever the more passionate and hot-headed of the two. They both attended a public meeting in November in Milledgeville, and with Stephens standing right behind him, Toombs forthrightly declared that the security of the South depended entirely on the Democratic Party. An editor describing the scene commented that "for the future, we shall regard these gentlemen as Democrats, and as Democrats we shall treat them."[25] That did not make them secessionists, nor were they, for their new party was a national one—the only national one—but the shift in priorities brought about by circumstances within and beyond their control had certainly put them on the path to a crossroads at which their characters, feelings, and emotions could force them and others within the democracy to make a choice, a road that might even separate them.

The journey began sooner than anyone expected, for like most of the previous legislation designed to end the sectional controversy, the Kansas-Nebraska bill only heaped fuel on the old fires. Soon there was a rush of men from both North and South, slave and free states, to settle the new territory and Kansas first, which sat immediately west of slave state Missouri. It was a rush for power, to build a majority one way or the other that could control the eventual fate of slavery. When elections were held for the territorial legislature, thousands of Missourians swept into Kansas to cast illegal ballots that resulted in a proslave majority. That legislature immediately moved to weave slavery permanently into the fabric of the territory, even banning nonslaveholders from civil office and clearly intent on forcing an early constitution. Outraged free state men set up their own rival rump legislature and tried to outflank their opponents by sending Congress a petition for immediate statehood. It was the beginning of several years of what the nation called Bleeding Kansas.

Through all that ensuing turmoil, Stephens and Toombs found themselves caught up in the maelstrom, Toombs especially helping give spin to the storm. Along with Pierce and the Southerners in the party, he supported the proslave legislature; and in a stirring address that ignored the fraud in the legislative election, he asserted that the settlers be left alone to decide their affairs for themselves until they framed a constitution and applied for statehood. Soon Toombs would be supporting a Senate bill for statehood. Little Aleck was in the gallery and applauded his friend's address. "He is unquestionably the ablest debater and most eloquent man now in that body," Stephens declared with no little hero worship in evidence. "For originality of thought and power of expression he has no equal." Toombs's recent purchase of $30,000 worth of Texas land for speculation only added to his interest in western matters.[26] For his own part, Little Aleck leaped into the debates in the House when the issue was presented, with the conundrum of two competing territorial representatives arriving from Kansas, one from the slavery legislature and one from the free state group and each expecting to be given a seat. He argued that Congress could not decide this issue and did not have the power. The compromise and the recent legislation left it entirely with the settlers of the territory. Congress's refusal to stay out of the matter, forced by the antislavery majority, infuriated him.

Tempers flared throughout the Capitol. In May 1856 South Carolina congressman Preston Brooks went into the Senate and attacked Massachusetts senator Charles Sumner by surprise with a cane to retaliate for a highly insulting address made three days before, beating him senseless. It was an act of base cowardice that did not much miss becoming an assassination, though Sumner eventually recovered. Yet Toombs stood by and made no effort to halt the assault and later declared in the Senate that Sumner had it coming. "Sumner takes a beating badly," he quipped. "Yankees seem greatly excited about Sumner's flogging. They are afraid the practice may become general."[27] Stephens, too, condoned the attack, for it was what his own temper might very likely have led him to in the face of sufficient provocation. Of course it was never surprising to find the two friends in agreement, but for them to be in unison in sanctioning an act so indefensible and cowardly showed the direction in which events were driving them. Their defense, like Brooks's, was that the vile Republican Sumner was not the social equal of the South Carolinian and that therefore Brooks was entitled to give him a surprise beating rather than challenging him to a fair fight on a gentleman's terms.

From the extremism of his approbation of the Sumner attack, Toombs swung rapidly to perhaps his finest effort at statecraft. Rarely one to author or introduce new legislation of his own—he left that to Stephens—he worked with Douglas to quell the uproar by a proposal to take a census of the Kansas inhabitants, under federal oversight, and register genuinely qualified voters. That electorate should then choose delegates to a convention to frame a constitution to be submitted with an application for statehood, with or without slavery as the convention so chose. Toombs and Stephens met to discuss the measure, and the result was that Little Aleck introduced virtually the same legislation in the House a few days later. Both assumed that a majority of proslave men who were genuine residents would decide the issue in favor of Southern rights. Toombs's bill passed the Senate handily, but the House virtually ignored Little Aleck's version and instead narrowly passed a bill that recognized the rump free state legislature as legitimate and approved its application for admission. It failed in the Senate, however, and thus both bills went to oblivion, sadly, because Toombs's measure might actually have relieved the tension.

With Kansas igniting emotions everywhere, the country went into a presidential election and the first test of the Democrats against the burgeoning Republicans. The two Georgians, predictably, favored the reelection of Pierce at first, but soon it became apparent that his support for repeal of the Missouri Compromise all but killed his chances among Northern Democrats. While Toombs continued to favor the incumbent in spite of his liabilities, Little Aleck shifted toward Douglas. Neither of the friends attended the nominating convention, and they may have been surprised when James Buchanan emerged as the eventual nominee. Stephens felt no disappointment, for he found Buchanan solid on the Kansas question, and Toombs readily accepted him. By August they were both at home engaged in a surprisingly bitter and close campaign to put Georgia in the Democratic column in November. Many of the former Whigs and Constitutional Unionists had sided with the Know Nothings, who had their own nominee in former president Fillmore. They fought bitterly, meeting Toombs and Stephens repeatedly on the stump, and especially taking the offensive against Little Aleck, making him coequal with Douglas in responsibility for the Kansas bill and taking advantage of ambiguities in some of his arguments to accuse him of favoring squatter sovereignty. It became so bitter that Stephens challenged Benjamin Hill to a duel and was infuriated when the man refused to fight him. Worse, his antagonist managed to make something of a fool of Little Aleck on the stump and in the press when their correspondence was published. They were not reconciled for a quarter of a century.[28]

The reward for the friends' efforts was Buchanan's handy victory in Georgia and in the general election as a whole. It was the end of the Know Nothings, but the Northern Republicans, committed to halting the spread of slavery, though eschewing to espouse attacking it where it already dwelled, garnered an amazing vote for a new party in its first national election. That did not bode well for the future either of the Democratic Party or of protection of Southern rights. Nor did matters improve when Stephens and Toombs returned to Washington in December for the next session. Like Toombs, privately Stephens had expected that Kansas would eventually become a free state simply because he thought population, climate, and geography did not favor slavery's introduction. Thus he publicly declared that the election of Buchanan would settle the Kansas controversy and so was free to admit that in fact he had been fighting for a principle, and not for Kansas. It was a serious misjudgment, for he admitted that he had misled Southerners by espousing a false hope, and he soon found himself attacked for betraying the South. Toombs had announced his opinion many months before, free then to pursue the principle as well but without any deception. Little Aleck quickly backtracked in the face of a minor storm and then endured a wrenching personal loss when Linton's wife died and he had to battle his brother's near-suicidal despair.

The only good news came in March 1857 two days after Buchanan took office. In the landmark *Dred Scott* case, the Supreme Court rendered a decision that Congress did not have the power to bar slavery in the territories. It was what Stephens and Toombs had been arguing in politics for more than twenty years, and Little Aleck had, in fact, attempted to exert some influence through friends close to the Court to produce just such a ruling.[29] The North erupted in indignation, for the decision was a further repudiation of the Missouri Compromise and an assertion that any new territory anywhere could be made a slave state. That made the true difference between popular and squatter sovereignty even more important and the battle for Kansas that much more vital as a testing ground. The proslave legislature, which Pierce had recognized as legitimate, was even then engineering an election for a constitutional convention to meet in Lecompton in fall 1857. In protest over the blatant vote-rigging that took place, free state men boycotted the election, and as a result the convention predictably produced a document including slavery.

When it was required to be submitted to the people of the territory in referendum, the question on the ballot was so phrased by its managers that the option of accepting or rejecting the constitution itself was omitted; only the option of excluding or not excluding slavery in the future, but not those slaves already in the territory at the time of adoption, was to be determined. Free state men once more boycotted the referendum, and so the Lecompton Constitution passed overwhelmingly. A few months later another referendum was held in which voters were to decide on the constitution itself as a whole, and this time the proslavery forces boycotted what they knew would have been a defeat, and so the constitution was rejected by more than 98 percent of the ballots cast. Here was a pretty mess: two referenda, each shunned by one faction or the other, producing two exactly opposite results.

Stephens and Toombs stood behind the administration on

Lecompton. "We now have the Kansas question in full blast," Little Aleck wrote in February 1858, and he feared that admission under Lecompton would fail in the House, though much hinged on the president and Buchanan did not help. Stephens called on the president on February 2 and found him weak and worn and much more willing to be persuaded by others than was good for a chief executive, with the Georgian quite happy to do as much persuading as possible. In the light of what had happened in the two referenda, Stephens opposed the notion of submitting the slavery question to a popular vote at all, but Buchanan endorsed such a policy even though Stephens insisted that he reconsider. The president decided to make the first ballot supporting slavery an administration measure, in hopes of settling the issue and keeping the South appeased. Instead, he made the Lecompton question the center of controversy for the next year and a test of Democratic Party loyalty between himself and Douglas, who found it a violation of popular sovereignty. In short, he split the one and only remaining national party just as another sectional party was on the rise and making political capital out of every moment of the sectional turmoil over the territories.

Stephens could see the effect within days, as Northern Democrats began to break ranks, failing to stand with their Southern compatriots on Kansas's admission. On the evening of February 4 he looked on as tempers rose to such a pitch that a general brawl broke out among some thirty or more members, and the fighters aligned themselves along purely sectional lines. "All things here are tending to bring my mind to the conclusion that the Union cannot or will not last long," he lamented the next day. He gave way to despondency again. "I am wearing out my life for nothing," he moaned to Linton. If they could just admit Kansas, he believed he would retire from politics for good, but that of course was just transitory gloom.[30]

Toombs and Stephens both faced pressure from home that enhanced their support of Buchanan, for Little Aleck's own Georgia Platform required the call of a state convention if Congress interfered with slavery in a territory, and congressional rejection of admission for Kansas under Lecompton would constitute such interference. The purpose of a state convention could only be to discuss the mode and manner of resistance, most likely secession. The en-

suing debate pitted Stephens and Toombs against Douglas, though
neither broke with him politically or personally, and it seemed to
drag on interminably, until Toombs complained in the Senate that
the whole business of the nation was being held hostage to Kansas.
He even suggested that if they admitted Kansas under Lecompton,
there was nothing to prevent that state from subsequently amending its state constitution to exclude slavery after all. In short, Kansas
could be a free state any time it so chose, and all this uproar was a
waste of time. Finally, the admission bill passed the Senate in
March.[31]

The House proved a harsher battleground, even with Stephens
himself directing the administration forces. He had a hard time getting the measure's friends to attend the House to be ready for a vote
when it came, and just as much trouble in bringing it to a vote.
When he got his ballot, however, the administration lost by a slim
margin when the House voted on an amendment to refer Lecompton back to Kansas voters for another referendum on the full constitution. The revised bill had to go back to the Senate, which in
turn rejected it, and then the two chambers played ball with the bill,
bouncing it back and forth for two weeks before they agreed to refer
it to a joint conference committee to break the impasse. Little Aleck
himself was appointed to the committee; thus he could really bring
his best abilities to bear.

It was plain that the Lecompton Constitution itself now had no
hope in Congress. Instead, the Georgian devised a solution that
saved face for the administration and yet met the sense of Congress
that Lecompton should go back to the Kansas voters. He drafted a
new measure resubmitting the charter to Kansans but attached what
can only be called a bribe. If Kansans approved Lecompton as written, with slavery, their new state would receive 4 million acres of the
public lands for the state to use or sell as it saw fit. If they rejected
Lecompton, then the whole issue of statehood would go in
abeyance until its population rose to 90,000, a probable delay of two
years. In effect, he changed the object of the referendum from a
choice on slavery to one on land grant. Stephens wisely kept his authorship of the bill quiet, for by then he was a lightning rod for criticism from opponents on all sides. Indeed, Rhett, though no longer

in Congress, immediately began digging for information on both Stephens and Toombs, in order to portray them as traitors to the South in the *Charleston Mercury*. Consequently, Little Aleck had the bill introduced by William English. Subsequently known as the English bill, it passed both chambers by the end of April, but not without much effort by Little Aleck in the House and considerable aid from Toombs as liaison with the president.[32]

It was a questionable victory, for in August Kansans decisively rejected Lecompton. Still, if Kansas was not to come in then as a slave state, neither could it become a free state for another couple of years. And the administration had managed to appease both those who demanded that popular sovereignty be given a fair chance untainted by corruption and the Southern extremists, who had at least the satisfaction of the referendum not being tied to slavery, thus honoring the *Dred Scott* decision that Congress could not interfere in the matter. One unequivocal benefit of the result, however, was that Kansas almost immediately ceased to be a source of provocation. Toombs looked on when Buchanan signed the English bill at the executive mansion and spoke on peace and harmony to come with this legislation. His friend Stephens was too exhausted for ceremonies, however, and simply went home. Besides the cost to his principles in the twisting and turning he had done over Kansas, he also found himself widely attacked by fellow Southern Democrats for standing by Douglas during the controversy, for the so-called Little Giant had become anathema in the South because of his opposition to Lecompton. Stephens and Toombs also finally broke with the opportunistic Cobb, now secretary of the treasury, because he had supported the administration in opposing Douglas. Kansas, it seemed, had the power to dissolve almost anything except the bond between Little Aleck and Bob Toombs. But what Kansas could not do, its underlying catalyst of slavery and sectional agitation might.

The remainder of Buchanan's administration was a shambles after Lecompton, with most of the Southern wing of the Democratic Party in open war with Douglas, who made little secret of his presidential aspirations for 1860. Formerly more moderate men became increasingly strident, even Jefferson Davis, who demanded on the floor that the South be given constitutional guarantees protecting slaves in the territories in the face of the loss of Kansas, despite the fact that he and many others had maintained previously with Toombs and Stephens that Congress had no right to legislate on slavery. No one, it seemed, had a monopoly on inconsistency. Davis and Toombs had already had another argument on the floor over the Georgian's opposition to a bill to increase the regular army, when Toombs asserted that it was easier for a black man to become white or a leopard to lose its spots than it was for any standing army "to be a friend of liberty." Toombs's continued support of Douglas was another wedge between them. For his part, Stephens decided once again, and finally this time, not to seek reelection. That, at least, sent him back to Washington for the short winter session in 1859 with some sense of relief. Politically, at least his burden would soon be taken from him. His final battle on the floor was over the admission of Oregon, which Southern extremists stoutly resisted in revenge over Kansas and because it would be a free state. Showing the best that was in him, Little Aleck rose above partisanship to give a stirring address on patriotism and the inevitability of progress. They were secure in their slave states, thanks to the Constitution. The balance of power with the free states was already gone and had been since the admission of California. There was in effect a strict set of rules for the admission of new states, and Oregon met them. There was no way for a good American in good conscience to stand in its way.[33]

It was his last appearance in the House. On March 5, 1859, he boarded a boat on the Potomac to begin the journey home. He stood on the deck looking back at the unfinished new dome on the Capitol, when a fellow passenger asked if Stephens might be thinking about returning to that building as a U.S. senator some day. No he was not, the Georgian replied. In future he was to be only a bystander. Indeed, he never expected to see Washington again, unless the sectional unrest resulted in disunion and war, and he should be forced to stand by Georgia if it seceded. In that event, he could imagine the possibility that one day he might come back, but as a prisoner of war.[34]

Toombs, too, had hoped to return home at the end of the session, not in retirement but at least to a peaceful season with his family. Instead, neither of them enjoyed much leisure, for the coming state elections sucked them into the whirl of politics at the local level, as national events could touch them even at Crawfordville and Washington. Little Aleck inadvertently made himself the center of controversy when he gave an ill-advised public address in which he tried to assure Georgians that they had nothing to fear in the Union, that simple demographics always meant they were going to lose Kansas to the free state faction, and what the South needed to do to protect itself from such losses in future was to seek a reopening of the slave trade. The more slaves they could import, the more white Southerners would become slaveowners, and then there would be substantial numbers who could emigrate to the new territories and compete more effectively for control. At least, this seemed to be the intent of his address, and there was no mistaking his call for acquisition of Cuba and perhaps northern Mexico, as further sources of new slave states. Never before had he avowed either foreign acquisition—Cuba he hoped might be purchased from Spain, but he did not say how more of Mexico might be gained except by conquest—or reopening the slave trade. It raised an immediate outcry, even from Southerners, for none but the handful of extremists like Rhett favored importing more slaves, and recent filibustering adventures in Central and South America had put foreign attempts at conquest in a bad light. Rarely did Stephens so misread the sentiment of his own people, yet clearly in his desire to find some causes for optimism and to dampen sectional apprehension in the South, he had taken a giant misstep.[35]

Toombs thankfully refrained from commenting on his friend's speech, if he in fact found anything objectionable in it, but he was more engaged in something else. Howell Cobb, with heavy backing from his odious brother Tom, was flagrantly politicking to get the Democratic nomination for himself in 1860. Identified heavily with the Buchanan administration in which he had served, the elder Cobb seconded the attacks on Douglas, helping make him increasingly unpalatable in the South, and then suggesting that as the next nomination rightfully ought to go to a Southern man, he was ready. Cobb was always an opportunist, and even many Georgians found

him unsavory, but when John Brown and a small party of abolitionists attacked the arsenal at Harpers Ferry, Virginia, in October
1859, announcing their intent to foment a massive slave uprising
that might have led to widespread mayhem and murder in the
South, millions in the slave states saw the raid as the natural out-
growth of Northern agitation against slavery and perhaps the first
act of greater outrages to come. Toombs denounced Brown and his
Republican sympathizers, Little Aleck no doubt felt similar outrage,
and the state authorities voted an appropriation to increase its militia while announcing that it was ready to unite with its sister states
to demand protection from the Washington government, or else
secede.

John Brown did more to unite the South than two generations of
secessionists, and Cobb moved to capitalize on the hysteria. In a
move to help stop the Douglas movement at the 1860 nominating
convention, he sought the backing of the forthcoming state convention for himself but did it in so clumsy a fashion that he succeeded only in splitting the state's fragile Democratic Party firmly
into Douglas and administration wings instead. Then Toombs and
Stephens found themselves the objects of repeated feelers and lures
from Cobb seeking their support. As the two most influential Douglas supporters in the state, their siding with Cobb could go a long
way to reuniting their followers on his candidacy. Stephens simply
refused to be drawn out in the matter, and Cobb was further angered when the press and the Douglas wing of the party started a
new chorus of "Stephens for president" calls, which Little Aleck also
ignored. In fact, as far away as Washington Toombs heard people
speak of his friend as the ideal electable Democrat, for it was assumed that Douglas could never get the coming nomination. As a
Douglas man, Little Aleck could expect strong support from Northern Democrats, and yet as a moderate Southerner and frequent
champion of slave states' rights, he could hope to carry the widespread moderate majority in his own region.

The problem was, for all his ambitions in the past, Stephens
genuinely did not want the nomination or the presidency and tried
repeatedly to take himself out of contention, but at the same time
he delayed doing so long enough that Cobb would not have a chance

to try to fill the vacuum. As for Toombs, true to form he allowed the
Cobbs to think that he would back Howell, supposedly even saying
that he was the only man fit for the presidency at the same time that
he privately urged Stephens to change his mind and make a run.[36]
His motive, no doubt, was simply to put off the Cobbs with flattery
and equivocal assurances while working on his friend to reconsider,
but in the end Stephens would not budge. His strategy may have
worked, for when the state convention finally met, it refused to endorse Cobb and decided to send an uncommitted delegation to the
national convention. In Washington by this time, Toombs had little
or no role in the business but was still urging Stephens to let his
name be used as a candidate. Failing that, he would support R. M. T.
Hunter or even Douglas, but increasingly he expressed the feeling
that no matter whom the Democrats nominated, he would be destined to defeat. If they could not find a candidate acceptable to both
sections, he said in December, "I see no safety for us, our property
and our firesides, except in breaking up the concern." Nor should
they wait for the North or the Republicans to commit some overt
act, for then they would be on the defensive: "We should prefer to
defend ourselves at the doorsill rather than await the attack at our
hearthstone." To Stephens he complained that in Washington, "It
is a mere Gallipago's turtle business," every faction moving slowly
in its own direction. He decided to make a speech early in the New
Year, making what he called "a clean breast" of all the evils and dangers facing the country and the remedies as he saw them. "I shall
not withhold the truth because it may be unpalatable or even dangerous to anybody or any section," he promised. Ominously, he
added in a note to his friend that even during the holiday season
in Washington, Northerners and Southerners, Democrats and Republicans, had stopped gathering together socially.[37]

It was in such a frame of mind that Toombs had made one of his
most celebrated speeches in the Senate on January 24, 1860, after
Douglas introduced a bill in reaction to the Brown raid, proposing
federal protection to each state from invasion by the citizens of another. Toombs rose to speak in support of the measure but then
went on for ninety minutes to lament that matters had gone too far
for such palliatives. Fundamental principles of the Union were

being attacked, the rights of slaveholders threatened, and even their homes were subject to assault by fanatics from the North. "The instinct of self-preservation arms society to their defense," he declared. "The bargain is broken," he said, and the Republicans had broken it. Restore respect for Southern rights and the Union could continue, but on no other terms. "It is vain, in face of these injuries, to talk of peace, fraternity, and common country," he thundered. "There is no peace; there is no fraternity; there is no common country; all of us know it." He called on Georgians to honor their pledge in the Georgia Platform to resist when their rights were assailed. "Defend yourselves!" he fairly shouted. "The enemy is at your door; wait not to meet him at your hearthstone; meet him at the doorsill, and drive him from the Temple of Liberty, or pull down its pillars and involve him in a common ruin."[38] Toombs had obviously warmed to his doorsill metaphor. Whether or not he regarded himself as the Samson to pull down those pillars, however, he did not say, not yet.

Not since 1850 had Toombs spoken so threateningly, and many observers missed in all the bellicose rhetoric his reaffirmed promise to labor as hard as anyone to find a way to save the Union. Indeed, his speech came in support of Douglas's conciliatory proposition, though few could overlook his forthright implication that a Republican victory in the coming election would be cause sufficient for secession. Stephens applauded his friend, thinking he had followed exactly the right course between defending Southern rights and staying loyal to the Constitution and the spirit of the Union as originally framed. Toombs had his critics, too, from those who remembered that only a few months before he had said the state of the nation was not so bad as to require extreme action—a statement made before the Brown raid changed forever the political landscape—to others who said that if the dangers before them were so grave, then it was foolishness to wait until a Republican victory in November to act.[39]

As if to punctuate the inability of anyone to soothe the sectional nightmare, Davis offered resolutions asserting that no legislature, territorial or congressional, could decide on slavery in the territories. Rather, those legislatures should be bound to protect slave property in the territories. Only upon becoming a state could a people determine the final issue. It was an administration sellout to the more extreme Southern position, a final blow to Douglas by Buchanan, and a red flag to the North. Predictably, it aroused a furor, and true to his promise to strive for the Union, Toombs broke Southern ranks by opposing the measure—perhaps taking a little pleasure in thwarting the priggish Davis in the offing. The Georgian knew it was folly to try to get Congress to pass a slave code such as that proposed and that it would only drive Northern Democrats from the party. Declaring the "naked folly" of such a course, he fought it unsuccessfully, for a party caucus finally adopted a variant of the resolutions, though several Southerners, including Toombs, boycotted the meeting.[40]

"We are all at sea here about politics," Toombs thus groaned in March. "It is sad to see the divisions in the South, especially those in the Democratic party to which the South must mainly look for aid in her present emergency." He thought his section was entitled to the party presidential nominee this time around and could think of half a dozen men whom he thought had a chance to unify the Southern vote, if only the potential candidates could get along among themselves. He did not say who they were, but undoubtedly his old schoolmate and friend Senator Hunter of Virginia came to mind, and certainly Stephens, who was still trying to halt the talk of a candidacy. And undoubtedly Toombs considered himself suitable. The only acceptable candidate in the North was Douglas, yet Toombs knew that Southern enmity toward popular sovereignty and ire among Northern administration Democrats would combine to beat the Little Giant if he were nominated. As a result, the Georgian gloomily concluded, "I do not think we have any chance or rather a very poor one for the next election." Added to that, he was convinced that Yankee abolition fanatics would not stop their spread of influence until they took over the government. It must lead to a "smash up," as he called it, and warned friends that "we should begin to set our house in order to meet the approaching difficulties." It was his doorsill argument again, and there was no mistaking his meaning.[41]

The turmoil came to a head in the Democratic convention in

Charleston in April, and the meeting proved to be a shambles. The slave states managed to control the majority report for a platform, but Douglas's supporters took control of the debate and the vote and succeeded in passing their own platform instead. At that, six slave states walked out and assembled on their own, followed the next day by Georgia, and the convention broke up without a nominee. When it reassembled in Baltimore in June, the convention fell apart again over competing delegations from several slave states that sent groups committed to the Douglas platform and candidacy and other delegations backing the original Southern rights platform. Predictably, the anti-Douglas forces bolted again. In their wake the remainder nominated Douglas; the bolters assembled at Richmond and chose John C. Breckinridge of Kentucky.

Toombs and Stephens watched these fiascoes from afar, yet an outcome most observers would not have expected was in the offing as a result of the turmoil. Little Aleck deplored it all and still clung to the hope of some accommodation. Stephens held fixedly to the principal of nonintervention by Congress, for that was still the law of the land, and in it was all the protection the South could need. By demanding something more aggressive, by calling for positive congressional guarantees and protection in a slave code, the slave states themselves would be authoring the ruin of the Union by claiming what their Northern compatriots in the party could never accept. "There is a tendency everywhere, not only at the North, but at the South, to strife, dissension, disorder, and anarchy," he declared after the Charleston breakup. What was about to happen to the country was not about insoluble political differences but about extremism, fanaticism even, and the petty ambitions of small men with "no loyalty to principle, no attachment to truth for truth's sake." The Rhetts and Yanceys of the section were putting the South on the road to disaster simply to serve their own selfish ends, he complained, and he was largely correct.[42]

In a break with his friend, Toombs saw in the turbulence the realization of his predictions of the last few months. Almost overnight after the Charleston breakup, he abandoned not only hope for compromise but also his stated and apparently sincere intention to work for peaceful accommodation. Indeed, he had advised the Georgia delegates at Charleston to walk out, having clearly stepped over the line even before the convention assembled. Just the day after Stephens appealed to Georgians in an open letter asserting they still had no cause to look to disunion, Toombs wrote his own open letter. "Look to the preservation of your rights," he warned. The Union was the greatest danger facing the slave states, and he forthrightly repudiated his long-held adherence to nonintervention, since he had decided to join those who demanded that Congress protect slavery in the territories. He even wrote to Stephens to inform him that "I do not concur with you as to the extent of our obligation to maintain *non-intervention.*" It was virtually the first time in a quarter-century of friendship that either had openly notified the other of political disagreement, but then Toombs had always been more changeable than his friend.[43]

Unfortunately, they disagreed frequently thereafter, not only on the degree of cause for Southern resistance but also on the action to be taken, Toombs's instinct for overstatement and confrontation clashing increasingly with Stephens's measured and consistent attachment to the Union.[44] Inevitably, difference led to distance. Indeed, before the nominations of the Baltimore and Richmond meetings emerged, Toombs reversed his own past course and for the first time actively discouraged talk of his friend as a candidate, claiming that Stephens's health was so bad that a campaign would kill him.[45] Clearly, however, the real reason was that their growing differences convinced Toombs that his closest friend was no longer a suitable candidate for the protection of Southern rights. Once the groundswell of emotion, frustration, paranoia, and his own hyperbolic nature took sway, Toombs seemingly propelled himself toward the secessionist camp. Sadly, it also opened a gulf between these two Georgians. If two men who had loved each other with a bond that excited the admiration of their friends and the enmity of their enemies could no longer hold together their friendship, despite all they had done in the past twenty-five years, how could the Union possibly stay together when the old bonds were breaking under the weight of suspicion, acrimony, and hate?

4

Founding Fathers

They were together again for the ride to Montgomery, to the great relief of each and to the chagrin of some of their enemies like Thomas Cobb. Stephens to the last minute did not want to leave home. He distrusted too many people in the new movement and feared too much its outcome. An old Whig could not change his spots overnight. Even an improvement in his health—or more likely a bettering in his own usually gloomy assessment of his health—did not help. Just the day before he had told a friend, "My word for it, this country is in a great deal worse condition than the people are at all aware of." It probably did not improve his mood when he saw who was already on that train. Most of the South Carolinians were there, including the prejudiced eccentric Thomas Withers; James Chesnut, still an unknown quantity; and even an obscure Florida delegate whose presence Stephens never even noticed. It did not augur well for the new confederation-to-be when poltroons and nonentities were to be its founding fathers. Stephens feared even more some of the individuals who were already in Montgomery, especially Rhett of South Carolina, so anxious to dominate the proceedings and make the new nation his own monument that he had rushed to arrive ahead of the others. "They are selfish, ambitious, and unscrupulous," Stephens grumbled. [1]

Toombs, always more affable and easygoing, preferred to regale his fellow passengers with stories and bon mots during the ride rather than indulge in Little Aleck's foreboding. But then that was in his nature. Even his deep concern for his only surviving child, Sallie DuBose, many months pregnant and very ill at home, could not dampen his spirits entirely. Stephens was a man who lived life inside himself. Toombs lived it on the outside, and larger than life if he could. If he felt any misgivings, he kept them to himself. But then he had little cause for apprehension. He had embraced secession heartily, even when it led to the still-healing rift with Stephens. This train was carrying them to a new Southern destiny. Moreover, he had not ignored the predictions of those who foresaw a special destiny for Bob Toombs in Montgomery. Though no one knew just how coming events would unfold, whether the delegates would consult and then return with recommendations to their conventions and legislatures for the formation of a new confederacy, or whether the delegates would themselves seize the initiative and frame a government, as Stephens felt they must, it was bound to be based on the Constitution they were leaving behind. That meant a congress and a president. Georgia was sending the largest delegation to Montgomery, and Georgia was sending the only statesmen of truly national stature. When the delegates chose their president, whether at the outset or later, many, including Stephens, expected the office to go to Toombs, an expectation that he shared himself. What cause, then, for gloom?

The president-to-be and Little Aleck passed much of the trip with the Chesnuts, James and his diarist wife Mary, who were more pleasant and congenial company than Tom Cobb or Francis Bartow, when he boarded the next morning. Though Toombs held forth with his usual charm, inevitably most of their conversation turned on the days ahead. Both friends stood in agreement that the delegates had to act immediately. They must not just talk in Montgomery. They must not stop, as many suggested, at drafting a constitution and then sending it back to their states for debate and amendment and ratification. That could take months, and in the crisis time was everything. They must go beyond the consultative authority granted them by the state legislatures and constitute themselves a provisional congress for some definite period like a year, actually frame a new government under a provisional constitution, establish and man the necessary executive departments, choose a president and vice president, and set the new nation in motion at once, including raising an army for defense. With that under way, they could then act more deliberately in framing a more perfect permanent constitution and refining their structure before the provisional government should expire and the regular one take office.[2]

Undoubtedly Toombs's ears pricked up when Chesnut turned the talk to the presidency and told them that the South Carolina delegation was determined not to put forward anyone from its own ranks but that they looked to Georgia to make a nomination. Any candidate must be a moderate, not too extreme a secessionist, which eliminated the fire-eaters like Robert Rhett of Charleston or Montgomery's own William L. Yancey, and not too reluctant a former Unionist, which in Stephens's mind—though he did not say so—eliminated himself. Toombs was the perfect fit, moderate enough not to frighten away the large Unionist element in the seceding states, yet not so moderate that the ardent secessionists could not stand with him. Few other Southern leaders of high stature filled that same requirement, except for Jefferson Davis of Mississippi, and perhaps Charles Conrad of Louisiana, but even Conrad was not well known outside his own state. Some might think Howell Cobb a possibility, too, but for many he had changed his political coat too often, and too expediently, to be trusted. At one point, when Toombs was distracted in conversation with others, Little Aleck straightforwardly proposed his friend to Chesnut as the proper nominee, at the same time taking himself entirely out of consideration, or so he thought.[3]

Fate, and the miserable condition of the West Point & Montgomery Railroad, almost robbed the convention of the choice of either Georgian. They had changed trains at West Point, Georgia, and were lumbering through central Alabama on the morning of February 3 when half an hour before noon, and just three miles from Montgomery, the train jumped the track at more than twenty miles an hour. Ordinarily the two passenger cars would have been immediately behind the engine and tender, but for some reason this day only one was there; the other, with Stephens and Toombs, rode at the rear of the train behind the two baggage cars. Every car but the last one left the track. Miraculously, among the debris of baggage and chickens and stunned passengers from the front car, there were no fatalities or serious injuries. Yet some could not help but wonder what might have happened in the days ahead if both passenger cars had been at the front, if Toombs's and Stephens's car had left the track. Had they been killed, or even incapacitated, what might have been the outcome of the Montgomery convention?[4]

When they reached Montgomery two hours late, the Georgians went to the Exchange Hotel, where most of the arriving delegates would board. Toombs was content to take a room there, though he would have to share with others, but in keeping with his private nature, Little Aleck had already arranged to rent a private suite in a nearby boarding house, with his own parlor and fireplace and a bedroom. No sooner was he unpacked, however, than he walked back to the Exchange, which had already become what one newspaperman called a "conversational parliament." With the convention set to begin the next day, the business of politics was already well begun in the Exchange bar. Over juleps and cigars the delegates began to frame their new nation.

Soon it became evident that some delegations came with their own prior agenda. Mississippi wanted the convention to adopt the U.S. Constitution, commission all the representatives that the seceded states had withdrawn from Congress in Washington immediately to constitute their new congress, select Jefferson Davis for president, and then go home. Louisiana, on the other hand, suggested that they frame a provisional constitution and government, elect a president, and then work out a permanent constitution and present it to the several state conventions to ratify or reject, but without doing anything to put a government in immediate operation, for the convention itself should then dissolve and go home.

So far as Toombs and Stephens were concerned, neither approach addressed the immediate need for action, and significantly, a number of these delegates from other states came with special letters of introduction to Little Aleck in particular, tacit recognition that his reputation for reason and intellect already predisposed some men to seek his counsel and perhaps even to defer to his judgment.[5] Perhaps, too, some knew—or expected—that the Georgians would come with their own proposal for organization. Being the powerhouse delegation—their ten delegates made up fully one-fifth of the convention—and with Georgia geographically the vital bridging state between the Atlantic seaboard states and the Deep South, it was inevitable that everyone would have to take account of the Georgians' views. And Stephens and Toombs knew that better than anyone; thus they had come with their own plan, soon called the "Georgia project." As the lobby conversation unfolded, they proposed the most comprehensive and immediately practical plan, and the most dynamic. The convention that met the next day must go far beyond its constituted authority and seize power, declare itself the provisional congress, frame its provisional constitution, and establish the governmental departments itself, choose a president and vice president, and commence operation as a new nation immediately.

The boldness of the plan was breathtaking. The delegates had no elective or appointive power to do this. They would be acting entirely on their own initiative, and at the risk that their states—especially the skittish Georgia and Alabama—might repudiate what they did. They would raise taxes, start an army and a navy, frame provisional and permanent constitutions, and establish foreign relations, all without a jot of lawful authority. They would choose and install in power a president for whom not one Southern citizen other than themselves would have had an opportunity to vote. In seeking to redress the shortcomings of democracy they had suffered in the Union, they would establish and operate for a brief period the most undemocratically conceived ruling body ever seen on the continent. Not one of the Georgians took credit for the plan. Neither of the Cobbs, Howell or Thomas, had the courage for such a leap. Bartow had not the sense. There were others in the delegation whose initial views and characters are not sufficiently well understood to determine if the plan originated with them. But its boldness and daring, almost to foolhardiness, was certainly redolent of Toombs.

He had a reputation for rashness, but those who knew him well knew also that this was largely conversational bluster. "What I say, I mean," he would boast, though even he had to admit that he often gave way to exaggeration and intemperance in his speech. Yet his associates also knew that there was a difference between what he said and what he did. "Notwithstanding all he may say in the highway, he is the wisest and safest man in counsel," fellow Georgia delegate Martin Crawford declared. Toombs was the man, he said, "when anything is to be done."[6] Toombs could grasp a great problem and conceive a solution to match, as he had done so many times before. In the current emergency, he could see that the greatest risk was really the least. Time worked against them. The more they delayed, the more time the conservative and wavering elements they all feared in their states would have to try to prevent any assertive action. A cold iron would not burn; the South had learned that repeatedly since the days of Nullification. The iron was hot and they must strike. Nor would he have been Toombs if he did not take counsel of his own ambitions and realize that boldness favored his own prospects for leadership. He may already have been taking it for an accomplished certainty that he soon would be a president. Not bad for a man once expelled from college.

His eloquent and able advocacy of the Georgia plan suggested that there was some of Little Aleck in the proposal as well, certainly in encouragement to Toombs if not in actual authorship. One who came so reluctantly to secession in the first place would hardly seem a likely candidate for this sort of revolutionary seizure of power, for in the plan the Georgians proposed the slave states would have accomplished their independence from one central federation only to find themselves committed—without authority—to another. Yet there was nothing out of character in Little Aleck's so readily and earnestly endorsing such a scheme. He may have resisted secession to the last moment in Georgia, but once it came he embraced his state's new destiny apparently without reservation, despite accusations from some doubters that he was and always would remain a reconstructionist, secretly dedicated to bringing the seceded states back into the Union in return for some constitutional guarantees from Washington that would meet their demands on protection of slavery in the territories. Indeed, Stephens never escaped those accusations, especially from the rabid fire-eaters like Rhett. Yet nothing in the Georgian's actions or utterances gainsays his absolute dedication to the success of the new experiment in democracy, and he was too intelligent not to see at once, though from a different vantage, the same great truth recognized by Toombs and others. They must act boldly and immediately. Half-hearted or irresolute measures must doom them just as much as delay. That Stephens was committed to the Georgia plan is above question, for it was he himself who moved that his state convention endorse it before the delegation left for Montgomery.

Thus, as the delegates smoked and drank and argued in the Exchange, the two Georgians were united, and most of their delegation with them. Fortunately, their plan was close enough to the Mississippi and Louisiana proposals that the majority of delegates from those states were willing to be persuaded. Some of the Alabamians, too, willingly came over, especially from fear that any delay would allow time for their opponents in the Unionist northern part of the state to mount a serious opposition. Only South Carolina balked, and that was chiefly Rhett, whose own delegation soon rejected his objections and came over. Florida, though then and thereafter inclined to follow Rhett, had but a single delegate present yet and thus was little better than a cipher. By the evening of February 3 it was decided. When they walked up Market Street the next day and convened in the senate chamber of the Alabama statehouse, they immediately formed themselves into a congress, completing two revolutions within as many months.

The dominance of the Georgians seemed beyond challenge. There was no serious question from anyone when they proposed Howell Cobb be selected to chair the convention and, when they assumed their role as a congress, that he be elected its president. After all, he had been Speaker of the House of Representatives some years before, a governor of Georgia, and recently secretary of the treasury. As such, he had held the highest national offices of any of them present, and that alone dictated that he deserved the honor of presiding over their body, though in their provisional and uni-cameral body, he had little real power. Even his enemies like Toombs and Stephens could afford to accord him that little honor. Besides, some observers believed that doing so would only further remove Cobb from any consideration for an office of real power, their new presidency.

It had been a long day, yet before breaking up to return to the bar or to try to coax some sleep from the symphony of snores and coughs echoing in the overcrowded bedrooms of the Exchange, the delegates made more decisions, planning in advance the resolutions to be introduced the next day, and who was to make them. They could not risk spontaneity; every move they made would be publicly scrutinized, and thus success depended upon the appearance of a smooth and united group of delegates welded to a single purpose. The problem was, as Stephens was the first to recognize, that many of these delegates had never sat in a congress or even a legislature before. Moreover, some of the state delegations came bound by their conventions to vote not as individuals but as a single state unit. That presented insuperable parliamentary problems, while the in-experience of some members only promised further confusion on rules of order. Little Aleck approached Cobb before they broke up and proposed that their first duty the next morning was to appoint a committee to draft rules of order to govern their deliberations. Cobb instantly agreed. Stephens then said he preferred not to be appointed to such a committee, perhaps fearing any appearance of self-interest since the committee had been his own idea, but just as likely merely showing one more example of that assumed air of dif-fidence that he so often used to cloak his genuine ambitions. Cobb heard the request, but made no comment.[7]

Little Aleck walked back to his boarding house that night for a late supper, and so he did not hear the continuing drink-fueled speculation at the Exchange bar over whom they should choose for their president. It ranged wide at times, but most of the speculation centered on Davis and Toombs, and to a lesser extent on Howell Cobb and Stephens himself. No doubt Toombs took some part him-self, his conversation more animated and dynamic the more he drank; and the more he heard assurances from delegates of their support for him, the more seriously he took his chances. Indeed, as more and more delegates said they looked to Georgia for their president, the more it became apparent to him that he would be himself the only Georgian generally acceptable. Within a few hours, if not already, he regarded the office as his for the asking.

Little Aleck spent a quiet night by contrast, and when he awoke early on February 4 to a brisk fire warming his room against the sub-freezing temperature outside, he followed his ancient habit of writing letters first, while his servant Pierce kept the fireplace glowing. When he walked up Market for the opening gavel, he wore the huge woolen overcoat that always seemed to enshroud him like a cocoon, and once he reached the second floor senate chamber he would still have felt a chill in the ill-heated statehouse. But the atmosphere was certainly ablaze with anticipation, with journalists and lobbyists and citizens from all across the South there to witness the proceedings. Old friends introduced themselves to Stephens anew, especially delegates just arrived that morning. Toombs, always surrounded by a crowd, held forth in booming tones as he shook hands and slapped backs. For both the Georgians, it was all too reminiscent of the opening of another congress in another capital.

From the first gavel everything went according to plan. The delegates elected Cobb unanimously to preside over them, Toombs helped elect a permanent secretary, and then Stephens arose for the first time to make good on his suggestion of the night before. He moved that Cobb appoint a committee to draft rules of conduct for them, and the motion carried, but then Cobb appointed Stephens himself to chair the committee. His motive in doing so is obscure. There was little affection between the two. Perhaps Cobb simply enjoyed having the power to deny Little Aleck's request. But then he might well have considered that having a Georgian in charge of producing their rules would give their delegation just that much more influence over the management of the congress. Whatever the case, Stephens could hardly object, and once Cobb appointed the committee, the meeting adjourned, pending presentation of a report from the rules committee.[8]

Despite his earlier request not to serve on the committee, Stephens cannot have been entirely surprised, for he actually came to Montgomery armed with a copy of a parliamentary manual written by Thomas Jefferson, and with the procedures of the U.S. Congress permanently imprinted on his memory. Before leaving the statehouse he met briefly with those composing his committee and appointed a time to meet in deliberation, then returned to his boarding house and immediately set about drafting a working paper to provide a starting point for their discussion. By the time his committee was shown into his parlor later that afternoon, he had finished a set of thirty-three basic rules of order that, with only a few emendations, would govern the future deliberations, not only of this provisional congress but also of the permanent one that followed.

Recognizing the sensitivity of many Southerners who feared the tyranny of the majority that had already in the past overridden the rights of the states, he took into account the fact that some state conventions had instructed their delegates to vote as a unit. He then proposed that all delegations should do so. Although there were thirty-seven delegates from six states present at the moment, Little Aleck provided that all votes in the new congress should be by state. Thus Florida's little voice, with only three delegates, would be just as strong as Georgia with its ten. Moreover, to ensure that in such a system the smaller states could not tyrannize the larger ones by taking advantage of such a procedure, he also proposed that only legislation with an unequivocal majority should pass. All ties would result in defeat of a measure, making it virtually impossible for anything to pass without at least one or two of the larger states being in favor. If the delegates in any delegation could not produce a majority to determine their state's vote, then they could cast no vote. And in a final blow at possible majority excess, as well as in the practical interest of seeing that legislation could be enacted despite the absenteeism that always plagued such bodies, he proposed that even a single member of a delegation could constitute a quorum for voting purposes. Of course, that did the raise the possibility of the constitutional absurdity of just four men, one from each of four delegations, being able to determine their state's votes and thus to pass or defeat legislation against the opposition of full united delegations numbering as many as eighteen delegates from the two remaining states. He could hardly suspect then that this very provision would later play a decisive role in one of the major decisions to be made by this congress, one that would impact the entire history of the new nation they were founding. Yet it was the natural logical extension—or illogical absurdity—of the South's thirty-year fight against the tyranny of simple majority rule.

Little Aleck proceeded to the daily conduct of the congress, modeling it largely on that of the U.S. House of Representatives, with a daily reading of the previous day's journal, the handling of unfinished business on the calendar, a call of the states for any new business and the presentation of memorials for relief of their constituents, reports from the standing and special committees, and then the scheduled business for the day. In debate, he limited each delegate to speaking twice on a measure; the delegate was to stand beside his desk and be seated when finished while all others were to observe a respectful and decorous silence. He wanted none of the uproar and confusion that so often attended and impeded the Washington Congress, a nice idea in concept, but one that simply ignored the nature of politicians. Stephens even struck a blow at a parliamentary device he had always disliked in Congress, the so-called previous question. It only served to close off debate and require a vote on all pending amendments to a measure, followed by a vote on the measure as a whole. It was used too often to stifle free views and to kill a measure rather than to allow a fully informed decision. In his rules he eliminated the offending tactic altogether. In its place he proposed simply calling the question, which provided only for a vote on any motion currently on the floor, and without preventing any further amendment. Cobb was to enforce the rules and settle points of order, and there would be no appeal from his rulings.

In keeping with his concern for decorum, Stephens even included a rule that members were never to use profane or intemperate language. Bills were to receive three readings before coming to a vote, with amendments allowed only on the second and third readings. Concerned as they all were with the appearance their deliberations might present to the outside world—and more especially to those wavering sections of their own new confederation-to-be—

he empowered Cobb to determine when and where journalists were to be allowed into the hall. More important still, he provided means by which they could clear the hall at once and go into secret session. Stephens knew all too well how much division and disagreement there was in this body, and how crippling it would be to their cause for their enemies foreign and domestic to be able to seize upon it. They must keep their internal arguments and dissent to themselves if they were to present a united front. Secrecy was the only means to accomplish that, and to add further force to this he added a rule providing for expulsion from congress of any member who divulged to the outside world anything that transpired when they were in secret session.[9]

When the rest of his committee arrived that evening, Little Aleck presented them with something of a fait accompli. Although some members proposed minor changes, and there was some general discussion on many of his points, his rules mainly passed without objection when they took a committee vote. That done, Stephens went out in the chilly night air to a local printer and paid to have type set and fifty copies run off to distribute to the congress the next morning. When the time came to assemble on February 5, Little Aleck was there early and placed on each delegate's desk a copy of "Government of this Congress, Rules for the government of this Congress."[10]

The rules were the first order of business when Cobb called the delegates to order, and they passed them almost without comment. Little Aleck himself sat silent during the brief debate, and those watching him—for his authorship of the rules was hardly a secret— wondered at a man so small he seemed more a boy but for his wrinkled and sagging face and the clothing that hung limp from his bony body. "What in the name of wonder did they send such a man here for?" a journalist noted on his pad. "Where did he come from?" But then after the passage Stephens rose. "We are a Congress," he declared, the first in the body to call them such on the floor, and those looking on found wonder changing to awe. This little giant, declared one witness, was "every inch a man."[11]

Whether by accident or design, Stephens had assumed a de facto position of leadership in the body. His part in forming and supporting to victory the Georgia project, and his domination of their rules, gave him a moral power that no doubt surprised some who did not know him and frightened others like Rhett and Thomas Cobb who intensely distrusted anyone who had come to secession reluctantly. But this reaction did not stop the Georgian from riding the wave of his momentum. He proposed that the delegates meet thereafter at noon each day, and he, too, proposed that all subsequent references in debate to their body should be to "the Congress" and not to the "convention." Though he may have resisted coming to this pass, having arrived, he appeared to embrace the moment as unreservedly as any of them. When they passed a resolution calling for a committee of two from each state to frame a provisional constitution to put the government in operation, Georgia naturally put forward Stephens.[12]

It was perhaps significant that the other Georgia member on the committee was not Toombs, but Eugenius Nisbet. Though it was yet in the early days, Toombs had been uncharacteristically quiet in the Congress and apparently after hours as well. The fact that he had higher expectations no doubt accounted for his not thrusting himself forward in the chamber, and some of his fellow delegates' hopes for him equally accounted for their failure to name him to the constitutional committee. They must not be seen to attempt too much dominance, and since they continued to get reports that most of the other states expected to support whatever presidential nominee Georgia should put forward, they would do well to keep Toombs available and out of any potentially contentious or acrimonious debate such as could be expected in framing their organic law.

The constitutional committee convened for its first meeting that evening at six o'clock, and significantly they met in Stephens's parlor at Elizabeth Cleveland's boarding house. The venue no doubt reflected in part the likelihood that they would not find a quiet or secure spot at the Exchange, but there was also no denying that in gathering at Little Aleck's hearth, it represented a tacit admission of leadership for the Georgian, even though Christopher G. Memminger of South Carolina had been appointed to the chair. Even had it not, Stephens from the first asserted a leadership both in their discussion and in the subsequent drafting.

They wrestled for six hours that first night, Stephens hearing anew all the arguments over what sort of confederation they ought to be, what powers they should assume, if any, and whether or not they should act preemptively or merely frame suggestions to be acted upon by their conventions and legislatures at home. Once again some members argued that they had not the authority to make themselves a congress or to draft anything, but Stephens fought persistently and ultimately won the point that they had to act immediately and decisively or they were lost. Joined by Nisbet and by both the Alabama members, and soon by the Mississippians, Stephens's view finally prevailed.

It was with some difficulty that they got past that and settled down to the work with which they were charged. Virtually all agreed with Stephens that they should take as their model the U.S. Constitution. After all, most Southerners never had a problem with that document, only with what was being done under it by the growing Northern majority. Hanging their provisional charter on that established frame would greatly simplify their work, for they need not assemble an entirely new constitution but only reform those parts of the existing one that they found objectionable.

To save time, and recognizing that this was a provisional constitution that would last only for a year until being replaced by a permanent one framed with less haste and more deliberation, Stephens suggested that they make the whole document simply a long list and include within it every section without reference to organization. Even that would prove a taxing chore. "I shall wear myself out here," Little Aleck worried at the end of the first session, and he had seen more than enough to fear the divisions within the group. He frankly distrusted many of the delegates, especially the extremists like Rhett and Tom Cobb. Ambition and selfishness in such men posed an even greater hazard than the North at the moment, though he anticipated the inevitability of a clash there, too. One aspect he seemed not to anticipate was the effect of his own ambition on himself and the new nation in the days ahead. More than most of them, Little Aleck possessed a strong self-awareness, yet even his stopped short of fully appreciating how much of himself he was going to try to insert into their experiment, and just how he would react when disappointed.[13]

Stephens's committee—and everyone perceived it as his committee—met again the next morning, then again after the brief noon session and long into the night. He took the measure of his colleagues, and they of him. Rhett's cousin Robert Barnwell of South Carolina found that he liked Little Aleck better than any of the rest, a man of candor and courage in spite of what Barnwell perceived as a willingness to deal and compromise like a politician instead of standing immobile on policy, as should a true statesman.[14] They settled on six articles for their document and took as much verbatim from the U.S. Constitution as they could. They eliminated much that was not immediately necessary and that could wait for their permanent charter. Meanwhile, much of what they added came from Stephens himself.

He, like Toombs, admired the parliamentary system of the British, in which cabinet positions were filled by appointment from members of the House of Commons. Whether it was Little Aleck's idea, or whether he was acting on his friend's suggestion, he managed to eliminate the existing prohibition on members of Congress simultaneously holding cabinet portfolios. From the British system, too, Stephens borrowed a solution to the generation-old Southern complaint against Congress's appropriating money from the Treasury to encourage particular industries or to fund internal improvements that seemed always to favor Northern interests at Southern expense. He placed, with virtually unanimous support, a statement in their document that Congress should not have the power to initiate any appropriations whatever, except those for its own expenses. All other appropriations must come from the executive through one of his cabinet ministers.[15]

Undoubtedly, Stephens supported a continuation of the abolition of the foreign slave trade, for that was a position shared by all but the extremists like Rhett. With a slave population already approaching 4 million, the South did not need the trade, nor did they need the opprobrium that the other nations of the world attached to it. They would have enough to deal with in their foreign relations in the resistance of European nations to the very existence of slavery itself. They did, however, insert a powerful fugitive slave law. Some other issues, such as the manner of admitting new states, they glossed over, leaving those, too, for the permanent document to come.

It was almost midnight on February 6 when the meeting finally adjourned, but they had finished their task, and Little Aleck once more bundled up in his voluminous coat and walked to the office of the *Montgomery Advertiser* to awaken the printers and put them to work setting the type and printing copies for debate the next day. When George Shorter began pulling the type from their cubicles in his composing room, he became the first person outside the committee itself to discover that they had decided not to address a means of electing a president and vice president, and for logical reasons. The Congress already intended to choose a president as soon as this constitution was adopted, but that officer, like this document, would be only provisional, to be replaced within a year by a regularly elected chief executive chosen by means specified in the permanent constitution. Given the circumstances, for the moment they did not need to bother about that because it was already decided informally that their provisional president would be chosen by a majority vote of the states represented in Montgomery.

What Stephens and his committee, and Shorter as he set his type, could not know was that elsewhere in the city the process of choosing that president was already under way, in circumstances and by means that none of them would have expected. Every night the lions of Montgomery society gave lavish dinner parties for the assembled delegates and other dignitaries who filled their city, and few delegates declined an invitation. Almost at once the citizens formed their opinions about the characteristics of the different delegations, and Georgia became known quickly as "the most boisterous." It was an adjective that could hardly apply to the diminutive and retiring Stephens, but it fit Toombs like a second skin, and most likely he more than any other was responsible for the impression. The last few evenings, while Little Aleck wrestled with the constitutional committee, Toombs had taken a stand in the Exchange bar and all but held court, regaling journalists and other delegates from his bottomless fund of anecdotes and amusing stories. "What a jolly rotund celebrity Toombs is," one newsman declared of the man he called the "Bibacious Georgian."[16]

Of course, his fellow delegates were assessing Toombs all the while, considering him as one of the front-runners for their soon-to-be-filled provisional presidency, and the Georgian himself knew full well that he was being judged. Thus he devoted extra effort to his famous conviviality, his eloquent political pronouncements, and his famous bon mots. He wanted the presidency and expected it, not least because whoever should be chosen for the provisional office could well anticipate succeeding himself under the permanent charter. The groundswell in his favor had been growing, though Mississippi was pushing hard for Davis. The outcome might depend upon whom Georgia chose to nominate, but his own delegation was so secure in the knowledge that the others would accept any nominee they put forward that they had not yet themselves met to consider the matter. Besides, with Stephens and Nisbet virtually closeted all day on the constitutional committee, there was as yet no real opportunity for them to caucus.

Certainly there was division and dissent among the ten Georgians. The two Cobbs detested Toombs, as did Bartow, and Tom Cobb at least had hopes of electing his brother. The problem was, however, that everyone else on the delegation distrusted Howell and would never have agreed to nominate him. That left only Toombs and perhaps Stephens as acceptable alternatives, and Little Aleck had already protested, whether sincerely or not, that he was unsuitable and did not want the post. Thus simple logic dictated that if Georgia were to achieve a majority vote for any nominee when it caucused, it could only be for Toombs, who could easily grab the laurel despite the minority opposition of Bartow and the Cobbs. Without having said so—for it would be intemperate and unwise—Toombs himself took this for granted by the evening of February 6, and so did Stephens. Indeed, their near-complacence in the matter also helped account for the failure to try to bring their delegation together in caucus.[17]

Little Aleck and his committee, as was their custom, had taken a break for dinner in their deliberations that last evening, and he went with Toombs and others to dine. What he saw worried him. Every night since arriving in Montgomery, Stephens had seen his friend enjoy rather more liquid conviviality than was wise. However aware his friends were of Toombs's inability to handle much alcohol, Toombs himself rarely seemed to take it seriously, or else was so easily swept up by a drink or two that he lost the ability to reflect on his behavior. Little Aleck lamented that he had seen Toombs too "mellow" for three nights running and may well have been concerned when he returned to his committee meeting after dinner. Toombs said he was going to a party being given by one of the South Carolina delegates; Stephens watched his friend depart the table "tighter than I ever saw him—too tight for his character & reputation by far."[18]

When Toombs arrived at the party, he found a good number of the delegates present, and with them a flowing punch bowl. Given the head start he had from dinner, and his innate weakness, he soon made a fool of himself. The other delegates found him "flighty," irrational, perhaps even "monomaniacal," as Stephens had seen him on other similar occasions. Tom Cobb, though hardly objective about him, was probably being honest when he spoke of Toombs as being "pretty high from wine" on some occasions in Montgomery, and this was one of those times.[19] The effect was bound to be disastrous for his hopes, especially considering that some of these men had seen him slightly inebriated on previous evenings. Those who had not still must have heard stories of the Georgian's behavior. His performance demanded that they reassess their willingness to accept him as provisional president, should Georgia nominate him, and even among the embarrassed fellow Georgians who favored his nomination, his behavior called for a serious reconsideration. As president, as commander in chief, as chief diplomat in their efforts to take a dignified place among the nations of the world, the Toombs they saw at Chesnut's party would be an embarrassment, a humiliation. By the time they left the party, a number of the shocked delegates had already changed their thinking. Happily his friend Little Aleck was not there to see it, but he heard about it soon enough. "I think that evenings exhibition settled the Presidency," he lamented. Toombs had drunk himself out of the office.[20]

Toombs himself awoke the next morning blissfully unaware of
the dramatic turn of events he had set in motion the night before.
Like the rest, he appeared at the statehouse just before noon, ready
to deal with the proposed new provisional constitution, which was
still being printed and would not arrive for hours. Indeed, to open
the debate, Memminger rose and read it to the Congress from a
handwritten draft, and then little Aleck moved that they postpone
debate until the printed version arrived so they would each have a
copy, which would not be until the evening. With no alternative,
they simply adjourned until the next day, February 8. What else
could they do but wait?

One matter they could address was the suddenly altered dynamics of the coming presidential election. Even while Toombs remained unaware of his virtual elimination, leaders among the delegations began casting about for an acceptable substitute, one not
too radical and not too conservative, and possibly to his own surprise, and possibly to his chagrin, Little Aleck found their gaze suddenly turned toward him. In fact, some of the delegates had been
thinking of Little Aleck from the start, the Louisianans having been
advised by their former governor that Stephens was the best man.
If Georgia was to have the presidency—which most still took for
granted—the odiousness of Howell Cobb and the behavior of
Toombs left only one alternative, and better yet, Stephens almost
exactly fit the requirements for a unifying centrist. The radicals like
Rhett would deplore him, of course, but Rhett deplored everyone
but himself. The great mass of Southerners were moderates, many
of them still clinging to a hope for reconciliation and reunion with
guarantees of Southern rights. Little Aleck fit their temperament.
Moreover, he had been one of the two most distinguished and influential Georgians in Washington for nearly a generation, a man
of national reputation in an era when there were too few Southern
statesmen whose stature extended even throughout their own region. Within hours of Toombs's misstep, rumors hit the streets that
Georgia, Mississippi, and even South Carolina (excluding Rhett, of
course) might smile on a Stephens candidacy.[21]

The matter went in abeyance for several hours the next day when
the convention assembled to hear the report of Little Aleck's com-

mittee. Memminger read it to them, but then Stephens surprised them with a motion to postpone debate until the next day, since there had not been time to get the document printed. Unspoken was the possibility that he wanted that extra day for his committee members and others to cajole some few recalcitrants like Rhett. Far more important than principle at this point was unity, or at least a semblance of unanimity, before the public at large; and if radicals started picking the proposed temporary constitution apart, the ensuing debate could cost them an embarrassing and divisive delay and perhaps prejudice the chances of their movement itself ever being anything more than temporary. Once again, Stephens revealed himself the supreme master of parliamentary tactics.[22]

That evening he could have become a personage even greater. While waiting for the printed draft of the Provisional Constitution, virtually everyone speculated on the presidency, and in no time the Georgian went close to the head of the list of possibilities. A well-timed telegram from Washington informed them that representatives from those slave states not yet seceded wanted Stephens to head the new government, and even a radical like Louis T. Wigfall of Texas argued that only Little Aleck could unite them, bring the conservative border states like Virginia and North Carolina out of the Union, and give them fair prospect for success. "All for the cause, and the best man for it," Wigfall wired. By evening the reporters in Montgomery were sending out telegrams to their papers advising them to look for the election of Stephens.[23]

The next morning, February 8, Toombs, still thinking he was first in line, and Stephens, not yet aware he was even in it, returned to the statehouse to deal with the Provisional Constitution. Before leaving, Little Aleck wrote to a friend, "We are now in the midst of a revolution." None could say where it would lead, or for better or worse, but he felt no doubt that their momentum was carrying them, and if the debate on the constitution did not raise too many obstacles, they could hope for success. Little Aleck's wisdom in closing debate the day before meanwhile became apparent. With the exception of the members of the constitutional committee, and the oral reading of it the day before, the rest of the convention saw the document for the first time when they took their seats that morning and found copies on their desks. They had only limited time during the open session to note objections, and then immediately on going into secret session they began its consideration. As a result, Stephens had minimized the opportunity for consultations and combinations to form during the previous evening. There were still objections and amendments proposed, but he had circumvented the likelihood of an organized opposition that might have delayed or even killed adoption. Little Aleck himself started the amending, changing the suggested name of the new nation from the Confederate States of North America by removing the word North, thus putting the name in its final form. Thereafter it looked at first as if the document would see hard going, but after a couple of sticky debates, the balance passed smoothly, though the delegates sat well into the evening.[24]

Lawrence Keitt of South Carolina looked at Stephens that evening as he sat at his desk writing letters during the less interesting parts of the debate. Already Keitt thought he saw a resemblance to a spider as Little Aleck sat spinning his silk web, feeling the tremors of movement, and acting to stop or exploit opportunities. "His speech is the concentrated sense of that whole house," Keitt said a few weeks later, "the brains of Congress double-distilled."[25] He stepped to Little Aleck's desk during a lull in the debate and asked him to leave the chamber for a few moments. Once outside in the rotunda, the Carolinian came to the point. South Carolina's delegates were almost all agreed—excepting Rhett, of course, who preferred himself for the office—that Georgia should have the highest office. Toombs had blotted his chances. Cobb was unelectable. Would Stephens accept the presidency? Louisiana favored him, and Florida had indicated that it would vote with South Carolina. Assuming that Georgia would present Stephens, that could be four states out of six, a clear majority, with only Mississippi and possibly Alabama committed to another candidate, Jefferson Davis. Perhaps he had only to accept, to become president of the nation he had himself styled the Confederate States of America.[26]

Despite his dismissal of presidential talk in 1856 and 1860, Stephens hesitated. He still preferred Toombs, despite his friend's faux pas at the party, and no doubt said so to Keitt, as well as reminding him of the reasons that mitigated against himself as president, since he had never been a leader in the movement that led to secession. But he did not want to see Howell Cobb in the office, and if everyone insisted on a Georgian, then Cobb was the only likely one left, and he was the only man of any national stature available other than Davis, both having been cabinet members in the Union. Rather than see Cobb get the post, and if Stephens could be assured that his election would be unanimous for the sake of unity, and not just a simple majority, then he would agree.[27]

He later claimed that when he and Keitt walked back into the chamber, he thought Toombs was still first choice, and that he offered himself only as an alternative second choice. Sitting next to his friend Martin Crawford of Georgia's delegation, he detailed what had just occurred and started to waver. He should not be chosen, he said. If the new nation were likened to an infant babe, it should be cared for by its mother, one of those who had struggled for its birth, not someone like himself, who could be a "stepmother" at best. "Someone who has been identified with the cause should be chosen," he whispered, adding that he would support almost any nominee. Across the hall a jealous Tom Cobb saw Stephens return in close conversation with Keitt and grumbled, "Stephens is *looming up* for President."[28]

The delegates passed the rest of the Provisional Constitution late that night and took a unanimous vote at midnight. That done, they scheduled the election of the president for noon the next day, but then a proposal came from William Porcher Miles of South Carolina to take a vote immediately. He never explained his motive for such a suggestion, knowing that his own state had not yet caucused to decide whom to support and probably aware that neither had Georgia and probably others as well, except Mississippi. Yet Miles was one of the Carolinians who seemed to lean toward Stephens, and it is probable that Keitt told him of his conversation with the Georgian as soon as he returned to the chamber that evening. Anticipating that Georgia could not put forward Toombs, and that no one but Tom Cobb and Francis Bartow would support Howell, Miles may have expected that the Empire State would settle on Stephens as its nominee before he could change his mind. It is just possible that by bringing it to a vote then, before a concerted movement could gel around any other candidate, Miles hoped that Keitt's scenario would then unfold, Stephens outpolling Davis. Then, since the deliberations were being conducted in secret session, the one or two states that did not vote for Stephens on the first ballot would be under considerable pressure to change their votes to make a public show of unanimity, meeting Little Aleck's condition. The convention defeated Miles's motion, however, and without realizing it, in so doing they all but ended Stephens's brief four- or five-hour candidacy.[29]

All the delegations but Georgia went into caucus immediately. Confidant that the presidency was theirs, the Georgians decided to wait until the next morning. During the hours in between, and for the first time, some serious politicking took place. Tom Cobb went to some of the delegations and told them Georgia would nominate Howell in the morning, an outright lie, in the expectation that they would fall in line as expected. Instead, the delegates in South Carolina, Florida, and Alabama were so repelled at the idea of Cobb that they quickly seized on the only other man being put forward, Jefferson Davis. That virtually decided the matter, and when Tom Cobb sounded the delegations the next morning, expecting to find a groundswell for his brother, he discovered instead that his stratagem had backfired and the election was all but in Davis's pocket. Later that morning when the Georgians did meet, Stephens nominated Toombs to be their candidate. They were about to vote when Tom Cobb spoke up. Disappointment at brother Howell losing out was at least mollified by having stopped Toombs or Stephens, and he announced what he had learned from the other delegations—without saying a word about his own role in making it happen.

Toombs was stunned. It was the first inkling he had that he might not be elected, and the news generated the greatest disappointment of his political life. He could not believe his ears, nor could his friend Stephens. The Georgians sent Crawford to visit the other delegations to see if it was true, and if not to sound their views about a Toombs candidacy. At the same time, and to his credit, Toombs said that if four states were for Davis, then he would not allow himself to be put in nomination and thus inaugurate a floor fight. Their president must be chosen on one ballot, unanimously if possible. Then remembering his friend, he also proposed that if Georgia lost the presidency, it should have the next highest office and proposed Stephens for vice president. "What do you say, Aleck?" he asked. The other Georgian knew what he would like to say. No one had ever enjoyed being vice president in the Union, and there was no reason to expect anything different in the new Confederacy. It was thankless, powerless, and he would be working under Davis apparently, a man to whom he had never been close, and one not noted for working well with subordinates. But Toombs pointed out that a moderate like Stephens in the executive branch would be helpful in binding the more reluctant citizens, especially in the border states, to the cause. There was no argument against that, and so Stephens agreed. Besides, as vice president he would preside over the Senate after they drafted their Permanent Constitution, and that might give him scope to exercise the sort of parliamentary influence for which he was justly famous. When Crawford left, the dejected Cobbs and Bartow sat in glum silence, their chagrin at Howell's losing out on the top honor as great as their disgust over Stephens winning any honor at all. Within minutes Howell Cobb simply stood up and walked out without a word. Tom followed him, and Bartow soon after. The five who remained went through the formality of nominating Toombs unanimously in case Crawford returned with good news, and in case he did not, they also contingently, and unanimously, nominated Little Aleck for the second office. Then they adjourned.[30]

Toombs learned the news when Crawford found him in the Exchange Hotel, and took it well. Immediately, he summoned the others and held them to their pledge to drop his own nomination and submit his friend's. That done, Crawford and Toombs walked to Stephens's boarding house to give him the news.[31] An hour later they were in the statehouse once more, and after some preliminaries they took their oaths under the newly adopted Provisional Constitution, then cleared the galleries and went into secret session for the election. Rather than be placed in the awkward position of voting for himself, Stephens left his seat and went to the empty spectators' gallery. It took half an hour. At the call for nominations, only Jefferson Davis's name was placed before the delegates, and then came the roll of the states. One by one their chairmen stood and cast for Davis. Ironically, Georgia may have cast its vote for Howell Cobb, once it mattered not at all, but merely as a compliment to his service as president of the convention; then it immediately changed its vote to Davis for unanimity.[32]

That was all. They were now embarked on the most perilous journey of their lives as a people and as Southerners. Toombs, so widely expected to lead, had lost what he wanted more than anything else in life and had no position at all. Little Aleck, expecting nothing, suddenly found himself with an office he had never wanted. For the moment at least, and perhaps far into the future, they needed one another more than ever.

Disillusionment

If any tension had remained from their recent estrangement, Toombs's disappointment wiped it away.
The two friends seemed to become closer than ever before, and in time Toombs moved in with his friend at
his boarding house. On February 18 Stephens walked
to the Exchange to meet Davis and ride with him in a
carriage in the inaugural procession to the statehouse,
now to be the capital of the Confederacy. Stephens sat
beside Davis on the front portico as the new president
took his oath, and then went inside to swear his
own oath as vice president. That done, Davis asked
Stephens to call on him later that day, which boded
well. Though the two had never been more than ac-
quaintances in Washington, it appeared that the new
president might be the collegial sort who would seek
and take advice. Giving advice had been one of Little
Aleck's strengths for years. When people did not heed
him, however, he often did not take it well.

Little Aleck somewhat self-importantly told friends
that he intended to use his influence on Davis to persuade him toward the best possible cabinet appointments, and when he called that afternoon he no doubt

went expecting to be consulted. He found instead that Davis had already offered posts to William Yancey of Alabama and Robert Barnwell of South Carolina, but both had refused, and instead of asking for advice on filling a range of portfolios, the new president only asked what office Toombs would accept. Not ordinarily sensitive to such matters, Davis realized how close Toombs had come to being where he now sat and understood his disappointment. Toombs deserved the highest office he would take in compensation. Rumor already spoke of him as secretary of state, though Stephens thought him best suited to be secretary of war, but he responded only that Davis should give Toombs his choice. Knowing the Georgian's facility for financial affairs, Davis might have preferred him for Treasury, but in the end proposed the senior cabinet post and asked Stephens to carry the offer of the State Department to his friend.[1]

Stephens found Toombs at their lodgings and was in the act of discussing the offer when a messenger delivered an urgent telegram from Georgia. Toombs's daughter Sallie had gone into labor with her first child and become seriously ill. Tenderly devoted to his family as he was, Toombs almost went to pieces briefly, then immediately packed a few things and rushed to catch the evening train east. There was no more talk of cabinet posts for the moment. Several days later, however, Davis sent a telegram to Toombs reiterating the offer, but again Toombs declined, this time explaining that he was a legislator by experience, not an executive. Moreover, he expected Virginia and North Carolina to come into the fold soon and asked if the president had not better hold a high office open for some son of one of the border states. Besides, he had already been appointed to the committee to frame their permanent constitution, and that was where he felt he could do the greatest good. Unsaid, of course, was his lingering resentment that it should have been he giving out the offices, not Davis. At least he was forthright in acknowledging that he had not the temperament for bureaucracy or an office job. But Davis enlisted Stephens in his aid, and he in turn brought the Georgia delegation to bear, and all started applying pressure to Toombs to accept. It was, after all, the third highest office in the nation, and if Toombs did not take it, Davis might be forced to give Georgia's spot in the cabinet to one of the Cobbs.

Finally, Toombs relented and sent word to the president that since his daughter's health had improved he would agree to take the post, but only temporarily, until the border slave states made their decisions on secession. Once the Confederacy was fully formed, however, he would resign to make a place for someone else. There was no glory to be won shuffling paper in an office, and probably already Toombs thought ahead to leaving the cabinet for the field to lead troops, if it came to war.[2] Reactions to the appointment were generally favorable, though Tom Cobb, with only his role in preventing Toombs from achieving even higher office to console him, speculated that the other Georgian's vaulting ambition made him dangerous. Calling Toombs "the great I am," he believed him just capable of someday attempting to overthrow Davis in a coup and to install himself as leader.[3]

Ironically, as incumbent in the second highest office in the South, Stephens had virtually nothing to do. The Provisional Congress was a unicameral body, presided over by its president, Howell Cobb. Anticipating that the permanent constitution, when framed, would virtually copy the U.S. Consitution, Stephens could expect in future to be president of the Senate. Until then, however, his only active role in the new government continued to be his seat on the floor as a delegate. When he returned to Montgomery, Toombs, too, still held his seat and his place on the framing committee, but he also had to set up the offices and organization of the new State Department. He showed a quick disposition to delegate, so much so that subordinates deplored his lack of attention to detail. Since the president had the constitutional prerogative to appoint diplomats and to dictate foreign policy, Toombs had little unilateral authority, and he was not a man for taking orders. Most days his office as secretary of state, just one floor above Davis's in the new government office building near the Exchange, sat vacant, and Toombs himself dismissed his position as so meaningless that he could carry its business in his hat.[4] When applicants for office approached him, Toombs dismissed them flippantly, saying it was quite useless. Occasionally he took off his hat and pointed to it, asking, "Can you get in here, sir? That's the Department of State, sir!"[5]

Instead, it would be in the Congress that Toombs, too, would concentrate his energy, and even before they undertook their new constitution, he and that body first turned their attention to money to finance the new nation. Given his reputation for a keen grasp of sound and conservative fiscal policy in the U.S. Congress, it was no surprise that he was appointed chairman of the finance committee or that he continued to hold the post even after his appointment to State. Initially, the new states offered loans or made outright gifts to the new government, but that would only get them through the interim. First, the Congress authorized up to $15 million in loan certificates to be put on the market and subscribed by citizens. Then they voted to begin printing and circulating Treasury notes that, though used as currency, were also interest-bearing loans.

From the outset, however, Toombs and Stephens believed that the greatest monetary resource of the Confederacy lay in its cotton. In Davis's very first cabinet meeting, his attorney general, Judah Benjamin, suggested taking Southern cotton and shipping it overseas to sell for money to buy munitions and to establish credit, and Toombs and Stephens backed the idea. Little Aleck wanted the government to buy up every available tuft of cotton in the South in return for interest-bearing bonds. Instead, on the advice of Treasury Secretary Christopher Memminger, Davis did not act, believing that withholding cotton would sooner force Britain and France to grant diplomatic recognition and perhaps military aid; the president preferred a cotton embargo. His critics, Toombs and Stephens chief among them, never forgave him for disagreeing, and in later years even exaggerated considerably their earlier support for the cotton scheme, their certitude of its effectiveness perfected by hindsight.[6]

Unfortunately, Toombs soon showed his disdain for the State portfolio, and it became general knowledge. Never one for restraint in his remarks, if he was not taking off his hat and inviting people to jump into it, he told them that his job consisted of being polite and hospitable to foreign nations, but not one of them would talk to him. On his own, he would have offered a host of concessions to lure recognition, and one newsman joked that if it would help the Confederacy, "he was for an alliance with Satan himself."[7] One evening before Davis took office, and when too much at the wine, Toombs even declared that Confederate policy on tariffs would be "free trade with all the world," but he only made policy when in his cups.[8] The decisions were up to Davis, from appointing the first envoys to Europe, to the details of their mission. He left them almost powerless, whereas Toombs would have given them wide authority to conclude treaties without the delay occasioned by communicating with Montgomery. It was with some dismay that he admitted, when asked, that the Confederacy's first foreign mission had no real powers at all.[9]

It also fell into Toombs's hat to oversee—again without authority—the negotiations that Davis tried to open with Washington to adjust the differences between the two nations and to agree on some settlement for the takeover of Union military and government installations in the seceded states. Davis at first asked Stephens to head the mission, and it made good sense. Sending the vice president ought to cloak the mission in the fullest priority possible; moreover, Stephens had been a close friend to incoming president Abraham Lincoln, which might help. But Little Aleck declined to go. He thought the mission a waste of time, and fully expected war, not peace. As a result, he did not want to expose himself to responsibility for an attempt doomed to failure. Davis sent others instead, and indeed they did fail. A few days later when Stephens also refused to go to Arkansas to represent the government before a state convention considering secession, Davis must have begun to wonder just how much cooperation he was going to get from the diminutive Georgian. As for Stephens, he showed his pique when the president did not follow his suggestions on other men to choose for those missions in his stead. If Davis were going to ask his advice, he ought to take it, Little Aleck thought, grumbling, "I fear the appointing power will not act with sufficient prudence, discretion, and wisdom."[10] Their relations were not off to a good start, and the bulk of the blame had to rest with the vice president.

Stephens and Toombs believed that the North would never yield their forts and arsenals in the seceded states, making a conflict all but inevitable, and there at least they were in agreement with Davis. Yet at least a show of good faith effort at negotiation must be made.[11] Clearly there would be war, it being only a question of who would fire the first shot. The impending conflict made even more vital the

framing of the organic law of the new nation, and that is where the
Georgians spent the bulk of their energy, rather than in their
sinecures. Toombs had been appointed to the committee to prepare
for debate a draft of a permanent constitution, and that pleased
him, for he believed getting that document properly framed to be
more important than any other issue before them except their actual independence itself.[12]

On all sides general agreement dictated that the U.S. Constitution serve as the model, for it had been nearly perfect but for some
weak points that had allowed the Yankees to pervert it and usurp
powers under its cloak. Thus the basic format of their new charter
would be easy to plot, and even much of its language a verbatim borrowing. Rhett, the chairman of the committee, arrived with his own
draft prepared as a working paper to get them started. Toombs, who
had his own ideas, and no love for Rhett, may have been displeased
when the committee first met on February 11, just two days after he
lost the presidency, and the chairman introduced his working draft.
But soon it became evident that the other members came only to
work from the Constitution as a starting place, and thus the Carolina extremist was not going to dominate their deliberations.

They argued over matters great and small. Disagreeing with his
friend Stephens, Toombs wanted to call the new nation the Federal
Republic of America, a matter of little moment, but also pressed
hard, and unsuccessfully, for a pet idea he shared with Little Aleck
of following the British parliamentary system of cabinet appointments being made from among sitting members of the Congress.
Toombs did speak for fiscal responsibility by inserting, with no opposition, a provision that, unlike the old system, their Post Office
Department must be self-sustaining within two years. Day after day
they went through the old charter sentence by sentence, and it was
only as they were coming up on the really tough issues that Toombs
learned of his daughter's illness and had to leave. He did not return
until four days before the final report was to be submitted to Congress but thereafter was present for what proved to be a long and
sometimes hot debate.[13]

It was slow going, sometimes only ten lines of the document getting treated a day. An impatient Stephens repeatedly pushed for

night sessions in order to finish sooner, no doubt counting as well on exhaustion to make the men more amenable to action and less to endless debating. "We lack statesmanship of what I consider of the highest order," he grumbled after just one day. "We have but few of any real forecast." Perhaps that was only because so few agreed with his sense of urgency and the need for unity. Indeed, having had no influence on the preparation of the original draft of this document, Little Aleck took control as he had so often in the U.S. Congress. The logjam of endless debate and niggling had to be broken, and on March 2 when the next sticky issue threatened to bog them down, he moved that it be deferred until they had finished with the rest of the document. Time and time again he rose to propose this same tactic in the days ahead, and it worked. Their deliberations ran much more smoothly. All the while, of course, the pile of unfinished clauses grew larger, but Little Aleck knew human nature well enough to expect that by the time they had finished the rest of the constitution, the members would have such an investment in it, and such a habit of compromise—as well as being exhausted and anxious to get home—that the disputed issues would be settled quickly and with a minimum of acrimony. Once again he showed that when it came to understanding parliamentary rules and the dynamics of an assembly, this little man was truly a giant.[14]

The debate was often tense, sometimes amusing, and just as often dull. "No body looking on would ever take this Congress to be a lot of Revolutionists," Stephens observed after four days of debate. He even revised briefly his usually gloomy assessment of the character of most of the delegates, asserting that as a body they were the finest group of men he ever sat with. Another day or two, however, and they were selfish and querulous lightweights, depending on his mood, as he complained of "debate debate—no end of debate." Toombs moved yet again in the debate for elimination of the clause prohibiting cabinet members from also holding elected seats on the floor. It had always been Little Aleck's measure, and when again Toombs failed, Stephens himself tried, but failed to get the votes.[15]

Toombs himself came up with a new measure, at least to him, when he proposed inserting a specific prohibition of internal improvements, of spending federal money for the encouragement of any local industry by road building, canal construction, or laying railroad track with government subsidy. Years earlier, as a Whig, he had supported such expenditures as being in the overall national interest, but in this more conservative environment, and no doubt aware that for some time to come the Confederacy, even if successful in gaining its independence, would be hard-pressed for cash, his old instinct for conservative fiscal policy suggested that such an exclusion would protect the Treasury until it was more securely funded. Ironically, where the issue of internal improvements had once inflamed the South in past decades, by 1860 it had all but ceased to be an issue; and Toombs was reawakening it unnecessarily, perhaps simply hoping to use their constitution as a means of retroactively settling all past problems as well as those present. But Little Aleck himself moved yet again to postpone when he saw the old antagonisms over internal improvements starting to monopolize the debate. They had enough real issues to divide them without reaching back through memory to find more.[16]

Then they hit upon the section that prohibited the African slave trade. It was always an emotional issue. To extremists like Rhett, it implied a stigma on slavery itself, which he found intolerable. Indeed, there had been a substantial movement in the early 1850s to reopen the slave trade, and though it had failed, many people still felt sensitive about an issue that touched their sectional pride and honor. For their part, Stephens and Toombs were lifelong believers in slavery, both in the political and moral correctness of the institution, and even in the benefits it provided to the blacks themselves. The white race was superior; on that they were in perfect harmony. Toombs had laid out his views in the matter in detail just five years before in a speech that, typically, he delivered in the heart of abolition country, Boston. Black subordination was "normal, necessary, and proper," he argued, and advanced the interests of both master and slave. He did not dwell on whether it was right for slavery to have been started in America. It was a fact with which they must deal, and since blacks were by nature unable to govern themselves, and certainly could not be allowed into society on an equal footing with whites, the only alternative was some form of servitude, which kept the social order and peace intact and at the same time provided food, clothing, shelter, and occupation for beings presumably otherwise unable to take care of themselves, especially in competition with whites. Unlike many, he did not oppose education for slaves, and he certainly favored teaching them the ways of Christianity.

Moreover—and borrowing an old argument of the extremist Rhett—he averred that slavery provided the unique circumstance of an economy in which capital and labor were one and the same, thus discouraging waste while promoting efficiency and ensuring that in his own interests the slaveholder would care for and nurture his labor force rather than exploiting the blacks, as labor was in the North's factories. Toombs was a prominent slaveholder himself, owning a large number of them on his several Georgia plantations. For his part, Little Aleck agreed on every point, adding that the institution was sanctioned by the Bible; thus it must live as long as Christianity. He did, at least, concede that it was not the happiest situation for the slave himself, yet the black was better off as a slave in the South than as a free barbarian in Africa, enjoying a better standard of living, access to religious instruction in the true faith, perhaps education, and a degree of health that gave him a dramatically increased life expectancy. Despite all the problems posed by slavery—and to Little Aleck as to Toombs, those problems were exclusively political, not moral—it was the best relationship between white and black that could be found.[17]

Yet both of them opposed reopening the slave trade itself. Stephens always opposed the idea, and even in his controversial 1859 speech he had not specifically advocated it but merely observed the seemingly undeniable truth that unless a large influx of slaves came into the South from abroad, thus expanding the number of slaveowner voters who could emigrate to the territories, there would be no more slave states coming into the Union. Toombs had not been as vocal against the trade in the past, but their ideas were in accord; and when Rhett attempted to soften the prohibition with an amendment to the existing clause, everyone who opposed a reopening voted to table the measure. Yet in the Georgia delegation, only Toombs and Stephens voted against tabling, which would have killed it. Apparently, they felt that this was one battle that ought to be fought out rather than avoided, but they were outvoted.[18]

The next stumbling block was the manner of electing the president, for few had liked the electoral college system of the U.S. Constitution, but here again, Stephens moved postponement and prevailed. On and on went the talking, Stephens musing at one point, "If I could find a '*mute*' I should fall in love with him."[19] Then, as they approached the end of the document, they appointed a select committee to study and report on the postponed legislation. To date Toombs and Stephens stood with Rhett, Tom Cobb, and a few others, as dominant in the framing debate. Now they were going to need every bit of their persuasive powers, for they had come to the issue, surprisingly enough, that proved to be the hottest one of all, what Stephens himself called the "Great Debate" over admission of new states into the Confederacy.[20]

Little Aleck had persistently feared that someone, probably from South Carolina, would propose excluding free states from applying for admission, and the Carolinian William Porcher Miles did so. Stephens jumped up at once and tried to postpone this, too, but the Congress wanted to debate the issue then, not later. The problem was simple. Admit free states, and there was the possibility that new territory that might be acquired by the Confederacy could give birth to states in regions where slavery was impractical. It was even feared—or expected—by some delegates that states of the Old Northwest like Indiana or Illinois might one day want to leave the Union and join the Confederacy, which offered more common economic interests and considerable political sympathy. Allow this, and theoretically one day the free states might outnumber the slave states, and the Southerners would be right back where they started. It would be reconstruction in reverse, and by their own doing. The debate ran all day, and often hotly, Little Aleck giving his best effort yet in Montgomery and then using parliamentary tactics once more. After Miles introduced his amendment, one attempt to soften its content failed, and then Tom Cobb introduced an amendment of his own that prohibited free states and instantly called the question, to cut off debate. By four states to three the amendment passed,

Toombs and Stephens splitting their votes in a rare disagreement as
Little Aleck voted in favor and Toombs against. But then an Ala-
bamian, possibly at Stephens's request, moved to reconsider the
vote—essentially to take it again—someone called for the question,
and Georgia demanded a voice vote. Men began to shift, and the
vote to reconsider carried, Toombs voting with his friend in favor.
Then came the actual reconsideration ballot, again a voice vote, and
Stephens himself demanded the question and an immediate vote
without debate. Three votes changed in Louisiana, and two, including Toombs, in Georgia shifted, changing the state tally to two
in favor, four against, and Georgia divided. Cobb's amendment was
defeated, and that effectively ended the debate on prohibiting free
states. "We had the most exciting debates of any in the convention,"
Stephens declared that evening.[21]

The next day, March 9, was to be the last of the debate, and
Stephens felt sick to his stomach all day for fear someone would
bring up the statehood issue again, or dig in on one of the postponed matters that they must handle. To his surprise, and as he had
hoped all along, the Congress dealt with almost all the matters
rather quickly, anxious to finish their work, adjourn, and go home.
Toombs dropped his internal improvements amendment in favor
of one by Rhett that passed easily. Predictably, Rhett did try to introduce again, as an amendment to another clause, a prohibition
of free states, but Stephens cut him off by tabling, which failed by a
near vote. Seeing his support slim at best, Rhett withdrew his
amendment and another member offered a substitute, and Little
Aleck quickly called the question. Three states voted in favor and
three against, with one evenly divided, and by Stephens's own rules
of procedure, that meant failure. Once having feared that they
would never succeed in framing this document, at last the Georgian
could see a successful end in sight. The contentious issue of re-
forming or doing away with the electoral college never came up.
They were done.[22]

Toombs and Stephens had much to be proud of. Rhett accounted for several of the more significant provisions in the final
draft, though he lost on those most important to him. Although the
Georgians introduced much less in the way of changes, they—and

especially Stephens—had managed the debate and the after-hours negotiating as much as any, and more than most, in order to produce a document that improved on some facets of the U.S. Constitution, even if it was less than ideal on others. In balance, Little Aleck still thought the original document superior, but given the range of tempers and expectations in this Congress, especially from Rhett and a few other extremists, he regarded their success as keeping the new charter from being any worse than it was. "I see many dangers and breakers ahead," he confided to his brother the day after they finished. Still, it seemed a remarkable achievement all the same. No wonder he was exhausted.[23] It was big work for little pay, an exhausted Stephens joked the day after they passed the Permanent Constitution. Teasingly, he told one of the innumerable office seekers who accosted him that he had no appointments to give but that the fellow could have his congressional seat, which would be "cheerfully bestowed," and he offered to throw in the vice presidency as well.[24] Toombs bore the weight of the debates lightly, as he always did, his good cheer unfailing, especially with his daughter out of danger and himself sometimes visibly "glowing" from wine.[25]

Other events could arouse the big Georgian's ire, and though he controlled himself during most of the constitutional debate, in the regular business sessions of the Congress, especially it if touched the province of his finance committee, his response could be aggressive. The tariff had been a much contested issue in the Union for three decades until it finally died away in the 1850s, but still it could arouse passions. Most Southerners wanted to move closer to free trade, and Toombs had his committee at work for two weeks revising and enlarging the list of commodities on which duty should be reduced or eliminated entirely. Then an ardent free trade member from Mississippi rose and offered a resolution that the Congress should do what the committee had already been doing, implying that duties should be all but eliminated entirely. Toombs rose in response and somewhat impatiently noted his resentment at being instructed to do what he was already doing, and then addressed the call for drastic cuts in the tariff. He might have made a flip remark a few weeks earlier, when in his cups, about the Confederacy opting for free trade, but he told the delegates that "such a reduction would be unwise in the last degree." He pointed out that they were even then trying to raise their military and naval forces, their Treasury was as yet only a few millions in gifts and loans, and the tariff was their only other source of revenue. The South Carolinians, free traders all, would not be persuaded, and leaped into the discussion. Finally, someone announced that Toombs's committee report would be submitted in two days, and that should have ended the matter. Instead they kept on, even after the president repeatedly declared them out of order and tried to quiet them, Rhett, Withers, and others riding tenaciously one of their favorite hobby horses and Toombs letting his own rising anger contribute to the heat of the moment. Compared to this, the constitutional debate had been almost a relaxation. Since the debate got out of hand in open session, it was also the first time that spectators had a chance to see anything other than the heretofore carefully maintained façade of perfect unity and accord, and it seemed only natural for Toombs to be in the middle of it.[26]

After passing the Permanent Constitution, the Congress rushed through some other imminently important legislation in order to adjourn on March 16. They had to return to their state conventions, report on their activities, and submit the new charter for ratification. Alabama did so even before they adjourned, but other states, especially Georgia, might not move so quickly. On the last day Stephens and Toombs signed the new Constitution along with the other delegates, and Little Aleck left for home almost immediately, but his friend was unable to go home as quickly, thanks to his other official duties. Toombs, who had enjoyed staying with Little Aleck, Judah Benjamin, and a few others in their boarding house, began looking for a house to rent so he could bring Julia to stay with him. Stephens had found himself as content in Montgomery as he ever was anywhere away from Crawfordville and Liberty Hall. He became something of a local sight to the thousands of tourists who came to the new capital to seek jobs or to gawk at the government and great men. Many wondered at his size and wizened face, thinking he looked more dead than alive until he spoke. Casual passersby took to calling on him at his lodgings at all hours, merely out of curiosity and to have a look.[27]

At least being an object of curiosity had given Little Aleck something to do, for his official duties had provided almost no occupation other than attending Davis's cabinet meetings. There were numerous parties, and the two friends generally went in company, but the particular etiquette of Montgomery's social set often left them somewhat baffled and on more than one occasion unfed, when they accepted dinner invitations for a certain hour, only to find that the meal would not appear for hours and they had to leave for other appointments. One evening after leaving a home without being able to dine, Toombs and Stephens amused each other with speculations that the Montgomery hosts must have concluded that these men who came but never stayed to dinner were socially inept "crackers."[28]

Ironically, Stephens had often made political capital of his common birth among the "crackers" at home, and that was what helped him gain the stature and influence that required him to stump Georgia in favor of the new Constitution. He started making speeches as soon as he entered Georgia but delivered the most important in Savannah on March 21, when he addressed the convention itself, and there, as in his address that hinted at reopening the slave trade, he uncharacteristically went too far. After reviewing what had brought them to their current state of affairs, and pronouncing the new Constitution a much more perfect document than he thought it in private, he turned to slavery. A few days earlier in Atlanta he had hinted at his theme when he said that "African *inequality* and subordination, and the *equality* of white men" were what he called "the chief cornerstone of the Southern Republic."[29]

In Savannah he went further, saying that their new government's "foundations are laid, its cornerstone rests upon the great truth, that the negro is not equal to the white man; that slavery—subordination to the superior race—is his natural and normal condition."[30] Not until afterward did he realize—though he never accepted—that he had compromised much of the effort of the past weeks to portray secession as a movement to protect the rights of the minority and to defend state sovereignty, not as a crusade to preserve slavery. Ordinarily Stephens would not have come out so stridently, despite his own firm belief in the rightness of the institution. But given his concern over the division of opinion in Georgia on ratification of the new Constitution, he appealed to the one issue that he could expect would bind virtually all Georgia voters together, and that was slavery. Equate the new government with the preservation of the institution, and he could show Georgians that a vote for the one was an act to sustain the other. At least his misstep did not prejudice ratification of the Permanent Constitution, for the convention had done that several days earlier, just as Alabama had not taken the risk of submitting it to a popular referendum for fear of rejection. His duty done, and perhaps to escape the controversy created by his speech, Little Aleck happily went home to Crawfordville for a few weeks of rest and isolation.

In Montgomery, Toombs attended to the mundane and uninteresting business of preparing documents to allow the European commissioners to depart for England and France, as well as acting as a conduit for the stream of conflicting information coming in from the commissioners sent to negotiate with the new president, Lincoln. Most days, other than reading dispatches, there was little for him to do, and visitors at the State Department were likely to find him sitting idly discussing politics, recounting old stories from his days in Washington, and simply entertaining any caller with his inexhaustible fund of wit.[31] He needed his sense of humor, for the boredom and his sense of being powerless only tended to exaggerate his discomfort at working under Davis. Soon people could see the formality with which they treated one another. The fact that they had come close to a challenge to a duel years before did not help, nor did their differences over fiscal and diplomatic policy contribute to harmony.[32]

At least Toombs was centrally located so that he could know the latest from Washington, where their commissioners got mixed signals from the Lincoln government, one moment thinking the Yankees would evacuate Fort Sumter and the next that they would attempt to resupply or even reinforce the garrison. By early April Toombs saw in the dispatches that Lincoln and his cabinet were not in full accord, and there began to be hints that they might be deliberately misleading Montgomery in order to delay. Toombs assured his commissioners that if it came to a confrontation and the Confederacy had to take Fort Sumter forcibly to prevent its being reinforced, they were ready, and privately he wrote to Stephens that the military preparations he saw under way in the North suggested that Lincoln would not back down.[33] While Toombs had hoped for peace, Stephens all along assumed the South would have to fight to be independent; finally, on April 8 Toombs received a telegram from Washington that the commissioners were breaking off negotiations, convinced that they had been misled.[34] The focus of activity then shifted from State to the War Department, and Toombs could only look on as frantic activity in Montgomery betokened imminent confrontation. Davis met daily with his cabinet, and the meetings ran long into the evening as they discussed what they should do. Davis argued that they had to demand Fort Sumter's surrender or take it by force, before a supply fleet being sent by Washington could reach it and perhaps land more men and weapons as well as food. Toombs apparently argued for guarded calm, concerned that the Confederacy not fire the first shot, which could injure their position before the world as having no hostile intent and wishing only to be allowed peacefully to leave the Union.

On April 9 Toombs raised the heat in a cabinet session and later claimed that he warned that "the firing upon that fort will inaugurate a civil war greater than any the world has yet seen." Pacing to and fro in the cabinet room, the Georgian borrowed from the poet Longfellow when he argued that "the shot that is fired at Fort Sumpter will reverberate 'round the world.' " They should move slowly and deliberately. "At this time, it is suicide, murder, and will lose us every friend at the North. You will wantonly strike a hornet's nest which extends from mountains to ocean, and legions, now quiet, will swarm out and sting us to death. It is unnecessary; it puts us in the wrong; it is fatal."[35] It was strange talk coming from the man who had for years threatened war on the floors of Congress, the Hotspur who only three months earlier had asked the Georgia convention to give him the sword; and it may have been hindsight. Or else in the moment of crisis, when the resolution of the bluster and threats of a generation of Southern men were about to be tested, restraint suddenly took over at the realization of what they were about to do.

Toombs sat with the president and cabinet all day April 11, moni-

toring the flow of telegrams coming from Charleston, where a surrender demand had been sent to Fort Sumter. The fort's commander refused to surrender but then said he would be starved out
anyway in a few more days unless resupplied. It was a last glimmer
of hope short of hostilities, which should have pleased the newly restrained Toombs, and Davis authorized Charleston to await a definitive statement of when the fort would give up, before opening
fire. That done, Toombs and the rest left the cabinet room, no
doubt for a sleepless night at their lodgings or, more likely, a long
session at the Exchange bar. The next morning a telegram arrived
from Charleston. The fort's response was unsatisfactory, and Confederate commander General P. G. T. Beauregard had opened fire.
Further reports of the progress of the bombardment came in
throughout the day, and that evening crowds gathered and called
on their leaders for speeches. They roused Toombs from bed at his
boarding house to get him to say something, and by then, the die
cast, his old bellicosity had surely returned.[36]

The next day came a telegram announcing the fort's surrender
and no one hurt. Montgomery went into euphoria, and the government with it, but hard on the good news came the necessity for
urgent and energetic action. Davis sent a wire to Stephens to return
to Montgomery immediately, and he arrived on April 15 in time to
join Toombs for dinner with the Davis family and others, and to
hear his fellow Georgian once more optimistic, declaring that everything seemed to be going smoothly.[37] Then came news that Lincoln
had issued a call for 75,000 volunteers to put down the rebellion,
meaning that the Union would try to force the South back into the
fold. That could only mean war.

In the days ahead, Davis feverishly worked to increase their small
but growing armed forces and also to acquire arms from any sources
available, including sending an agent to England to buy overseas,
but Toombs then and thereafter seriously dissented from the president's policy, thinking it too cautious.[38] Then came word that Lincoln's proclamation for volunteers had finally started to push the
border states over the line. Virginia was ready to secede, and its convention wired Toombs that they would soon be out of the Union.
Two days later they were, and the word reached Davis when he was

meeting with Stephens. "It will probably end the war," Little Aleck ventured with rather unusual optimism.[39] In cabinet that evening Davis revealed the request from Governor John Letcher for representatives to be sent to Virginia to conclude an alliance, which would lead to statehood, of course, and the president once more asked Stephens to serve as his envoy. Again the Georgian tried to get out of it, but this time gave in when the rest of the cabinet, including Toombs, insisted that he go. He left that same evening.[40]

Little Aleck reached Richmond April 22 and immediately called on Letcher, and the next day he appeared before the state convention urging an immediate treaty with the Confederacy and speedy adoption of the Permanent Constitution and consequent application for statehood. They quickly drafted a treaty, and Stephens signed on behalf of his government; then as an inducement for the convention to approve the treaty—and it was by no means certain that the deeply divided state would do so—Little Aleck suggested that Richmond might soon assume even greater importance in Confederate affairs. The hint was taken. The convention approved the treaty, and then Letcher wired directly to Davis with an invitation for the new nation to move its capital to Richmond. Such a move made sense on several levels, political as well as military, and had already been discussed in Montgomery as a possibility. His mission done, Stephens left just a week after he had arrived. He ought to have been buoyed by the addition of the Old Dominion, especially since North Carolina must surely follow, and probably Tennessee as well. All along the way back to Montgomery he saw signs of the martial spirit and enthusiasm of the people, and yet he felt gloomy and pessimistic. "If one general battle ensues," he mused, "it will take many more to close the strife." On his arrival in Alabama, Chesnut's wife found him so gloomy on their prospects that she accused him of being only "half-hearted" for the cause.[41]

The next three weeks in Montgomery were almost as hectic as the first ones had been, with war preparations racing ahead. On April 19, after showing it to Toombs first, Davis addressed a message to the specially called session of Congress, one of the last times he would consult his secretary of state for his opinion on a state paper.[42] The sudden pressure of business driven by the certainty of war shortened patience and tempers in Congress. Arkansas seceded, raising Stephens's depressed spirits—he tried to cover his gloom by making sword-rattling speeches on the trip from Virginia that could have matched Toombs's, predicting even that Confederate boots would soon be marching on the streets of Washington itself.

The two men felt immense concern over financing what lay ahead. "The revolution must rest on the treasury," Toombs told his friend. "Without it, *it must fail.*" Little Aleck agreed, asserting that "independence and liberty will require money as well as blood."[43] Once more they came up against their disagreement with Davis over funding policy. Davis still would not use cotton in the way they wanted. He saw it as a political weapon, and they regarded it as financial power, useful only when converted to cash. Unfortunately, Southern bumper crops in recent years meant there was a glut on the foreign market at the moment, which defeated Davis's hopes of influencing recognition by withholding cotton but also seriously weakened Toombs's and Stephens's plan, since prices overseas would be low even if Britain and France wanted to buy any cotton. But neither of the Georgians ever recognized the flaw in their thinking, especially as the years advanced and they drifted ever further from the president. Davis did authorize a produce loan by which growers would turn over cotton and other agricultural produce to the Treasury in return for bonds, and the government could then sell it to raise hard cash. Toombs even stood in accord with Tom Cobb, for once, in support of the measure and then put pressure on members of Congress to use their influence to get their planter constituents to subscribe. It raised far less than its originators hoped, but it was a start.[44]

Finding himself powerless as secretary of state, Toombs was receptive to a proposal from the otherwise disliked Rhett that would empower their agents abroad to conclude commercial and navigational treaties granting favored nation status with preferential tariff rates—virtually free trade. Toombs spoke on behalf of the proposal before the foreign affairs committee, but when it went to the floor of Congress, opponents killed the bill with amendments.[45] It may have been even more frustrating that when the president did ask Toombs to take some action, it was more as an errand, as when he asked him to intercede with the obstreperous Governor Joseph Brown of Georgia, who seemed to make it his life's work to interfere with the operation of Confederate authority in his state. Toombs loathed Brown, and Stephens only tolerated him because of Brown's blatant—yet unperceived—flattery.

The two Georgians were most often seen on the floor of Congress, which took on such an air of bustle and noise that Little Aleck complained he could hardly think. Old jealousies and animosities came out under the pressure, Tom Cobb thwarting candidates put forward by Little Aleck for appointments. One evening in May Toombs and Stephens had to intercede to prevent a duel between two other fellow members of their own delegation. Toombs himself got into an argument with fellow cabinet member Secretary of War Leroy Walker in the latter's office on May 22. He thought Walker incompetent—as did many—and apparently told him so. Regardless of the doleful impact it would have on Confederate diplomats—*his* diplomats—in their efforts to paint the Confederacy as an innocent victim with no goals of conquest, the Georgian wanted Confederate forces assembling in Virginia to march into the North and take the war to the enemy on his own ground. His brief flirtation with caution exhausted, Toombs wanted to take the war "into Egypt," but Walker could only reply that such policy rested with the president and was out of his hands, as indeed it was.[46] Stephens had no use for Walker either. "He'll 'do and do and do,' and at last do nothing," Stephens complained. "Toombs ought to have been there," he told a friend. "He is the brains of the whole concern."[47] It was a sentiment hard to justify when measured against the actual impact Toombs had made, except when working in tandem with Stephens on the floor of Congress. Almost the entire cabinet was coming under fire for being too slow or ineffective, and Davis himself received considerable pressure to replace the members, Toombs himself later saying that "the first Cabinet was a queer crowd" with his usual hyperbole, even claiming to have suggested at one point that they all resign.[48] His motive, if he did so, could have been to make way for better appointments, but just as likely he could have seen the threat of such a mass resignation as a way to coerce Davis into adopting policy more to the Georgian's liking. Yet no one complained of Toombs. But then, given the knowledge that foreign policy was the ultimate responsibility of Davis, perhaps no one expected Toombs to be able to do anything.

Stephens, for his part, was none too happy with Davis. Stephens never actually demonstrated what there was in Toombs's record to justify an assertion that his friend would have been the better man for the office—it owed more to hero worship than to anything else—but he would forthrightly complain to friends that the president was too slow to act. Indeed Davis was deliberate and sometimes hesitant and indecisive, but then he shouldered a responsibility far above any other's. "Toombs would dispatch more in twenty minutes than he does in three hours," Little Aleck averred.[49] In fact, a growing opposition was appearing in Montgomery, headed by Rhett, Tom Cobb, Withers, and a few others. They had hoped to be a nation without parties, and having seen the turmoil of the old Whigs, Toombs and Stephens would have heartily agreed. But a faction was growing, based not so much on a cohesive set of policies as upon dislike for Davis himself. Toombs had never liked Davis overmuch, and his losing the presidency to him, and being reduced to little more than a factotum in the cabinet, hardly improved his attitude. Stephens openly admitted to friends that after their initial good start, he found himself less and less in Davis's confidence, without realizing that his own uncooperative attitude when asked to undertake missions of importance hardly encouraged the president to lean on him.[50] The Georgians themselves were not a part of the opposition, and far from it as yet, but where they were to stand in future depended on the course of the next several months of peace or war.

Certainly Davis and Toombs were still on sufficiently polite terms that the president was welcome in the Georgian's home. Early in May Toombs finally brought Julia to a newly rented house that soon became the center for government society. Naturally they entertained Stephens as their very first guest, and thereafter several times a week at afternoon tea or for dinner, the luminaries arrived, including Davis. If kept off the gloomy subject of the impending war, Little Aleck was an entertaining guest at the soirees, sometimes telling amusing stories, but of course Toombs himself was the bon vivant of the crowd, ever ready with a story at the expense of Tom Cobb, and even with the tale of his recent exchange with Winfield Scott, with whom he had tangled before. Hearing that Scott had said the Confederates ought to quit or that the blockade being imposed by the Union would starve them out, Toombs had sent the old general an ear of fresh corn in a box as evidence that they would have plenty to eat. In the box he included a card simply saying "R. Toombs."[51] Toombs and Stephens also appeared as guests at the president's rented house, and even foreign visitors mingled in the convivial crowd, a British observer finding Toombs to be "unquestionably one of the most original, quaint, and earnest of the Southern leaders."[52] Not all visitors were quite so welcome. A reporter for the *New York Herald* left for Montgomery before the firing on Fort Sumter, when Northern journalists still came and went at pleasure, but he arrived some days after the surrender to find an entirely different atmosphere. Fearing for his safety, he appealed to the secretary of state for a safe conduct out of the Confederacy, only to be told that Toombs had declared, "The *Herald* man may go to hell."[53]

Among the many open questions just then was how long the government and its society would remain in Montgomery. As soon as Virginia seceded, the movement to shift the capital to Richmond got under way. Davis favored it, and so did Toombs, and Stephens played a role in starting the move with his mission to Richmond. By May 9 Little Aleck was certain the move would be accomplished, though there was bound to be hot debate on the subject, and he was not disappointed.[54] After some debate Congress passed a resolution calling for adjournment on May 23 and to reconvene in Richmond on July 20. But the bill only provided for moving Congress and the president, not the executive departments. Toombs, for instance, was both a member of Congress and also a cabinet member. Where should he go? Davis returned the bill with his veto, and a revision was drafted to meet his objections. It finally passed May 21 with only minutes of their session remaining, and only after several members whose vote might have changed the result had already left to go home. "Whether it was wise to do so or not the future must prove," Stephens mused as he was leaving Montgomery the next day.[55]

The members drifted out of town on every train that departed.

Little Aleck left in a hurry, but Toombs had to remain behind to oversee the packing of his department's records and assets. He also helped to prevent news from getting out of Davis's departure, with no ceremony, on the evening of May 26. Toombs himself left on the same train, but already harboring a resolve. Regarding himself as nothing but a spectator in this government, and even the other cabinet ministers as "ordinary outsiders" in an administration that Davis controlled with an iron hand, he recalled his conditional acceptance of his portfolio. He thus determined not to stay on any longer than necessary to get the department established in its new home.[56] There were other ways to fight this war.

6

Loyal Opposition?

Perhaps Stephens and Toombs already had an inkling that their days of political influence in the Confederacy began and ended with their roles in getting what Little Aleck called "the concern" started, and in framing the Permanent Constitution. While Stephens went home, Toombs had to endure the long train ride to Richmond with Davis and his aide Louis T. Wigfall, whose intemperance and bombast made the Georgian seem moderate by comparison. Once it was discovered who was on the train, word went ahead by telegraph, and at a host of cities crowds gathered at the depots to call out the president for a speech; often Toombs had to go out and make one of his own, where audiences warmed to what they took to be his frank and confiding manner.[1]

The problem with Toombs was that he was too frank and far too confiding. He had no qualms about telling anyone and everyone of his dissatisfaction with his associates in the cabinet. Secretary of War Leroy Pope Walker was scarcely better than incompetent and completely dominated by Davis. Secretary of the Navy Stephen Mallory threw away money on frivolous

nautical enterprises that did nothing to advance breaking the growing Union blockade of Confederate ports, a constriction that kept
them from being able to ship their cotton abroad to raise the funds
needed to fight the war, and Secretary of the Treasury Christopher
G. Memminger was consistently doing too little too late to raise that
money. Only the attorney general and postmaster general escaped
his criticism, probably because their responsibilities were simply too
minor to attract his interest or disapproval.[2]

Not surprisingly, as the government settled into its new home in
Richmond, Toombs found himself especially unhappy with the
seeming fiscal lassitude of the regime. Their effort for independence would stand or fall on their success at financing themselves, he
told Stephens, and though almost all the others in the government
would have agreed, Toombs from the beginning felt that he was the
only one who saw the importance of sound fiscal policy, reflecting
his own lifetime obsession with conservative finance. Within days of
installing himself in his new office, he was already deeply concerned
about the Produce Loan enacted shortly before they left Montgomery. "It is of the last importance to us," he believed, and vitally
important that the people at large be encouraged with every persuasion available to the government to subscribe substantially. "We
can meet the exigencies of this contest," he told Stephens, but the
buildup for war was "assuming gigantic proportions." The Yankees
enjoyed enormous credit and could use it to field and equip almost
unlimited numbers of men, he feared. The South's only hope was
to mobilize every dollar of credit abroad that was possible, and the
Produce Loan was their only meaningful fiscal action thus far, in his
view.

True to his trust in his friend, Stephens devoted himself to promoting the loan in Georgia when he reached home, and Tom Cobb
did as well, though Toombs feared it was a half-hearted effort.
Toombs himself subscribed 100 bales of his own cotton in June,
worth perhaps $50,000 or more, to the loan, yet a month later still
complained that though he and Little Aleck and even Cobb worked
in its behalf, the loan seemed to get scant attention from Memminger, whose attention focused on other means of raising imme-

diate cash. Toombs urged his friend and others in Georgia to keep promoting the loan subscription vigorously. They must make speeches wherever possible and get their addresses printed in the local papers to make certain everyone knew their views. He even asked Little Aleck to try to circulate their speeches in other states, especially Alabama, Mississippi, and Louisiana, which were especially lax in subscribing. "If we do not do this, the Loan will flag, and if that flags we shall see the worst times we have yet seen," he said in dire warning. "Nothing is done while anything remains to be done in a financial question," he warned. "With the Loan, we can do anything in time; without it, nothing." Lacking confidence in Memminger's other measures, Toombs frankly asserted that if the Produce Loan failed to finance them successfully—as indeed it did—then they would have no option but to impose a high and rigid direct tax based on wealth or income, something Southerners had opposed in principle for generations.[3]

Nor was he happy with the president himself, not least because where Davis could have used his position publicly and personally to promote measures such as the loan, instead he scrupled to be seen speaking out to promote little if anything, leaving that to the discretion of his cabinet ministers. Moreover, he found Davis's deliberate way of working more than irritating. Toombs may not always have been wise or prudent in his decisions, but no one ever accused him of being indecisive. Davis, on the other hand, took his time making decisions, a lifelong habit, and if not vacillating, still he could seem indecisive as a result. "Davis works slowly, too slowly for the crisis," Toombs groused to Stephens. Naturally, Toombs disapproved of the Mississippian's handling of the office that should have gone to Georgia, or to this one Georgian in particular, but there was more substance than jealousy to his criticism. From the first, once his uncharacteristic hesitation at firing on Fort Sumter passed, Toombs argued for energetic action on every front, especially the military. The inept Walker scarcely attempted to inaugurate a systematic or adequate program of arms purchases abroad, and even as they were raising forces soon to total more than 50,000 in Virginia alone, he had bought a mere 8,000 rifles through his European purchasing agent. "Our foreign arrangements were tardy and insufficient," Toombs complained early in June, "wholly below our wants from lack of comprehension in the War Department."[4]

Regardless of the fact of there being a secretary of war, Toombs knew as did everyone else that Davis himself was running the War Department, reducing Walker to little more than a clerk, and thus Toombs held Davis personally responsible for their failure to be more prepared. "Davis has not capacity for the crisis," he complained, "& I see great troubles ahead."[5] Primarily, the Georgian disapproved of Davis's policy of standing on the defensive. "The North is acting with wild and reckless vigor," he told Stephens early in June, almost admiringly. By contrast, he arrived in Richmond to find Virginia so inadequately defended that he believed the only reason the Yankees had not taken it yet was that they had not tried. The growing shortage of weapons was only one problem the South faced, for the failure of Walker and Davis more assertively to coordinate the central government with the several governors meant that the states had a considerable number of arms going to waste at the same time that their growing army in Virginia was in desperate need. "We have got to rely greatly on private arms or be overrun," he complained, and delay only worked to the enemy's advantage. "We ought to fight as soon as possible," he argued. The Yankees had superiority in arms and equipment and numbers that the Confederates could not reduce by letting time pass. But the South had a greatly superior quality of soldiers, he believed, if only Davis would use them. They should withdraw as many men as possible from far-flung posts like Pensacola, where nothing was happening or likely to happen, and concentrate them in Virginia to make a bold offensive thrust. Maryland had sent commissioners all but begging the army to march into their state, and if it did so the Confederacy could hope to cut off and isolate Washington itself, perhaps even capture the federal capital, which might virtually end the conflict at a stroke.

But every day that they delayed, the disparity in strength grew greater. "It will take courage and energy to avert great disaster and we have far too little of the latter for the crisis," he lamented to his friend in Crawfordville. "I fear the trouble is getting too big for the grasp of some of our most reliable people." It was not difficult to surmise whom he meant by that. "Upon the whole we are in a terrific struggle and need all hands and all heads for the public course," he suggested. Given Davis's insistence on standing on the defensive, thus giving the enemy all the time he needed to prepare, Toombs was feeling increasingly unsanguine within just a week of arriving in Richmond. There was no sign from his agents abroad that European powers would do anything more than remain neutral, in short unwilling to offer recognition or military aid until the Confederacy had proven that it could win its independence on its own, thus needing no outside aid. That response, too, worked to no avail toward an aggressive military policy, for Davis had appointed to top command in Virginia General Joseph E. Johnston, whom Toombs found to be altogether too "leisurely" in his preparations.

Toombs argued his case for taking the war to the enemy to anyone who would listen and became so voluble on the subject that some observers thought him unwise. A few days before leaving Montgomery Toombs actually held forth in the war offices, with all the cabinet and a number of clerks around him providing the audience that was always certain to draw out the orator in him. "The *man* seemed to vanish, and the *genius* alone was visible," thought one who listened. They must attack now. All delay only put them at greater peril. "We must invade or be invaded," he argued, and they should themselves make the war as terrible as possible from the outset, in order to dissuade the Yankees from continuing the fight. He even bitterly denounced Governor Letcher of Virginia for his idleness in defending the state. Perhaps most intemperately, Toombs did not hesitate to say what he would do if he were president, and as if that implied criticism were not obvious enough, he then asserted obliquely that Davis had failed to take responsibility for affairs in Virginia quickly or emphatically enough.

A government clerk thought him "bold almost to rashness," not just in advocating his own policy but in actually denouncing the standing policy, with Walker himself standing there listening. The war secretary responded meekly that he did not make such decisions but simply carried out the wishes of the president and Congress; Toombs rejected this as mere excuse making. Even the policy of the executive and Congress in setting terms of enlistment for volunteers was faulty. Instead of taking 30,000 to 40,000 men at the moment for short terms of up to a year, the government should be enlisting one-half million for the full term of the war, however long it might last. It hardly mattered, for no one would listen, though certainly it did nothing for the Georgian's relations with Davis, who set that policy as he did all others. "The prospect ahead looks very gloomy," Toombs told Stephens. Navy Secretary Stephen R. Mallory, listening in to this and other tirades, concluded that their origins lay in "envy and ambition," and in resentment of Davis, and John B. Jones of the War Department concluded from Toombs's remarks in his office that the secretary of state would soon be looking for another venue for his efforts.[6]

Toombs hardly concealed his own designs in that direction, having announced long before that he regarded his cabinet portfolio as at best temporary. Scarcely a month after moving to Richmond, his grumbling became increasingly frequent and vocal. He told Stephens on July 5 that he would leave his department as soon as he could but needed to do it in such a fashion as to attract as little notice as possible. Otherwise, it might look as if he had left because of his department's failure to date to secure foreign recognition, and thus imply that he bore some of the blame himself. But that was exactly what he wanted to avoid, for he above all others realized that he had never had any significant part in setting foreign policy. He merely felt that he occupied his office in order to be there if necessary to share with Davis the responsibility for measures that he himself had never approved. "I am of no use in it," he complained to his friend.[7] With Governor Joseph Brown, Toombs was equally frank. This government was directed almost entirely by Davis himself, and the all-important military policy was being dictated by the president and his generals, too many of them old cronies and favorites appointed chiefly because they had been to West Point, which the Georgian had opposed long before when in the U.S. Congress. As secretary of state, the senior cabinet minister, he felt like nothing more than what he called a "looker on" in the proceedings of this administration, and the cabinet members as a whole were all but cyphers, little more involved in real power than the merest man in the street. He wanted out, and his reason for informing Brown, with whom he never had much of a relationship, was no doubt to try to enlist his influence in fulfilling a more active ambition that had been on his mind for months.[8]

It was characteristic of Toombs to keep his friend Stephens apprised of what he felt and thought throughout the months they were separated by the adjournment of Congress, for as vice president Little Aleck had no real function when Congress was not in session and in any case no desire to be in Richmond. Although ill as soon as he reached Liberty Hall, still he roused himself and spoke widely throughout his area in answer to his friend's clarion call on the Produce Loan. Like every other member of Congress, he was expected to promote the loan and to take pledges from planters personally, and he did so tirelessly until the coming July session in Richmond called him away. When he spoke in Washington in Toombs's absence, he raised subscriptions for fully $1 million in cotton. Yet he never had quite his friend's faith in the loan, simply because it raised produce but not necessarily actual money. He was ahead of Toombs on this, for Little Aleck actually favored a direct monetary tax and had for some time, one of the few opinions he had in common with Rhett.[9]

Toombs saw the growing discontent with some of the government's policies through lenses colored by his own jealousy and frustration, but Stephens kept account of the complaints through his wide correspondence with everyone from Governor Brown in Milledgeville to Toombs and others in Richmond. No one was free of bias, of course, and already Stephens could see Brown especially revealing his naturally contrarian nature and trying to enlist his aid in circumventing War Department regulations when it came to Georgia troops.[10] It helped that Stephens also did not have a high opinion of Secretary Walker, though it seems only to have diminished after the recent adjournment, influenced no doubt by Toombs's steady stream of complaints. Little Aleck, too, complained of the secretary's inefficiency and lack of resolve, of his being the tool of other men.

But unlike Toombs, Stephens sided with Davis when it came to staying on the defensive. If delay aided the North, it also gave the

Confederates more time to prepare. Especially in Virginia, he thought they should "avoid an encounter of arms as long as possible." Granted that the Yankees had occupied Arlington and Alexandria in May and were clearly building to move against Manassas, a vital rail junction some thirty miles south of Washington, still he favored waiting, even if the Union forces did launch their movement. "Temporary invasion is not conquest," he counseled. The foe might do a lot of damage to their property during such an incursion, he granted. "Still, so long as our army is preserved the work of the enemy is unaccomplished." For the time being, at least, the cause lived in their growing army in Virginia. To risk it in a rash invasion of the North risked losing everything. The longer they lasted, the greater the hope that the North would tire of trying to force them back into the Union. Meanwhile, they could withstand any privation or sacrifice if the spirit of their people remained high. Stephens saw better than Toombs just how tenuous was that spirit. The Confederacy rode high, in large part because it had not yet been tested in battle. He had learned the lesson of recent Southern history. Passions could heat Southerners' blood with remarkable speed, but any sudden setback could also bring out their deep-seated caution, killing a movement almost overnight, as it had Nullification and later the secession movements in 1850 and 1858. A defeat to their arms, especially on Northern soil, could kill the Confederacy overnight by dispiriting its people. Keeping their spirits high depended ultimately on the policy of the Davis administration.[11] Stephens also believed more strongly than ever that they would have to maintain that spirit for a long time. It would be no quick war, but a long one, in the end a test of will as much as of resources and manpower. If Confederates could accustom themselves to that fact and parcel out their élan for the long term, then they might achieve their independence.

Congress was to reconvene for the next session July 20, and when Stephens reached Richmond for the opening gavel he discovered what he probably expected beforehand, that at least one Confederate was achieving independence of a sort. Robert Toombs had resigned as secretary of state. That had been coming for some time, of course. Yet only Stephens and a few others knew that Toombs had another kind of service in mind. As far back as early May, Toombs had told associates that he wanted to raise a Georgia regiment as soon as that session adjourned and lead it into the army, just as Howell Cobb and other congressmen intended to do.[12] As the buildup of forces in northern Virginia foretold an impending battle, and as his frustration with his current position mounted, Toombs finally decided he could bear his inactivity no longer. Instead of applying to Brown for authority to raise a Georgia regiment as its colonel, however, sometime in early July he began to politick Davis for a field commission as a brigadier general.

At first Davis resisted for the very sensible reason that the Georgian was a lifelong civilian with neither training nor experience in the military. He could not stop Brown from making such men colonels, but the power of appointment of all general officers rested with the president, and it took considerable persuasion—more likely pressure—before Davis could yield his common sense to the logic of giving a civilian such a high command. As a prominent Georgian, Toombs in uniform would be a powerful inducement to his constituents and other Georgians to enlist; and in both the North and the South in this war, such "political generals" were often deemed to bring assets to offset their inexperience. Besides, Davis had heard good reports of Toombs's brief service as a captain in the conflict with the Creeks in 1836. Certainly the president would not miss Toombs personally if he left his official family, and the secretary of state's relentless criticism of administration policy would make his departure not unwelcome.[13]

Finally Davis relented and on July 19 appointed Toombs a brigadier general to rank from that date, subject to confirmation by Congress. Toombs notified Davis of his acceptance the next day, even as Congress convened.[14] The Georgian took his seat for the opening, introduced a bill from the ways and means committee that he chaired, and listened to a reading of Davis's message to the session. That done, they adjourned, and Toombs took no active role in their deliberations for the next two weeks.[15] On July 21 the first real battle of the war finally came at Manassas, along the banks of Bull Run, and fortunately for the Confederacy it was a dramatic— though hardly a decisive—victory. It achieved all that Stephens could have hoped, however. Winning boosted the always mercurial Southern spirit and bought them time while the Yankees retreated to Washington to regroup and rebuild.

Perhaps frustrated at already missing the first—and what some thought might be the last—battle of the new war, Toombs handed Davis his resignation as secretary of state three days later, July 24. The knowledge of his intent had been general in government circles for at least two days by then, and two days later the president formally accepted in a note that spoke in leave-taking of more cordiality than they had ever enjoyed when together.[16] At first Toombs announced his intention to leave Richmond five days later to join the army under General Johnston at Manassas, where he was assigned a small brigade of Georgians, the First, Second, Fifteenth, Twelfth, and Seventeenth Infantry regiments, the Fifteenth containing a company commanded by Captain Linton Stephens. But one delay after another kept him in the capital, perhaps not least the fact that Julia Toombs felt deeply distressed at her husband's going into the army. She actually wept in front of Tom Cobb even as she commended her husband for his patriotism in giving up a cabinet post to risk the rigors of the field and dangers of battle. Even through her tears she declared that she had never been more proud.[17] And though he had resigned from the cabinet, Toombs, like several other congressmen who had taken commissions, did not yield his seat on the floor. An important tax bill was pending, and ever vigilant in matters financial, he hoped to stay in his seat to see it passed.[18] Even then, observers could see that his heart and mind were elsewhere. He looked jaded, disinterested, his speech more careless than was his wont, as if he were anxious to be away.[19]

Indeed, Toombs was still in Richmond into August, and some people were hoping that he would not leave at all. His brother Gabriel implored Stephens to use his influence to persuade the new general to resign his commission and not go into the field. Toombs was just over forty, and the old robustness of youth had given way to some recurring ailments, including rheumatism that left one of his arms occasionally useless and a bout with something approaching pneumonia from which he was not yet recovered. Besides, Gabriel Toombs could see what his brother could not, that "my brother's zeal blinds his judgment." Having neither training nor experience in the military, his attempting to lead a brigade simply was unwise. "If anybody can change his purpose in this matter it is you," the brother told Stephens. "No mortal perhaps was ever more dependent upon another for happiness, than I am upon him," Toombs added, "so you can imagine what my feelings must be when I tell you I look upon his going in the army as an unnecessary sacrifice of his life."[20] Indeed, Little Aleck could well imagine the torture of losing a beloved brother. Since the day of Linton's enlistment, Stephens had been resigned to the possibility of losing him, all the while hoping that he would himself resign and return home to safety.[21]

Meanwhile, Julia Toombs soon resigned herself to her husband's action, and while waiting for him to go even entertained the Cobb brothers for dinner, Toombs himself appearing as jolly and garrulous as ever. He even quipped that since Julia had not presented him with a son who could enlist, he had to do so himself. The Georgian's actual inauguration as a soldier was not exactly auspicious. Before ever visiting his new command, he appeared with Davis, Wigfall, and others at a military review at the Richmond fairgrounds. Toombs himself got carried away with the pomp and excitement, started riding his horse somewhat recklessly, and was thrown. His foot caught in a stirrup, and he managed to hold onto one of the reins, but the spooked horse dragged him over the ground; when it stopped, trapped by the carriages, it began rearing up and down, Toombs himself caught underneath its hooves. Only by a miracle did he escape injury, but his pride was wounded enough to turn his face purple with rage. When finally he got clear, rumpled and covered with dirt, his face red and his hair flying in every direction, he remounted and rode back into the review.[22]

Toombs was involved with army politics even before ever assuming his command. A man in the Second Georgia, on the train to join Toombs's brigade, got into an argument with a South Carolina soldier and in the ensuing fight killed him. For the next several days Toombs engaged in a heated controversy with the Carolinians' commander, Colonel Maxcy Gregg, who demanded that the guilty party be turned over. Brigadier General Toombs in turn tried to give orders to Colonel Gregg, orders that the colonel seemed disinclined to heed. Toombs actually went to the president in the matter, and it took the intercession of several prominent men before the controversy was resolved short of a challenge between Toombs and Gregg themselves.[23]

Meanwhile, Toombs's nomination as brigadier went before Congress on August 1 and was confirmed four weeks later. In the interim, he usually took his seat on the floor but had clearly lost interest in legislatures, with battlefields beckoning. He spoke seldom and then only with real interest when trying to perfect his pet bill for a war tax to fund the issue of Treasury notes. After it passed on August 16 he did not take his seat again for the remaining two weeks of the short session but instead left almost immediately for Manassas.[24]

He left behind his friend Stephens, who as vice president replaced Cobb as president of the still-unicameral Congress. Like Toombs, however, Little Aleck seemed to be gone as much as he was in his seat. He had little enthusiasm for a position that effectively removed him, as delegate from Georgia, from the floor debate. Besides, with Linton in the growing army near Manassas, he was often out in the camps visiting his brother, and after the first great battle just as often went to visit the sick and wounded soldiers in their hospitals. Once Toombs joined his brigade, Stephens had the added pleasure of seeing his old friend when he made his visits to Linton.[25]

When not on a visit to Manassas, Stephens kept abreast of army affairs through his correspondence with his brother and Toombs, and neither sent back word of a rosy picture. Indeed, Linton became so disenchanted with army life that before the end of the year, and before seeing a single action, he resigned his commission and went home. Toombs stuck it out, however, but suffered no less disillusion. His conclusions about Leroy Walker's ineptitude seemed confirmed, and it apparently did not help at all that Stephens was boarding with Walker in Richmond, where presumably Toombs's friend could intercede in behalf of the Georgia brigade. Inefficiency and inactivity were everywhere manifest, and the new general's letters to the War Department on a variety of matters went unanswered. When Walker himself resigned that fall, Toombs felt greatly relieved and held higher hopes for the replacement, former attorney general Judah Benjamin.[26]

Equally frustrating, the army's commander seemed uninterested in fighting. Joseph E. Johnston was by nature a cautious man, hesitant to take action and fearful for the damage to his reputation should he fail. Such a personality was destined to clash with Toombs's from the first, and did. "Johnston is a poor devil, small, arbitrary and inefficient," Toombs complained to Little Aleck in September. Likening the general to Walker, Toombs declared that Johnston did nothing well and was merely interested in power for its own sake rather than in using it. "He harrasses [sic] and obstructs but cannot govern the army," Toombs complained. "I never knew as incompetent [an] executive officer," he grumbled, and did not hesitate to voice to Secretary Benjamin himself his dissatisfaction at having Johnston in command of the army at Manassas. Far too freely Toombs engaged in one of his famous bon mots when he openly quipped that Johnston "was only put in command to annoy gentlemen."[27] After only two weeks with the army, Toombs actually wrote to President Davis to request that he and his brigade be transferred from Johnston's command to that of General Beauregard, now in Virginia and also serving semiautonomously with a separate command under Johnston.[28]

Already Toombs was privately at war with his superiors, especially those like Johnston who graduated from the U.S. Military Academy. In April he had complimented Virginia's General Robert E. Lee even though he, too, was a West Pointer, but once he actually lived with the army, Toombs began to see everywhere around him evidence that these so-called professionals had not the stomach for his kind of offensive war.[29] Sarcastically he suggested that since Johnston had been to West Point, "I suppose he necessarily knows everything." Increasingly, the only justification he could see for their tenure was the favoritism shown by Davis, himself a graduate, for fellow Academy alumni. Meanwhile, the army under Johnston sat idle, doing nothing and unlikely to move, he feared. Rather, he thought the army actually dying, not by the physical loss of its soldiers but by the slow disintegration of a body of men stuck doing nothing. "Set this down in your book," he told Stephens at the end of Septem-

ber, "and set down opposite to it its epitaph, '*died of West Point.*'"
They had made a new government in Montgomery, but they failed
to use new materials in the building, and thus the old ills, including
West Point cronyism, had been incorporated. "We have tied the living to the dead."[30]

By the end of September Toombs was so exasperated that he told
Stephens, "I am now thro' with Richmond." At least Julia came out
to Manassas frequently, at every visit bringing friends and pots of
chicken soup for her husband and the officers, who included Tom
Cobb, himself having raised a Georgia unit that he commanded as
colonel.[31] But nothing relieved the monotony of inactivity or the
sense of time and opportunity going to waste. Never one to hold
back opinions just because of protocol, Toombs actually circumvented proper military channels on September 1 when he wrote directly to Davis, without going through his own superior, Johnston.
The army must move, and immediately, he told the president. Returning to a theme he had enunciated months before, he urged
that Johnston be ordered to invade Maryland, isolate Washington
from the North, and either force its surrender or force the Yankees
to fight them on ground of their own choosing. The loss of Washington, or a defeat on their own territory, he felt sure, would cost
the enemy so dearly in morale and international prestige that Lincoln would not be able to continue the war. He put his suggestions
to Davis with uncharacteristic tact and deference but emphasized
that the enlistments of the majority of their soldiers would expire
the following spring, and if Johnston did not do something with
them quickly, the army would simply evaporate. "We should," he
urged, "make the most of them now."[32] Toombs's suggestions bore
a marked similarity to plans being put forward then by Beauregard
for grand concentrations and invasions of the North and may well
have been influenced by that general, accounting as well for the
Georgian's request to be transferred to Beauregard's immediate
command. Typical of his reaction to almost all suggestions of
strategy, however, Davis virtually ignored Toombs's proposals, in
part because they conflicted with adopted defensive strategy, and in
part because Davis held such planning very closely as his own prerogative.

Though complaining of his superiors, Toombs at least had no complaints about his men. The camp experience was a new one to him, but he entered it with all the enthusiasm of the neophyte. In fact, he found it a pleasant change. "It is next to repose itself in comparison with the events of the last six months," he told Davis. "Upon the whole I like it." He spent his time studying tactical manuals and drilling his command by regiment and as a brigade and found it agreeable employment, "without adling [*sic*] the brain."[33] His regiments had their bout with measles, which attacked almost all new units, but the damage was fortunately slight, and his own health proved better than friends and family had feared. His men and his superiors found him a mixed blessing. His immediate brigade commander, General E. Kirby Smith, found the Georgian "coarse and unrefined verging upon vulgarity," nor did the uniform of a soldier hide from Smith the pervading "politician and demagogue" that lay underneath; but withal he thought Toombs jolly and likeable, and fellow generals found him a constant source of amusement and entertainment, both for his affected rusticity and his undeniably keen wit.[34] Observers soon regarded the Georgia brigade as one of the finest in the army, though the highest compliments predictably came from Georgia observers, who also lauded Toombs for his management skills. The soldiers in the ranks, many of whom were or had been his constituents in past days, found him courteous and respectful, "as accessible to the humblest man in his brigade as a mother is to her offspring," approachable, sympathetic, "a private's friend" who would not allow the military despots and bureaucrats to trample on their rights as citizens and gentlemen.[35]

But the frustration of inactivity told on the general. Indeed, he was something of a metaphor for that peculiar Southern character that Stephens so much admired and yet feared. Easily aroused to enthusiasm and passion, Toombs could just as easily cool from impatience, as he did now. That fall Johnston stationed the Georgia brigade at Munson's Hill, from the summit of which Toombs actually could see Washington in the distance, and yet they did nothing but drill.[36] "We have no chance of moving shortly," he grumbled late in September, "and I fear the whole campaign is thrown away, with this mighty army ready and willing to end the war if they had a man of sense and ability to lead them." Instead, they just drilled while Johnston fussed and planned, and Richmond dithered. "It is time Davis concentrated all of his army on the Potomac instead of frittering his strength," Toombs grumbled. When Johnston fell back from Munson's Hill to Fairfax at the end of the month, Toombs actually complimented the Yankee commander George B. McClellan for not taking the bait and following them, as the Confederates had hoped. The enemy, at least, had a real general, not a Johnston. "We are lying here rotting," he told Stephens. "We have lost more men by inactivity and bad treatment since the battle of Manassas than it could have cost to have gone to Balt[imore] and ended the war." Even when Davis came to visit the army and meet with Johnston and Beauregard, as he did early in October, Toombs believed that the generals misled the president by underestimating their own strength in order to avoid having to take action. "We appear to be chained to the rock of immobility," he lamented, "there to linger and complain and wear ourselves away." He doubted that they would do anything before the coming of spring, and he made no attempt to conceal his discouragement. "The prospect to me looks more gloomy than at any time," he told Stephens.[37] No wonder that by late November Toombs was speaking of resigning his commission.[38]

In Richmond, Little Aleck could do nothing to alleviate his friend's growing discontent. Rather, his own frustrations mounted at his own inactivity. Furthermore, he unwittingly became the center of a brief controversy as November approached. The provisional government was to last only a year before the implementation of the regular administration under the Permanent Constitution. That included calling for the election of a president and vice president, for Davis's and Stephens's incumbencies would expire with the Provisional Constitution in February 1862. There was never any real question of anyone opposing their renomination and election, but that fall critics, including Tom Cobb, began to make open accusations concerning Little Aleck's fitness. Cobb was certain that the vice president still hoped for an eventual reconstruction of the Union on the basis of some guarantees of security for slavery in the territories, and other critics soon joined the chorus.[39] In September an unsigned editorial written by Littleton Washington, a clerk in the State Department, appeared in the *Richmond Examiner,* in which he accused the Georgian of reconstructionism and excessive vanity besides, the beginning of a series of attacks on Stephens. There was considerable speculation as to who authored the diatribe, though Keitt of South Carolina tried to deflect the criticism in capital circles, and in the army Toombs felt indignant at the assault. "It will do you no harm," he counseled his friend, "but I would like to know where it came from." For Washington's sake it was well that Toombs never found out, or Stephens for that matter, for he was just as quick with a challenge, but when it became evident that the vice president would be reelected no matter what was said, Washington stopped writing the attacks.[40]

In fact, so little did Stephens value the vice presidency that he might have preferred that the charges stop his reelection, but in November the vote was almost unanimous. To Little Aleck that only meant another six years of tiresome debate in Congress, in which he could not participate, and a like time of being ignored by Davis, who now scarcely consulted him and often left him quite in the dark about executive policy. Of course, by his own uncooperative attitude in Montgomery, Stephens had largely brought it on himself, but in any event Davis was the least collegial of men, never disposed to share even his confidences, let alone his authority. Sad testimony to Stephens's isolation in the government is that one conference with Davis in November after their election was their first in some time as well as their last for more than a year, and in that conversation the Georgian was so out of touch that when Davis asked him for advice on appointing a commander for Georgia and South Carolina, Little Aleck's only suggestions were Johnston and Beauregard, despite the fact that both generals, especially the latter, were already out of favor with the president. But no one had ever told Stephens. The fact that he suggested them, rather, probably only served to make Davis even less inclined to consult him in the future, for already Davis's political opposition was gelling around dissident generals, and Little Aleck's innocent suggestion may have persuaded the president that his vice president was in league with his enemies. And though he probably did not realize it as yet, Stephens was on his way there. Within a few weeks of the election in November, his letters to his brother so spoke of disenchantment and disaffection from the administration that Linton for the first time began to burn them lest they fall into the wrong hands.[41]

A month later Stephens's health took a dramatic downturn that kept him semibedridden until February 1862, with the result that he missed much of the long last session of the Provisional Congress that commenced on November 18 and ran until February 17. Even then, his participation when present was remarkably limited, as he introduced just three minor housekeeping resolutions during the entire session and rarely if ever was in his seat for most of December and the latter half of January.[42] The ever-acerbic Tom Cobb remarked that when Little Aleck did speak on the floor, "philosophying largely and with oracular consequence," few listened with real interest "while a good many old fogies shook wise heads and wondered at his eloquence."[43] In fact, Toombs was much more active, frequently leaving the army during the idle weeks from late January through the end of the session to sit in Congress, where he helped frame bills limiting sequestration of enemy property and raising volunteers.

On February 5 he even worked with Rhett, coming increasingly into sympathy with his opposition to Davis, however much he may have disliked the prudish zealot personally.[44] Fearful that the army would dissolve in April and May when its majority of twelve-months' volunteer enlistments would expire, Toombs introduced a bill to call out the militia of all the states. He may have done so after consultation with Rhett and other dissidents who favored a massive conscription by the state governors to raise an overwhelming army, and though Toombs had in mind bringing one-quarter million men into the army, his bill called only for 50,000. The administration, on the other hand, was counting on patriotism to induce discharged volunteers to reenlist for the term of the war. Toombs admitted that he had no real expectation of his bill passing, but he hoped that by introducing it within days of the close of the session and the expiration of the Provisional Congress to highlight the crisis and put his sentiments and others who would not be returning on record, possibly as an inducement to the incoming Congress to take decisive action. When the bill came up for debate on February 13, the ensuing discussion became heated—no surprise, with Toombs seeing here his only real battle in months—and sometimes acrimonious over the next several days. Toombs had the last word in the debate himself when he gave what Rhett thought "a most eloquent speech" in which he called on Congress to witness, that "he, and those who acted with him for a vigorous prosecution of the war, had done their duty; and that the sole responsibility for the disasters which might ensue from our armies being too few and feeble to meet the enemy, rested exclusively with the President of the Confederate States." Having made his point, he then proposed to withdraw the bill. Rhett suggested that a direct vote had better be taken on the bill, but Toombs said it would be useless, because it was clear that it would not pass, and withdrew it in disgust.[45]

Toombs also began to vote with the president's opponents in attempting to overturn his vetoes and came out in strong opposition to Davis's plan to spend $1 million on what amounted to an internal improvement by financing the connection of two private railroads as a military necessity.[46] It seemed a contradictory position for a one-time Whig who had favored internal improvements, and especially from a man anxious to go to great lengths to build a massive army that would need the rapid communications that such a link could afford. Granted that their Constitution forbade internal improvements, Toombs had rarely been one to allow the letter of the law to impede the necessity of the moment, yet he increasingly positioned himself as a strict constructionist. The likelihood is just as strong that by this winter of his discontent, his political positions were becoming more and more predicated on antipathy to Davis than on any consistent principle. However much he may have detested Tom Cobb and distrusted Rhett, Toombs by the expiration of his term as a congressman had firmly planted himself in their camp, united by opposition to Davis's conservative war policy and by personal dislike—and certainly jealousy—of Davis himself.

For a time it appeared that the blustery Georgian might still cast his booming voice in the new Congress, for he allowed his name to be put before the Georgia state senate as a candidate for one of the state's two seats in the new Confederate Senate. The election took place on November 19, at a time when the general was already sufficiently disenchanted with Johnston and the army that he may have encouraged his nomination. In the Senate he might just be able to speak out and influence military policy in a way that he could not as a general, even one who could not keep his mouth shut or recognize the subordination of the military to the civil authority. There were two terms to be filled, one for a full six years, and another shorter one of four years. On the first ballot, Benjamin Hill won the full term handily, with Toombs well behind. In the ensuing four ballots no winner emerged for the short term, and then on another one Toombs finally got the majority needed. It was a humiliation that the general felt keenly, for in days gone by he might have been unopposed. Apparently, his well-known disaffection from the Davis administration, combined with many old political and personal animosities from before the war, worked heavily against him.[47]

Still, on being notified of his election, Toombs at first seemed inclined to resign his commission and accept the office. Then in early January he and Julia returned to Georgia for a visit. While there he energetically encouraged enlistments with a vigor that brought compliments even from Tom Cobb, but at the same time he was also no doubt assessing whether or not he ought to go into the Senate. By January 18, when he had returned to Richmond, he was halfway to a decision, declaring that he would not leave the army after all, nor would he decline his Senate seat, though intending to serve for only a short period of time. His reasoning probably had more to do with Davis than anything else, for he and the Cobbs were agreed that their true policy was to support Davis when they thought him right but to condemn him outright when they deemed him wrong, even though his friend Stephens seemed reluctant to join in the chorus. Indeed, by early February Toombs was actually asking Tom Cobb not to resign his seat in Congress but to stay and help in the fight against Davis's military policy. Never did Confederate politics make more unlikely bedfellows. He even joined with the two Cobbs in signing a public address to Georgians, calling on them to fight to the last man, even to annihilation itself, rather than yield to the foe. There were other pressures on him, too, for the Toombses had decided to give up the house they rented in Richmond, where Julia had hosted her usual series of dinners and entertainments, Stephens being almost a permanent fixture in her drawing room. She would be returning to their home in Georgia, making residence in the capital for Toombs that much less attractive.[48]

By mid-February Toombs finally made his decision and wrote to Governor Brown a rather crusty letter in which he declined his election, in the process complaining that its taking six ballots to elect him was such an insult that he felt no obligation "to sacrifice either my personal wishes or my conviction of public duty in order to accept it." It was self-serving to say the least, for Toombs took fully three months to come to such a conclusion, and if the vote had really been so insulting, his passionate nature more likely would have led him to reject the seat immediately; his talk for months of resigning from the army seemed to gainsay protestations of convictions of public duty. Typically, he had carefully weighed what was best for him and very likely held back his decision, pending some even more important event that just might develop.[49]

President Davis's cabinet had been under attack for months. Indeed, there were widespread complaints in the press even while the government still operated in Montgomery, and after the move to Richmond the criticism gained momentum in the months after the battle at Manassas when the army seemed to languish in northern Virginia, doing nothing. No one approved of Walker's performance, and when Benjamin replaced him the complaints only increased, especially in February 1862 when an embarrassing defeat at Roanoke Island, North Carolina, and two genuine disasters in the losses of Forts Henry and Donelson in Tennessee appeared to hand the momentum of the war back to the Yankees. "Our government is imbecile and obstinate," Tom Cobb ranted. Davis himself was "an obstinate fool," and Benjamin "a mean low sycophantic dodging Jew."[50] By March 1862 Toombs himself claimed that "Davis's incompetency is more apparent as our danger increases," fearing that only divine providence could help them, given such leadership.[51] As the criticism mounted, the critics capitalized on the growing impatience in the country and became themselves, for the moment, more prominent. Army Quartermaster General Abraham C. Myers noted late the previous fall that "Mr. Toombs it appears is in great worth with us down here, and means to pitch in right and left when he comes down," but added from his observation of Toombs's mercurial nature that "as he does not remain on the track very long, he must demolish his enemies in a few weeks." Toombs even found himself reconciled with General Johnston, who actually included him in strategy meetings, despite his junior rank, no doubt in part because Johnston himself was feuding with the president.[52]

With the dissatisfaction becoming intense, and much of the criticism coming from powerful Georgians, a movement began to try to pressure Davis into replacing Benjamin with someone more capable and less controversial, by offering the appointment of secretary of war to Toombs, of all people. Politically, it could have been a sensible move, for it would at once all but silence the Georgian, who was hardly likely to rail against his own administration, and it would also diffuse the chorus of antiadministration dissidents by putting one of their own in an important position. Moreover, Toombs was confining his interest in Confederate affairs almost exclusively to the army. Despite his bombast and bluster, his proven skills as a businessman and administrator most likely would have made a welcome improvement in the administration of that department to the extent that finance and materiel allowed. However, the assertion of some observers that he possessed a surpassing ability at planning military campaigns was nonsense, for Toombs was and would always remain a one-idea general, that idea being to concentrate and attack. His thinking in uniform was just as it had been when he was in Washington; whatever he boasted he would do would happen, regardless of the fact that his opponent might have other ideas.

The movement never took fire, however, chiefly because Toombs himself would have none of it. More than once he told his friends in Richmond that he would take no place in the cabinet again, and certainly not the War portfolio, for he had seen how Davis used Walker and Benjamin. And since there was a movement to make Lee general in chief, he believed that Davis and Lee together—both West Pointers—would effectively act as secretary of war, "no matter who is in the office nominally." Under such a state of affairs, he told Stephens, even Benjamin "will make them as good a head clerk as they can get." "I would not be Mr. Davis' chief clerk," he told Julia in March. "His Secretary of War can never be anything else." There seems at least the possibility that Davis himself contemplated such an appointment, but the Georgians told his friends in the capital emphatically to discourage any such action to spare Toombs having to decline, which could open him to criticism from Georgia for refusing a high post of honor and even for a want of patriotism.[53]

Yet still it may have served Toombs's purpose to allow a movement for his appointment to gain a little headway before he killed it himself, at the same time that he dallied about declining his Senate election, for there was an office he really did want. Despite never having heard a shot fired or having had any experience in active command, he decided by February 1862 that he was ready for higher position in the army, and he began pressing Davis to promote him to major general, which would entitle him to the command of a division rather than a mere brigade. That would put him on a par with generals like James Longstreet and Thomas J. "Stonewall" Jackson, genuine commanders who had earned their rank at Manassas. Toombs's ambition soon became general knowledge in Richmond political circles, and there at last his overall purpose may have been revealed. Davis certainly did not need to have Toombs in the Senate, with a constant forum to carp and criticize, nor could he have wanted him in the cabinet again, especially if forced to it by political pressure, which he always resented and rarely gave way to. Making him a major general would have circumvented those alternatives, and it would have been just like Toombs to float the Senate and the War secretaryship potentialities as threats to make what he really wanted, promotion in the army, seem painless by comparison. If so, however, it did not work, for by February 16 rumor in the capital said that Davis had declared he would not promote the Georgian.[54]

It can hardly be coincidence that only after Davis made it clear that there would be no promotion did Toombs finally write to Governor Brown and decline the Senate seat and at the same time discourage any further movement toward the War office, his gambit having failed. Toombs's bitterness was evident in the letter he wrote Brown, and to Julia he confided even more his unhappiness. "So far

as I am concerned, Mr. Davis will never give me a chance for personal distinction," he grumbled. "He thinks I pant for it, poor fool."
His only wish was for victory and peace, he assured her. "It may be
his injustice will drive me from the army, but I shall not quit it until
after a great victory, in which I shall have the opportunity of doing
something for the country." That done, he would resign his commission. "I have grievances enough now to quit," he said, "but I shall
bide my time." By late March Toombs had almost isolated himself
from Richmond entirely, hearing only from Stephens, but from him
constantly, with a steady stream of capital news, none of it to their
mutual liking as the Confederacy they helped to found seemed to
totter on toward destruction, if not by the enemy without, then by
its own leadership within.[55] Both Toombs and Little Aleck found
themselves, as much by their own devices and disappointments as
by circumstances and policy, in almost the same position they had
been in less than two years before in the Union, a part of a small but
vocal minority in opposition to a government they had intended to
love and revere. By mid-March, as Toombs gave up his efforts at manipulation and promotion, dark rumors emerged from the secret
sessions of the House that members had discussed deposing Davis.
Tom Cobb thought they would have acted if they had not lacked
confidence in Stephens, his constitutional successor, but that may
have been nothing more than Cobb's own pettiness and jealousy
speaking.[56] Still, it began to appear that the two friends had helped
to turn America upside down, just to find after all that instead of
ending the contest that endangered the South and slavery, they had
only changed opponents.

7

Enemies Front and Rear

It was typical of Toombs to be no more content with Johnston's management of the army than he was with Davis's of the government in Richmond. By late March, after months with the army, he had actually seen his commanding general once and could say only that Johnston was "polite and clever," though even that was an improvement over the Georgian's previous opinion. He was that complimentary merely because, no doubt, he blamed Johnston's most recent act of indecision on Davis. The Confederates had remained in northern Virginia for months after Manassas, months during which nothing happened in their front, while the enemy regrouped and rebuilt after the disaster it suffered in July. Expecting the Yankees, commanded by General George B. McClellan, to launch a spring campaign south toward Richmond, Johnston decided that he could not defend his advanced line and pulled his army south of the Rappahannock and then the Rapidan Rivers early in March. He did it without proper preparation, without even notifying Davis of his intent, and abandoned millions of dollars worth of vital equipment and supplies.

Toombs may have had no active experience as a battlefield commander, but he was more than sufficiently proficient as a manager of simple business and finance to be appalled at Johnston's action. For weeks he chafed as Johnston made the few advance preparations for the withdrawal he effected. Then Toombs and his brigade were pulled out of their Centreville position and marched south to a new camp at Orange Courthouse just below the Rapidan. "This has been a sad and destructive business," he complained during the march. Through confusion and inefficiency at army headquarters, his brigade's baggage, blankets, "and every imaginable useful article" were burned. He estimated that his command alone lost one-half million dollars worth of equipment, and allowing for his propensity to exaggerate, still it was an irreplaceable loss. The destruction or abandonment of many times that throughout the rest of the army appalled him. "Never was any business worse managed," he told Julia, confessing that during the withdrawal he was himself sometimes in tears at the territory they were giving up to the enemy without a fight, and the thousands of Confederate citizens being left to Yankee mercy. This was what came of giving high command to men from West Point, men who obtained their professional education at government expense, in a school that apparently taught them only caution and timidity. "I would rather have fought ten battles than thus to have abandoned these poor people," he complained. "We have got to fight somewhere, and if I had my way, I would fight them on the first inch of our soil they invaded."[1]

The discontent only mounted when officers began trying to tamper with the organization of his Georgia regiments. Toombs enlisted Stephens's help and influence—such as it was—with the War Department in order to prevent such intrusions. Then, once in his new camp at Orange, he renewed his carping when Davis and Lee visited the army on March 22. The good opinion he had expressed of Lee a year before had almost evaporated, for Toombs saw him as yet another West Point crony and tool of the president's. Indeed, the only professional soldier whom he liked was General Gustavus W. Smith, second in command since Beauregard's recent transfer west, and himself already at some odds with Davis. By the end of March, reiterating again and again to Stephens the need to con-

centrate and attack, in Tennessee if not in Virginia, Toombs's disenchantment reached new heights. "Davis seems determined to perpetuate inefficiency," he asserted. "We shall get our independence
but it will be in spite of him."[2]

Meanwhile, whatever confidence he had remaining in Johnston
eroded even more as his commander seemingly dithered. On
March 27 Toombs received orders to have his brigade ready to
march within a few hours for the Shenandoah Valley and the small
army commanded by Jackson. No sooner did he have the brigade
formed and on their way west when another order came to return
to his camp. That evening Johnston directed him to be ready to
march east to Fredericksburg the next morning, but no sooner did
he have the brigade's baggage and impedimenta loaded on wagons
and the men formed for the march than that order, too, was recalled. An hour later he got instructions to ready them for a train
to Richmond that evening, and predictably, just as he was about to
leave, once more the directions were canceled. "Here we are waiting for something to turn up!" he told Stephens, no doubt recalling
Micawber in *David Copperfield*. "We have been in the most curious
condition for the last twenty-four hours, I suppose, that an army
ever found itself in." It was just more proof, if any were needed, of
the inadequacy and dilatory tactics of West Pointers like Johnston,
so far as Toombs was concerned. "We are in the very crisis of our
fate," he told Stephens on March 28, even while he expected momentarily to be ordered to the capital after all, "and I see nothing
at Richmond which seems to appreciate and prepare for it."[3] Of
course, there was plenty of concern in the capital, and a great many
matters occupying Davis and others that they felt no need to share
with a brigade commander in the field, but Toombs could never accept that others knew what he did not.

There was the recurring problem for the Georgian. No one else
could see what he saw; no one but he knew what ought to be done,
or how to do it, and no realization of his own inexperience or ignorance in military matters offered inconvenient interference with
his certitude. With McClellan moving his army from Washington
down the coast to land on the Virginia Peninsula below Richmond,
to approach from the southeast, and with small Yankee armies

threatening the Shenandoah on the west and moving into the northern Virginia country they had just abandoned, he saw disaster looming. "The enemy are all around us," he complained on March 31, yet Davis did not seem to recognize the danger and would not rush reinforcements from other parts of the Confederacy in time.[4]

No wonder Toombs was more than ordinarily touchy. When his brigade did reach Richmond early in April, he apparently stormed into Johnston's headquarters to upbraid him over a technical matter involving the admission of Georgia soldiers into hospitals. When he left, Toombs fully expected to be arrested for insubordination, though Johnston apparently decided not to act in the matter.[5] Meanwhile, a rumor went through the capital that the Georgian had publicly cursed at Colonel William J. Magill of the First Georgia, which was not a part of Toombs's brigade, and that Toombs was to be arrested when Magill preferred charges.[6] This arrest, too, never came to pass, but such episodes were ample evidence that sooner or later Toombs's temper and impetuosity were likely to get the better of his good sense in his military relations, especially when he felt pressure or frustration.

At least Toombs enjoyed the panoply of war. Indeed, he sometimes made something of an exhibition of himself in the eyes of the professionals, as when he first brought his brigade into the capital. With crowds lining the streets to welcome the troops heading for the peninsula to stop McClellan and save the city, the Georgian marched his command down Main Street past the Spottswood Hotel, its galleries filled with ladies and the capital elite. Instead of simply leading the brigade, he led each of his several regiments past personally, one by one, himself riding back when one had passed in order to be at the head of the next, a blatant case of exhibitionism as most people except Toombs himself realized. "It was somewhat amusing," recalled one professional officer, "but a harmless entertainment." Indeed, the prevailing attitude toward Toombs among his fellow career officers was that "that luminous intellect embraced no soldier's talent." Application and study might have taught him the craft, thought Colonel Moxley Sorrell, "but the Georgian was for once and all a politician, and in the wrong shop with a sword and uniform on."[7] Sorrell's commander, General James Longstreet, agreed as to Toombs's naivete, summing up the Georgian's idea of strategy as "the general idea that the troops went out to fight, and he thought that they should be allowed to go to it at once."[8]

By mid-April Toombs and his brigade reached the Confederate defenses at Yorktown, under the immediate command of Major General John B. Magruder. There was no hope of stopping McClellan there, but Magruder and Johnston hoped to delay his advance while Johnston set up a strong defense line further up the peninsula. If Toombs wanted a fight, he soon got it, for just two days after his arrival, Magruder assigned him temporary command of another brigade as well, making him a nominal division commander, and ordered him to guard and defend a dam on the Warwick River, right in the enemy's path. On April 14 the Federals struck, and Toombs at last saw his first, admittedly minor, action. His men had no difficulty in repulsing the enemy probe, and he wrote to Julia with glee that one of his regiments had killed and wounded more than 100 of the Yankees.[9]

Yet it was a fleeting elation, for after that he and his command spent the next two weeks doing guard duty at the dam and seeing only an occasional skirmish. Instead of the all-out battle that he expected, the Yorktown operation turned into a siege, with its attendant tedium, grueling hours, sickness, and demoralization. Even having Tom Cobb's new Georgia Legion put under his command temporarily, making up his division, was not as satisfying as it once would have been, for their antipathy to Davis was making them allies rather than enemies. Moreover, inept and irritating as he was as a politician, Cobb was demonstrating himself to be a competent officer. Meanwhile, where once Cobb would have been incensed at being assigned as Toombs's subordinate, he now had no objection.[10] That attitude changed quickly, however. When Johnston arrived to take overall command personally, Magruder reverted to division command, and Toombs to that of his brigade, and within three days Cobb was disillusioned. "He talks as wildly as ever," he complained of Toombs. "It is astonishing how a man of his capacity and character will render himself so perfectly unreliable." Cobb found his fellow Georgian frustratingly imprecise in his orders and arrangements, lamenting, "I have found in two days that I cannot rely on a statement made by T[oombs]." Worse, Cobb thought that Toombs placed his headquarters an unseemly distance behind the lines, and for all his bluster, was starting to show a reluctance to expose himself to enemy fire.[11]

To be sure, the monotony and routine of the siege told on Toombs, nor did his manner and mood improve when Johnston abandoned Yorktown on May 3 and pulled back up the peninsula. Though some of his men were posted nearby, Toombs's brigade was not involved in the first real battle on the peninsula at Williamsburg on May 5, and during the next two weeks the Confederates fell back steadily without stopping to try to halt the Federal progress. Probably all that saved them from a severe beating was the fact that McClellan was even less anxious to advance and fight than was Johnston. The whole operation so frustrated Toombs that he easily overflowed his admittedly low threshold of restraint. "Davis has no capacity & his generals but little more than he has & if it be possible to ruin our cause by imbecility they will do it," he fumed on May 13, just after his brigade finished the hard retreat to the Chickahominy River, almost in sight of Richmond itself.[12]

He was equally frank with Stephens, to whom he had sent a steady stream of carping letters throughout the so-called campaign. The long siege at Yorktown, much of it spent with foot-deep water in their earthworks, had reduced his command by about one-third through sickness and exposure, "without any necessity or object that I could [learn, except] the stupidity and cowardice of our officers." They could have attacked and beaten McClellan had they but tried, he declared, "but as usual we burnt up everything and fled," and then lost over a thousand casualties during the withdrawal. "This is called generalship!!" he raged. In fact, everything seemed to irritate and disillusion Toombs. Congress had passed an act authorizing impressment of cotton and supplies from civilian growers for the army, and that outraged him, for he never forgot that he was a planter as well as a soldier. And his opinion of Davis only plummeted further as he saw the president apparently sustaining an incompetent like Johnston in high command. It was West Point favoritism again, of that he was certain. "Science will do anything but fight," he lamented in a direct reference to the West Pointers. "It will burn,

retreat, curse, swear, get drunk, strip soldiers—anything but fight."
It was so disheartening that he confessed, "I feel but little like fighting for a people base enough to submit to such despotism from such
contemptible sources."[13]

Toombs's remark about professional soldiers getting drunk was
singularly inappropriate, inasmuch as even before the evacuation
of Yorktown, there were stories that he took refuge himself from the
monotony of siege life in the bottle. Tom Cobb complained of it at
the beginning of May, and by the time Toombs and his brigade
reached the Chickahominy the problem had become open knowledge. "Toombs is drinking like a fish and making an ass of himself,"
Cobb complained, adding again that his fellow Georgian showed a
"disposition to shirk all positions of danger." As subsequent events
showed, anything like cowardice would have been quite out of character for Toombs, and the accusation may have reflected either
Cobb's lingering dislike of him, or else simply the fact that sometimes Toombs was too drunk to be on the front line with his men.
By now those close to Toombs were learning what Stephens and
many of his old political associates had long known. Despite his
hearty size and physique, Toombs's constitution simply had no resistance to alcohol. That simple glass or two of wine that helped cost
him the presidency the year before threatened now to compromise
him in uniform. No doubt it also helped, added to his innately independent nature, to make him a difficult subordinate. "His disobedience of orders is notorious," Cobb added, concluding that "his
military career is a desperate failure." Declaring the idea of Toombs
being a military commander "a farce," Cobb told his wife, "I have
sergeants in my legion in whose military capacity I have more confidence."[14]

If Cobb spoke hyperbolically, still there is no doubt that Toombs
was almost out of control, his intemperance with the bottle matched
by the recklessness of his speech. Certainly it helped that he missed
Julia and feared for her health. Some thought him all but encouraging mutiny—that was probably the liquor talking—but certainly
he let any and all know how he felt about Davis. When the president
and Lee came to visit the troops after they reached the Chickahominy, he sarcastically wrote Julia that this was a sure indication

that they were not to have a fight until the coming of the next winter. Rather, he expected they were simply to sit down in front of Richmond and protect the city while allowing McClellan all the initiative in the campaign. "The utter incompetency of Mr. Davis and his West Point generals have brought us to the verge of ruin," he declared. By the end of May, when Davis again visited the army, he and Toombs met in a notably chilly atmosphere. "Davis is polite and formal," the general confided, adding almost gleefully, "so am I."[15]

Undoubtedly, Toombs said too much to the wrong people. His verbal assaults on his superiors, military and civilian, were in danger of demoralizing some of his men, especially the officers with whom he most associated, and when word got back to Georgia of the general's constant harangue against authority, one of his old neighbors whose son served on Toombs's staff was furious. "I was sorry that Mr. T. ever entered the Army," lamented Adam Alexander, "for I know he can cooperate with no man or set of men, unless *he* is the ascendant. He yields his opinions to no one, no matter on what subject, & would insanely maintain them against a regiment." Finding Toombs completely unfit to lead a brigade, Alexander complained that "he is satisfied with no one, but himself, or those who submit to him." Some observers read into the general's intemperate harangues against Davis a secret desire to bring down the administration and to elevate himself to the president's place. Hearing a brief rumor that Toombs's disenchantment might lead him to resign his commission, Alexander could only say, "I hope in God this is true & that he will come home & stay here, and keep his seditious mouth shut."[16]

Toombs was becoming an embarrassment in the army's high command. When the first battle of any real substance came on May 31 at Seven Pines, the Georgian and his brigade had been posted well away from the main army and did not see action. It would be too much to say that Johnston intentionally kept the inexperienced and overly voluble Georgian where he could do no harm in the fight, but certainly Toombs chafed at missing the engagement. Johnston took a dangerous wound himself and was superseded by Lee, who at first seemed to take no notice of Toombs, but in the days following Seven Pines others certainly did. His drinking became the disgrace of the brigade. A soldier of the Seventeenth Georgia complained early in June that "there is no discipline or order in the whole concern and to cap the climax the brigade of which this regiment is a part is commanded by a drunkard, Robt Toombs."[17] Cobb also observed that Toombs's brigade "is becoming utterly demoralized and disorganized," while Toombs himself every day behaved more and more indefensibly: "He is drunk almost every afternoon and makes himself most ridiculous, riding like Jehu driving from camp to camp, and uttering horrible oaths." Cobb expected that Toombs's behavior and insubordination were bound to result in his being arrested soon, "and *I think he wants to be.*"[18] Of course Cobb, totally abstemious himself and compulsively holier-than-thou when commenting on others less abstinent, may have been exaggerating, but others observed enough of the same behavior in Toombs to ensure that Cobb was not inventing stories. Certainly word got to other ranking officers, and though they were less vociferous than Cobb in their condemnation of Toombs's conduct, there can be no doubt that his behavior cost him the respect of many. Unfortunately for Toombs, the one person not there to see his antics was Stephens, whose friendship so often served as an anchor to keep Toombs steady, for by then Stephens had gone home to Crawfordville and they could only correspond. Time after time in the past, when separated too long by distance or disagreement from Little Aleck, the bibulous Georgian gave way to the exaggerations in his nature, and never for his own good. Because of distance, Little Aleck may not even have known of his friend's disintegrating behavior.

Indeed, some of Toombs's actions could only be described as perverse, as if he intentionally dared not only the army but also his old constituents at home to question his behavior. The demands of feeding the growing armies already placed a huge strain on the agricultural resources of the Confederacy, and at the same time the tight Union blockade and Confederate embargo policy all but ended the necessity for continuing to grow cotton. In all the cotton states, therefore, planters were encouraged to convert their crops from cotton to corn, and citizens' groups arose everywhere to promote the policy. When the movement began in Georgia in April and May, Toombs privately denied any sympathy. Let those who stayed at home making such demands of planters like himself who were with the army come and fight instead. They would win their independence that much sooner, and then the issue of what a man should plant would become moot. "Let them take up arms & come with me to drive the invader from our soil & then we will settle what sort of seeds shall be put into it," he grumbled on May 19.[19] Nevertheless, and without telling anyone who asked, Toombs gave orders that 1,250 of his 1,810 acres of plantation be planted in various food grains that spring, with only 560 for cotton. The perversity of his nature would not allow him to admit that he had gone along with the movement, however, for fear anyone might think that he had been forced into making the change.[20]

Thus, rumors in Georgia erroneously told of the general continuing to plant cotton as before, and soon came attacks in the press charging him with "selfishness and criminal indifference." In Randolph County a public meeting of citizens passed resolutions condemning his behavior, as well as that of others, and then called on him to divert slave labor from his plantations to the Chattahoochee River defenses instead, as did many other planters. Toombs exploded when a telegram brought him the resolutions. He would not divert a single slave, he declared. As for those who tried to force him to change what he did with his own property, they were "cowardly miscreants." He dared them to rob him of his slaves in his absence but promised, "You cannot intimidate me."[21]

His behavior was almost puerile. The Committee of Safety in Randolph County responded that his attitude demonstrated "that inflated egotism for which you have acquired some notoriety, and abounds with evidence that if written under *sober* reflection, you have lost all proper appreciation of what is due from a gentleman and a soldier," evidence itself that stories of Toombs's drinking were well known at home. "You are presuming too much, sir," they continued, when he indulged his vaunted talent for "defamation and detraction." Neither his past career in politics nor the onetime adherence of his old political supporters could shield him in this crisis from condemnation for his conduct.[22] All of this criticism appeared in the Georgia press, and before long Toombs realized just how bad it made him look, and no doubt the veiled reference to his drinking especially stung. Immediately after receiving the first barb from the committee, Toombs went to Tom Cobb and asked if he approved of his action in refusing to divert his laborers. That Toombs would seek reassurance from Cobb, of all people, showed just how deeply he felt the sting of the committee's reproach and his own inner suspicion that he had not behaved well. Cobb, however, gave him no comfort.[23] Still, perversely, Toombs did not release to the public the fact that he was complying handsomely with the call to divert cotton land to grain.

The public and private embarrassment over the cotton business, the months of indecision and cross-purposes with the army, frustration at missing the only real battles so far at Williamsburg and Seven Pines, the timidity and ineptitude that he saw in the West Point officers and of course in the president himself mounted dangerously, with alcohol pushing Toombs toward a crisis. General Lee, meanwhile, wisely turned to the shovel and spade to fortify his army in defenses around Richmond in the face of McClellan's powerful, if glacial, advance. The idea of digging holes in which to take cover instead of advancing out in the open to attack incensed Toombs, and he made no attempt to conceal his contempt for this additional evidence of cowardly West Point "science."[24] Indeed, for some time he had complained all too openly about the general's policy of falling back ever since Yorktown. "Toombs was making a great noise," one Virginian noted, "& said he came there to fight and if there was any more retreating, he would take his brigade to Georgia & defend that state."[25] Ironically, on first being directed to erect defenses, Toombs suggested in a meeting of Lee's generals that he pull his brigade back some distance to the rear to what he thought a better position, which amused Longstreet, who thought Toombs's suggestion "strange," given that "he was known to have frequent talks with his troops, complaining of West Point men holding the army from battle, digging and throwing up lines of sand instead of showing lines of battle." General Daniel H. Hill teasingly suggested that Toombs would better be used by advancing his brigade to fire on and break up the parties digging earthworks for the enemy, a playful suggestion that Toombs might have been seeking to get away from the foe, and a remark calculated not to win any affection from the Georgian.[26]

When he did turn his attention to fortifying, Toombs clearly either had no concept of what he was to do, or else made no effort to learn from others. Experienced officers—who would have been West Point trained, and thus not entitled to teach Toombs anything—knew that the best defenses were made of solidly packed earth, which simply absorbed the impact and explosion of cannon balls and shells, but Toombs put his men to work with axes felling trees, using the logs to make his breastworks. When Lee inspected Toombs's line, he saw what any trained engineer would have seen, that enemy artillery fire hitting the logs would shred them and turn their flying splinters into deadly missiles doing more harm than good. "When General Toombs gains a little more experience," Lee said with visible amusement, "he will be convinced that *earth* is a better protection against cannon-balls than logs."[27] If Lee said it in Toombs's hearing, it was just one more reason to resent those West Point scientists.

During the lull of early June, Toombs's brigade engaged in sporadic picket firing with the enemy across the ground between them, but then Toombs either proposed or agreed to an informal truce with the Yankees in his front, whereby they would not fire on each other and instead allow the men to meet and exchange tobacco and coffee, and especially newspapers. It was a common enough practice, but then Toombs's division commander, the West Pointer Magruder, ordered it stopped on June 13. This hardly endeared Magruder to his subordinate, and apparently there was already some strained feeling between them. "There is much bad blood among these high officers," Cobb said that same day in speaking of Toombs, Magruder, Major General Daniel H. Hill, and others, "many jealousies and back bitings." Toombs's own past behavior left little doubt as to which of them was the most jealous and backbiting.[28]

What Toombs never understood or countenanced was that his was the sort of behavior and attitude least calculated to advance the army's cause when and if it did come to what he most desired, a major battle, and now it was coming. Having completed the fortifications to protect Richmond, Lee decided to take the offensive and attempt to drive McClellan away from the capital and off the peninsula entirely, if possible. He began the attack on June 25 in the first of what became known as the Seven Days' Battles, though Toombs and his brigade were not engaged on the first two days. But then on June 27 Lee determined to strike at McClellan's position at Gaines's Mill on the Chickahominy. While Lee planned his main attack for the north side of the river, Magruder's corps, including the Georgians, was posted at Garnett's Farm on the south side. That morning Lee and Hill rode to Garnett's to discuss what should be done on this side of the stream. Lee did not want to bring on a general engagement there, and by the time Toombs and other of Magruder's generals arrived, it was already agreed to try to keep this part of the line out of action. Toombs became indignant. Cursing the eternal spade and shovel, he declared, "Damn West Point, they wont let me fight & if I can get nothing else to fight, I'll fight a nigger." He probably did not say this in Lee's hearing, but his intemperate remarks so disgusted Hill that he left the conference. Had Toombs been a part of Hill's command, he most likely would have put the Georgian under arrest on the spot.[29] Certainly Toombs did not endear himself to the North Carolinian.

That afternoon Toombs heard the battle open on the north side of the Chickahominy, where it raged for several hours. The enemy was positioned in his front at Garnett's, no more than a few hundred yards away, and yet he was to do nothing other than some desultory artillery dueling. But then at last came an order from Magruder, through the division commander, General David R. Jones, to make a feint attack in their front, the object being simply to tie down the enemy's strength without bringing on a general engagement and prevent him from reinforcing the hard-pressed Yankees north of the river. This would be the first time that Toombs and his brigade had been sent into an action, and Jones clearly did not entirely trust the Georgian to obey his orders to the letter. At the same time, believing that the Yankees were in considerable strength in his front, and despite his complaints to date about not being allowed to fight, Toombs himself objected to the movement, fearing the strength in his front. Consequently, whether because of Jones's mistrust or Toombs's own demand, the order for the move was put in writing.[30]

There seems little doubt that Toombs objected to the order, though whether because it was only a feint and not a genuine attack, or because he feared the losses he would incur, he did not say. Nevertheless, shortly before dark he took his brigade forward, with another brigade on his right, through a wheat field that separated the two armies by about 200 yards. The enemy fire soon became gallingly heavy, especially when the Georgians reached a slight rise barely more than 100 feet from the enemy works. They could go no farther, but Magruder sent orders to Toombs to hold that rise at all hazards. Toombs soon had his entire brigade engaged, attempting to send them forward again into a small ravine, but after about two hours he was forced to withdraw in the darkness to his original lines. Colonel W. F. McIntosh of the Fifteenth Georgia was killed in the fight for the ravine, and when the regimental surgeon informed Toombs on the battlefield, he broke down in tears. "I have been forced, by order of that damned Magruder, to send McIntosh, one of the best men God ever made, to his certain death," he sobbed.[31]

On finally witnessing real battle, Toombs was shocked at the losses, some 191 killed and wounded, about one-third of his command. Not surprisingly, the action got out of hand and became far more general, and costly, than Lee or Magruder had intended, and the responsibility had to be shared between Toombs for his inexperience, and Jones and Magruder for failing to enforce more careful oversight on their novice subordinate. But so far as Toombs was concerned, the blood of his Georgians was entirely on the hands of "that old ass Magruder," and he did not warm any more to his commander when Magruder soon tried to cover his own lack of oversight by claiming that Toombs had attacked without orders.[32]

The next day Toombs was in action again and once more complaining, as confusion in the high command led Magruder to order Toombs to send two of his regiments forward in a costly reconnaissance when McClellan appeared to be withdrawing from their front. This time Magruder tried to shift the blame to Jones, though Toombs came in for a share as well, but with the Yankees definitely retiring there was little time to waste on recriminations. Toombs

joined in the general pursuit but saw no action beyond skirmishing for the next two days until the evening of June 30 at White Oak
Swamp, when his troops just found the end of the battle and thereafter spent the night on the battlefield collecting and tending to the
wounded and slain. "It was a scene never to be forgotten," Toombs
told Little Aleck two weeks later. At last he was seeing war.[33]

But the real war began the next day. McClellan had placed his
army in a well-defended position on and around Malvern Hill, and
Lee hoped to drive him from the peninsula entirely with one well-
delivered hammer blow. Unfortunately, his own army was weary, his
high command not working entirely in unison. Magruder's command, including Toombs's brigade, was supposed to be pursuing
the Yankees closely, but instead Magruder mistakenly put them on
the wrong road and did not actually reach the pending battlefield
until well into the afternoon of July 1. After an artillery bombardment that failed to punch holes in McClellan's lines but that saw Magruder's own artillery badly mangled, Lee gave the order for an assault of almost his whole army in a line five brigades wide and three
to four brigades deep in places. As one brigade went into the foolish attack and was battered back, the next in line went forward.
Toombs's was in the third line, and like the others had to pass
through dense brush and briar-studded ravines to reach the front,
all the while seeing the road and the flash of the Yankee artillery on
the hill ahead of them. When finally they came into the open they
saw D. H. Hill's brigades ahead of them beaten back and three-
quarters of a mile of open field ahead of them, over which they had
to charge into the enemy fire.

Even a professional like Magruder could not control and maintain organization through that ground and in the face of that fire,
and an amateur like Toombs had no hope of doing so. When portions of Hill's command retired they passed through the Georgians
and inevitably disrupted their organization. The brigade began to
spread out, regiments strayed from the line of advance, and some
started falling back with Hill's men toward the safety of the woods
and brush from which they had just emerged. Toombs himself went
to the rear and tried to rally them and form them back into a useful organization, even taking the colors of the Second Georgia to

lead them back into the fight, but the task was beyond him.[34] As more men of other commands came up, they saw Toombs standing by the side of a path appealing to his men to stand, his arms flying wildly in gesticulation, yet it was evident that most paid no attention; and when they continued to retire, he went with them, no doubt still trying to get them to stand.[35] Meanwhile, Hill rode back to the Georgians to get them to come support his own faltering remnants. He could not immediately find Toombs himself and so started to rally some of the Georgians and lead them back into the fight. They were beaten back once more, and in the aftermath as Hill tried to rally them again, Toombs rode up from another part of the line where he had been trying to rally others.

Given the distaste he already felt for Toombs the braggart and malcontent, Hill was in no mood to be patient with Toombs the general who could not control his men. "Where is your brigade, sir?" he yelled through the din. "I told you that I wanted a fighting brigade, and your brigade will not fight. I knew it would not, and you are the man who pretends to have been spoiling for a fight. For Shame! Rally your troops! Where were you when I was riding up and down your line, rallying your troops?"[36] Hill, not given to verbal restraint himself, apparently even shook his finger in Toombs's face in admonition and all but called him a coward for not being at the front line, unaware that Toombs had, in fact, been rallying another portion of the command. Toombs responded just as heatedly and protested that he had been trying to get his men reformed to come to Hill's support, but Hill declared it was untrue and that he had been watching the whole business and saw no evidence of any effort by Toombs to get into the battle. At that, Toombs said simply that this was not the time or place to settle what had clearly become a deadly personal altercation and abruptly left to continue rallying his men, though the Georgians were so disorganized that several generals encountered them in places on the field without being able to reform them.[37]

The battle ended in a severe defeat for Lee, though McClellan was battered enough that he never fought again on the peninsula, and within a few weeks he evacuated. Toombs had no hesitation in admitting that his army had been beaten at Malvern Hill but could not refrain from declaring that his own army had been commanded "without skill or judgment." His near-megalomania over his own surpassing wisdom was such that even in front of the press he routinely declared that orders from higher authority "appeared to his superior judgment to be so clearly wrong, that he required them to be put in writing for his own vindication." Only Longstreet received his approbation for good performance. "Lee was far below the occasion," he averred. "If we had had a general in command we could easily have taken McClellan's whole command." Instead, he regarded the campaign as a barren victory without the decisive results he expected, and anticipating the reaction to his own inevitable criticism and second-guessing after the fact, he told Stephens, "All who will not sing peans [sic] to such blunderers and imbeciles will probably be crushed and dishonoured."[38]

What Toombs probably did not expect was that his own courage would be questioned as a result of Malvern Hill. Within days rumors of his altercation with Hill spread, and soon it was said that Toombs in fact refused to lead a charge when ordered, saying he was "not going to carry his men into that slaughter pen."[39] Obervers more in the know admitted that Hill was at fault for his ill-informed snap judgment of Toombs, as well as for his ungovernable temper and outburst, but still the opinion was common that, as Colonel Jeremy Gilmer observed, "as to Genl. Toombs generally, I do not think he stands very high with the provincal [sic] officers of the army." Almost no one seemed willing to speak on his behalf, no doubt Toombs's reward for months of carping at his fellow professional officers. The most commonly expressed opinion was that he was neither a good commander in camp nor in the field, and Gilmer was happy when a friend managed to get assignment away from Toombs's command.[40]

Even without murmurings of cowardice to impel him to demand an accounting, Toombs never would have allowed Hill's comments to him to pass unchallenged. Five days later, once the army had settled down, he sent his superior a note reiterating the substance of what had been said and demanded to know if his recollection of Hill's words was accurate and, if so, what explanation Hill had to make. Not one to avoid contention himself, Hill responded the same day essentially confirming Toombs's recollection, though denying that his comments were in any way a reflection directed at the Georgia brigade but were meant to apply only to Toombs himself. "It is notorious that you have a thousand times expressed your disgust that the commanding general did not permit you to fight," Hill added. "It is equally notorious that you retired from the field. These are the two facts of which I reminded you." It was hardly a response designed to mollify Toombs, who found Hill's language "violent and offensive."

Naturally, Toombs did not let it end there, and he responded immediately, accusing Hill of attempting to menace and intimidate him from seeking satisfaction for his insults, and Toombs now demanded that accounting, naming one of his colonels to act as his second in arranging a duel. Hill waited almost a week to reply and once more denied reflecting on the courage of Toombs's brigade; then he agreed that if he could be shown to have done Toombs injustice in his words on the field at Malvern Hill, he would apologize, promising that if he were to find that Toombs had in fact done all that a commander could and should do to rally his men and lead them into the fight, then his apology would be "cordial and complete." But in any event, he would accept no challenge, regarding it as contrary to the interest of the cause they both were sworn to serve and against the articles of war as well.[41] In his response, Toombs reiterated that he wanted satisfaction and demanded to know if Hill's refusal was only temporary, due to the pressure of events, or absolutely final. Typically, Toombs also said that though Hill might have sworn to abide by rules that prohibited dueling, he himself certainly never swore not to violate the articles of war that prevented serving officers from dueling. If that were the only impediment to a meeting, then he would resign immediately to remove the cause of Hill's sensitivity.[42]

Hill closed the correspondence with a final note on July 15, protesting that his last missive had been intended to be conciliatory. He reiterated that under no circumstances would he engage in a duel and repeated his offer to apologize publicly if satisfied that he was in error on the field. That said, he closed the correspondence, making it clear that he would engage in no further debate. The day before Hill's final note, Toombs had already written to Stephens telling him he intended to resign from the army "the instant I can do so without dishonour," possibly expecting that this was the only way to get his meeting with Hill on the dueling field. Besides, the glory he had expected had eluded him. The military reputation he had hoped to achieve, possibly to use as a political base to challenge Davis for leadership some time in the future, simply had failed to materialize; and he felt firmly convinced that there was virtually a conspiracy among Davis and the West Point generals to keep him from demonstrating that he was their superior in strategy and daring. "Davis and his Janissaries (the regular army) conspire for the destruction of all who will not bend to them," he complained, "and avail themselves of the public danger to aid them in their selfish and infamous schemes."[43] Mary Chesnut in Richmond heard him barking of "a conspiracy against him" among the army's high command, though she asked the obvious question that Toombs himself seemed never to ask, namely, "why?" But Toombs was past thinking logically in the matter. Mrs. Chesnut thought him "ready for another revolution" as he "curses freely everything Confederate, from a president down to a horse boy."[44] In the end, he could only strike out in one last petulant blow at Hill by going through the army camps and even to Lee's headquarters itself to denounce Hill as a coward and liar, and that, too, was done in the presence of a friendly Georgia newspaperman, Peter W. Alexander, who gleefully reported it through the Atlanta press.[45]

If anything more were needed to demonstrate to Lee especially that Toombs was an irritant he could do without, this petulant act served the purpose. He soon transferred Magruder away from his army entirely and shifted Toombs from Hill's command to Longstreet's. Probably only Toombs's remaining political influence in Georgia prevented him from being placed under arrest for unbecoming conduct. Certainly others expected such an outcome. "Toombs is denouncing Hill as a poltroon," Tom Cobb observed the day after Hill's final refusal. "I don't know how it will end, but I think you will hear that Toombs is under arrest in less than a week."[46] When that week had passed, with no arrest, Toombs still talked of resignation, and Colonel Thomas Jordan quipped that the

Georgian was stopped "like an ass between two bundles of hay," uncertain whether to resign and then horsewhip Hill, or resign and manipulate some Georgia member of Congress into leaving his post so that Toombs could replace him "and overturn the Government from the floor of Congress."[47] Before the campaign Toombs had promised his brigade surgeon to stay away from alcohol so as not to cloud his mind during the crisis to come, but clearly his erratic behavior evidenced a return to the bottle.[48] Cobb found him once more drinking heavily, "still making a beast of himself from liquor." It was a pity, said Cobb, "to see a great intellect debased by so contemptible a temptation."[49]

During the month following the end of the Hill imbroglio, Toombs remained near Malvern Hill, once again disdaining the spade and shovel work that to him so epitomized the professionals. "One engineer could find work for all the men that had been sent to hell since Adam sinned," Toombs said to Cobb early in August, "and according to scripture, tom," he added, "that is a big pile."[50] His dismissal of military routine almost got him in trouble with the only officer in the army as prickly as Hill, when one afternoon General Stonewall Jackson rode along his lines and found that Toombs had failed to place properly his advance outposts. Jackson found Toombs himself lying in the shade of his tent to escape the heat and promptly upbraided him with some severity, ordering the Georgian to remedy the oversight.[51]

All the while, Lee kept a wary eye on a growing Yankee army in northern Virginia commanded by General John Pope, and when it became evident that Pope intended to advance toward Richmond, Lee began to shift his army north to meet the new threat to the capital. Longstreet's corps got its orders to move on August 13, and many of those who remained in the Richmond defenses were not sorry to see the back of Toombs. Sarcastically referring to the Georgian's boasts about wanting to fight, and to Hill's suggestion that he had been anything but willing, Colonel Gilmer observed a few days later that the new campaign "will give him another chance to meet the foe, and shew his pluck, *if he has any.*"[52]

Unfortunately, Toombs's pluck did exactly the opposite, getting him into conflict certainly, but not with the enemy. With Longstreet's corps he arrived in the vicinity of Gordonsville, Virginia, as Lee began assembling to face the enemy, with the Rapidan River between them. A major battle was imminent, but protection of Lee's army was vital, for it was not at full strength yet. Longstreet ordered two of Toombs's regiments to go to Raccoon Ford on the evening of August 17. It was vitally important, for there were only two crossings on the Rapidan, and if the Yankees should gain possession of either of them, they might move on Lee before he was ready to meet them. Toombs previously had received orders from army headquarters to have his command cook and prepare rations to march on short notice. Despite what should have been an apparent urgency in that directive, however, Toombs had already left his command that evening and ridden some distance behind the lines to visit an old friend. Thus he did not receive Longstreet's order, which was carried out instead by Colonel Henry L. Benning.

When Toombs returned and found two of his Georgia regiments at the ford, he declared in a huff that no one but he had authority to order his men around. Moreover, seeing that being absent from their main camps prevented them from getting their rations prepared, and believing that another Confederate brigade was near the ford, making his presence unnecessary, he ordered his men back to their original position, perhaps sending word of his action to Longstreet in the process, along with a typically blustering assertion that it required no more than "an old woman and a broomstick" to guard the ford.[53] That was bad enough, but worse, by his action Toombs—who was mistaken about the other nearby brigade—left Raccoon Ford entirely unguarded, and not long after his Georgians left several regiments of Yankee cavalry rode across unimpeded and caused serious mayhem in the Confederate rear before they withdrew. Longstreet was livid. On August 18 he sent his chief of staff, Moxley Sorrel, to place Toombs under arrest for what Longstreet called his "usurpation of authority," a charge that Toombs believed did not formally exist under the articles of war, though his countermanding the orders of his superior officer without permission was certainly a serious breach of etiquette as well as of discipline.[54]

Longstreet, like most of the other officers of the army, had heard enough from Toombs to last a lifetime and was little inclined to be patient. Personally, he rather liked the Georgian and had said that if Toombs had been educated at West Point, "where he would have learned self-control," he might have been a distinguished soldier, "but his insubordination ruined him as an officer."[55] But insubordination in the face of the enemy was too dangerous to pass unpunished. Toombs immediately asked for permission to be excused the humiliation of accompanying his brigade without commanding it, and Longstreet acquiesced, giving him permission to go back to Gordonsville. The next morning, however, before Toombs could leave, he heard artillery fire in the distance that seemed to herald the opening of the battle and decided to remain with his brigade, riding in their rear. In violation of regulations for an officer under arrest, he wore his sword. Worse, when the Georgians went into camp that afternoon, he could not resist making them a speech that Sorrel said was of a "violent" nature, and Longstreet himself learned that Toombs had spoken "in anything but complimentary terms of his commander."[56]

Then it was that Toombs decided to ask Longstreet for a suspension of his arrest so he could fight with his men in the anticipated battle. Unfortunately, as he approached Longstreet, it was in sight of his Georgians, who saw their general about to beard the commander whom he had just condemned to them. They cheered Toombs on. Hearing that and knowing its meaning, an affront to himself, and seeing Toombs unlawfully wearing his saber, Longstreet charged him with breaking the terms of his arrest and disobedience of orders for not immediately going to Gordonsville and ordered him to leave the army at once. Lee himself apparently witnessed this scene, and Toombs a few days later thought it was the cheer of his men whose loyalty so incensed "the magnates Lee & Longstreet" that in jealousy they had him arrested.[57]

This time Toombs went back to Gordonsville, and there he remained for several days, fuming, writing to Stephens, and imagining everyone but himself at fault. "My zeal for the public service and desire to prepare my starving regiment for battle is my sole and only fault," he told Little Aleck. Once more it was the conspiracy of the West Pointers to hold him back, no doubt abetted by Davis, that lay behind his misfortune. "I must think it a pretext," he concluded, speaking of "the thousand lies which my enemies avail themselves of every occasion to propagate." He sent Stephens full details of his side of the issue and copies of his subsequent correspondence with Longstreet in which he tried to regain his command, so that his friend could defend him in the press, still incredulous that the whole episode had occurred, and entirely oblivious of how his behavior could have produced such a result.[58]

At least Toombs's repeated appeals to Longstreet to allow him to return to his brigade for the pending battle finally softened his commander's irritation, especially one plea that bordered—for Toombs anyhow—on outright apology and admission of error.[59] On Friday, August 29, as what was to become known as the Second Battle of Manassas began to rage on the old 1861 battlefield, Longstreet sent an order to Gordonsville directing Toombs to return to his command.[60] Toombs mounted his horse, Gray Alice, and raced for the battlefield, only approaching the contending armies toward the evening of August 30. He reached Longstreet's headquarters just as his commander was preparing a final assault and presented himself, hat off, sweating from the ride, and his horse thoroughly lathered. Longstreet said he was just about to send the attack order to Toombs's division commander, General Jones, and Toombs asked that he be allowed to carry it on his way to rejoin his brigade. Longstreet agreed, and Toombs galloped off, intoxicated with the drama and excitement of the moment.[61]

He raced toward Henry Hill, where Longstreet's command was preparing for the final action of the battle in attempting to drive the Yankees from the eminence and cut off their retreat. "Hurrah for General Toombs!" his men cried when they saw him, ahead of his staff, approaching their position. The Georgians raised their hats to him, and he raced past them cheering them on. He was on show again, and rode past every one of his regiments, standing in the stirrups to bow and wave his hat, attracting the cheers of each, and then on to deliver his message before riding back along the front of the division, despite the considerable stray fire coming his way from the enemy.[62] As he rode he yelled encouragements. "Go in boys and give the d——d invaders hell!" he shouted, promising he would lead them himself if the battle continued the next day.[63] Not content to leave it at that, he said to another group as he passed, "Go it, boys! I am with you again. Jeff Davis can make a general, but it takes God Almighty to make a soldier!"[64]

Just which Toombs thought he was, a soldier or God Almighty, he did not say, but he comported himself well as his brigade and others went in for the final assault just as he finished his dramatic, if histrionic, ride. During the advance, Benning may actually have commanded since Toombs did not know the positions or the ground, and in any case Toombs only got part way through the forward movement before he came upon a mortally wounded Yankee colonel leaning against a tree. It was Fletcher Webster, the son of Toombs's old friend Daniel Webster, and himself a politician turned soldier. It was an affecting moment. Recognizing Toombs, Webster called to him, and when the Georgian recognized him, he dropped out of the advance, dismounted, and knelt beside the dying Federal, giving him water from his own canteen. That done, Toombs left one of his staff officers to care for Webster and rejoined the advance. The Federals successfully repulsed the attack, for by then the Confederates themselves were spent from two days of hard fighting, and as they retired, Toombs returned to Webster's side. He spoke soothing and hopeful words to the dying man, then left once more to look after his command, and soon Webster died. That night Toombs sent a party to retrieve the body from the field, tearfully paying tribute to the son of his one-time political ally, and sent him through the lines under flag of truce to return the corpse to his friends and family.[65]

It was not the experience that the Georgian had wanted, but at least he was there to see his army in triumph, for the badly beaten Yankees soon retreated. Better yet, Longstreet, a more forgiving man than Toombs, chose to forget thereafter the business of the arrest and simply dropped the charges against his difficult subordinate. Indeed, the two men very quickly resumed quite friendly relations, Toombs having earlier tended to exempt Longstreet from his general condemnation of West Pointers for timidity.[66] In the two weeks ahead Longstreet certainly did what was best calculated to gain Toombs's good opinion, for he gave him an expanded command. Portions of the armies moved on to fight at Chantilly on September 1, but Toombs arrived only after the fight was over. Rather than pursuing the thoroughly defeated army before him, Lee allowed it to retreat to Washington, while he turned his attention to a long-held scheme to invade the North through Maryland, to take the war to the enemy's own ground. McClellan, back from the peninsula, had his own army there somewhere; but Lee expected he could steal a march or two on a foe who had already demonstrated himself considerably his inferior in the field and so sent Longstreet and Toombs's old nemesis Hill north across the Potomac toward Frederick, Maryland.

By September 14, vacancies and disruptions in his corps command structure led Longstreet to place Toombs, though only a brigadier, in temporary command of three brigades, including his own, making a substantial divisional command in the vicinity of Hagerstown. Thus Toombs missed the fight that day at South Mountain as elements of McClellan's army began to close on Lee, but late that evening he received orders to move west with his command toward Sharpsburg, along Antietam Creek, where Lee was going to concentrate his army for the inevitable battle. By dawn the next day, September 15, Toombs arrived to be assigned his place at the very southern end of Lee's long thin line along the creek, guarding the Rohrbach Bridge over the Antietam. At last the great soldier's destiny he so longed for had found him.

For a change, Lee's vaunted audacity—certainly not vaunted by Toombs, however—almost cost him dearly, for on the Antietam he found himself in a position with nearly half his army some distance away at Harpers Ferry, with McClellan and almost his entire army concentrated in his front. If McClellan pushed Lee away from the creek and Sharpsburg, Lee had the impassable Potomac at his back, his only line of escape or of reinforcement from Harpers Ferry being the road from the south that passed immediately behind the Rohrbach Bridge on his right. If the Yankees took that bridge and gained the road, they would cut off reinforcement and at the same time turn Lee's right flank. One concerted push then could force him back into the river and virtual destruction. Everything depended on that bridge. That being the case, assigning the troublesome and inexperienced Toombs to act as guard seemed at first a strange choice. In fact, however, Lee may have preferred to have more seasoned soldiers and more responsible commanders elsewhere on his line, where he expected to fight the battle. Moreover, the position at the bridge was so strong that even a small brigade and a less than desirable commander should be able to hold it. The Antietam did not appear to be fordable anywhere nearby, and the bridge itself was so narrow that any attacking Yankees could come across only a few abreast; even to reach the bridge the enemy would have to come along a road beside the creek that would expose them to unimpeded flank fire for 100 yards or more. Meanwhile, on the Confederate side a steep bank rose up from the end of the bridge, affording Toombs's men excellent defensive positions and a commanding view and range over the scene.

He needed that advantage, for by the morning of September 17 higher orders had detailed two of his regiments to another duty from which they had not returned, and he had only the Second and Twentieth Georgia, the Fiftieth Georgia on detail from another brigade, and a company of South Carolina infantry. Like the rest of Lee's army, Toombs saw some skirmishing and jockeying for position the day before and even took his men across the creek to occupy the high ground on the other side before Major General Ambrose Burnside's advancing IX Corps could get to it. They were still there the next morning when the rumble of artillery up the line gave hints that the main battle was getting started. Hour after hour Toombs could hear the battle growing in intensity to his left, knowing that eventually, inevitably, the Yankees were bound to make an effort to hit and turn Lee's right and get across the bridge.

Shortly after 8:00 A.M. pressure from the Yankees in their front began to force the Georgians back to the creek and the approaches to the bridge, and by nine o'clock they had crossed to the other side in the face of substantial skirmishing, Toombs knowing that his mere 500 men were no match for a Union corps that numbered 10,000 or more. Finally, just after nine, the first assault toward the bridge came and was easily repulsed as the Georgians, from their perches on the slope and in the trees and behind stone barricades, had a virtual turkey shoot before them when the Federals approached the bridge in full view barely 100 yards away. Fortunately, the sound of firing in that sector reached the ears of several dozen men earlier sent to the rear to get rations, and they immediately returned to the line to support their comrades, the only reinforcement Toombs had at the bridge itself that day. Soon another assault came at them, a stronger one this time, and at the same time Toombs saw his only support, a small division that had been guarding the fords below him, pulled out and called to the hard-pressed main battleline. Toombs's two regiments, the Fiftieth Georgia, three batteries of artillery, a little bit of Virginia cavalry, and one bridge were all that stood between the enemy army and Lee's rear.[67]

Toombs and his men turned back this next wave as well, the Yankees never reaching the bridge, though some, seeing it impossible, leaped into the creek instead and tried to wade across, only to be slowed into easier targets by the water. Only one of them reached the other side alive, and he was mortally wounded. With the assault beaten back, the Georgians rested, ate what they had, and awaited the inevitable next attack. It came around 10:00 A.M. but strayed from its target, though soon afterward yet another assault was launched in its place. Supporting Federal artillery gave the Georgians' positions a heavy pounding to soften their resistance. There were scarcely 300 of them left by this time, and the latest attack was four brigades deep. Regiment after regiment made the desperate rush along the creek road leading to the bridge, but none could reach it under the Georgians' withering fire. For three hours Toombs's little command had held the bridge against every attempt to take it, buying invaluable time for Lee, who was so heavily engaged on the rest of his line that he could hardly spare a thought, let alone a reinforcement, to support his endangered right flank, despite Toombs's now fervent plea for assistance.

About 12:30 P.M. the final massive assault came forward, and this time they reached the mouth of the bridge. Portions of eleven Union regiments were involved, many of them remnants of the earlier broken assaults now engaged in supporting the latest. Their fire was taking a heavy toll on the Georgians, but still Toombs held out. Only when elements of the attacking forces finally, and wisely, shifted out of sight north and south of the bridge and found undefended shallows were they finally able to get across. That put overwhelming enemy force both above and below Toombs's position, and when Toombs got word of the crossings he appealed yet again for reinforcement, but there was none to send. The Fiftieth Georgia gave way in the face of advancing Yankees from the south, but Toombs's remaining regiments just shifted their position to cover both the bridge and their exposed left flank, and continued their fire. Only when men ran out of ammunition did they pull back up the slope individually, and soon the pressure of the advancing enemy on his right made it evident to Toombs that if he did not pull out, the foe would reach the road in his rear and cut him off from the rest of Lee's army. About 1:00 P.M., feeling the slackening pace of the Georgians' fire, a Union regiment on the other side of the creek pushed toward the bridge again, many of the men going into the water and wading, this time with little fire from the heights opposite. They got to the bridge and began to cross, still under fire, but this time they crossed and actually engaged some Georgians at the other end hand-to-hand before capturing them. More of Toombs's men were overrun before they could get back up the hill, and others, out of ammunition and about to be overwhelmed, simply surrendered. Farther back on the slope, other Georgians continued firing, but the Second Georgia was down to no more than fifty men and the Twentieth was just as badly battered, and Toombs ordered them to retire at last. They had held up Burnside for nearly five hours and put more than 900 of his men out of action, at a cost to themselves of one-third or more of the two regiments engaged.

By 1:30 P.M. Toombs was pulling his remnants off to the southwest one-half mile back, to support General Jones's division and to protect the vital road connecting Sharpsburg with Harpers Ferry, Lee's line of retreat, and the road on which General A. P. Hill's massive division was any moment expected to arrive. Fortunately, the Fifteenth and Seventeenth Georgia arrived to rejoin their comrades in Toombs's brigade, for their fighting was not over yet. At least Toombs was able to rest his men somewhat and replenish their ammunition, for the Yankees wasted more than two hours in consolidating their bridgehead and building up for the renewed assault for the road. It was vital time during which Toombs and Jones met and planned their positions for receiving the inevitable enemy attack.

Then at 4:00 P.M., as the advance units of Hill's marching column came in sight, promising relief at the last minute at the most endangered spot on the field, Jones's division gave way in the face of renewed pressure from Burnside, once more leaving Toombs's brigade isolated. Toombs personally tried to rally remnants of Jones's demoralized command, riding frantically along their lines yelling for them to "stand firm." By the time the Georgians linked with Jones's remnant that was holding its position, the Federals had advanced within little more than 100 yards of the road and were even within the outer limits of Sharpsburg itself. Hill was known to be nearby, but he might still arrive too late.

There was nothing but Toombs's brigade and some of Jones's scattered men between the enemy and disaster for Lee's army. Toombs had always boasted that he could do great things if given a chance. However disappointing he had been up to this moment, given the one opportunity he had truly to affect the course of history, he acted every inch the leader he thought he was. He decided to attack the advancing enemy, though hopelessly outnumbered. If he could just stall their advance long enough, Hill could come up and join with Lee's battered right to save the army and the day, for the Confederates had been badly battered all along the line, and Lee knew he could not gain a tactical victory and wanted only to get his army back across the Potomac to Virginia and safety. Toombs bought him that time. Forming his remnants into a battleline in a field of high corn, he kept them concealed until the Yankees approached. When the Federals rushed forward, the Georgians took the enemy by surprise, poured several volleys into them, broke their line, and poured into the gap. Toombs himself was at their head, on foot for a change, and led a charge that recaptured some previously lost artillery. Less than half an hour after the attack began, and despite their numerical superiority, the Federals pulled back toward the bridge. The road and Lee were safe, and Toombs continued his advance toward the Rohrbach Bridge itself, joined by some of Hill's arriving units. Only the persuasion of Colonel Benning prevented Toombs from trying to push the Yankees completely across the Antietam. He had won enough glory for one day.

And considerable glory it was. Longstreet, though he did not personally witness Toombs's performance, later spoke well of what he had heard of it, saying that Toombs there made himself a fine reputation as a fighter. General Jones thought highly of the Georgians' stand, and Lee himself remarked on the "distinguished gallantry" of Toombs and his command. Before long the press, especially in Georgia, sang his praises as the savior of the day on Lee's right, and if home-state favoritism accounted for some hyperbole in the encomiums, still the fact was that Toombs had given his best performance to date. No one could rationally deny that had he fought with less fortitude, Burnside might have gained the west side of Antietam Creek hours earlier than he did. The potential for disaster that might have confronted Lee's fortunes can hardly be underestimated.[68] Certainly no one ranked Toombs's performance more highly than he did himself. That evening, when an officer came from Lee to survey the right flank, Toombs asked, "What was said of me at headquarters?" The reply was that the Georgians' stand was "the talk of the army." That was enough for Toombs to dictate on the spot a report of his great deeds to be delivered to Lee, boasting that he held the same ground he had held at the opening of the fight and even had seventy-five prisoners that he wanted to hand over to other troops whom he derisively called "cornstalks." Just as typically, he almost immediately began complaining again when a battery sent to his support that day was recalled. "General Toombs swore a blue streak at me," recalled the hapless object of his ire, "and cursed everybody, declaring that he never got a good battery that some one did not steal it away from him, and so on."[69]

Before the praise began to be heard, however, Toombs himself had one last encounter with the Yankees. Stubborn even in the face of near-defeat and disaster, Lee did not retire from the field on September 18 but stayed in his lines, daring a timid McClellan to attack him again with his entire army on the field. That evening Toombs sent orders to his advance pickets to come in to the main line, since there had been no activity in his front, and soon afterward a party of Yankee cavalry made a reconnaissance in the darkness. They came on Toombs and his staff, just as the Confederates were riding to meet with Benning. Toombs himself challenged the riders and demanded that they identify themselves. The Federals shouted through the darkness that they were friends, but one of Toombs's staff apparently saw something or spotted a false accent and opened fire. Immediately, the Yankees fired back, and a pistol ball hit Toombs's right hand as he held Gray Alice's reins. As the Federals rode off, reportedly shouting taunts at the "damned rebels," Gray Alice panicked and dashed off into the night, and it took Toombs some time to regain control, especially with his hand injured. Riding back to safety, he came upon the headquarters of a Virginia cavalry regiment and called on its surgeon, from whom he first got a drink and then perhaps some tending to the wound.[70]

It was not the sort of wound Toombs would have wanted, being delivered to him by an accident of his own carelessness after the battle was long over, rather than suffered in the heat of the fight, but that was only the first of his disappointments. He went ahead of Lee's retreating army the next day and reached Richmond September 27, where perhaps already he was hearing people speak of A. P. Hill as the savior of the battle, not himself. He remained in the capital only two days, visiting with Stephens and no doubt giving him in person an earful of his own exploits on the field and Davis's incompetency in the executive mansion. It was the first time the two had been together in months, and Toombs's days as a general in the field were really the first experience he had had in thirty years in which Little Aleck had not somehow shared. It may be more than coincidental that it was in those months apart that Toombs became more irrational and intemperate than ever before in his life.

The general left September 29 and was back at home in Washington, Georgia, by October 4, nursing more than just a wounded hand.[71] In his own mind, he more than any other deserved the credit for saving Lee's right during the battle, and thus saving the army itself, yet more and more he heard sung the praises of Hill, even though it truly was only Toombs's hours of resistance that made it possible for Hill to relieve Lee. Yet where was his reward? Moreover, at the time of the battle Toombs had been exercising, under Longstreet's orders, the functions of a major general commanding a division. Did he not deserve a promotion to recognize both that fact and his conduct at Antietam? Instead, the division he temporarily commanded went to George E. Pickett and with it promotion to major general, even though Toombs was several months senior to Pickett as a brigadier. And Pickett had not even been present at Antietam.

The explanation, of course, was clear enough to Toombs. It was the old conspiracy still at work. Pickett was a West Point graduate and a Virginian, and the Virginian Lee in the army and Davis in Richmond continued to look out for their own. Even when Postmaster General John H. Reagan approached Davis with the suggestion that Toombs deserved promotion, the president replied that he could not do so without recommendation from Longstreet and Lee.[72] Not surprisingly, though both paid tribute to the Georgians' hard fighting at the Rorhbach Bridge, those commanders had seen more than enough of Toombs's insubordination, carelessness, and inefficiency to know that he was unfit for higher command. By early December, his recuperation nearly over, Toombs told Linton Stephens of his situation in the army: "I am well aware that that scoundrel Jeff Davis will avail himself of any opportunity [to] drive me from it, with dishonor if he could." Nevertheless, he intended to continue in uniform as long as he could "with honor."[73]

In fact, Toombs began considering resignation early in November, coincidentally not long after Pickett got his promotion and the division command. Typically, however, Toombs thought long and hard about any move that would affect his personal career. He had done as he always said he would and stayed in the army long enough to be in a great battle and prove himself on the field, and that he had done. But having refused the Senate seat tendered him in 1861, he would have no position of any authority, civil or military, if he gave up his commission. In an attempt to remedy that situation, when Senator John W. Lewis resigned his seat, Toombs quickly went to Milledgeville and made a speech to both houses of the legislature, promoting himself as a replacement, but in the balloting that ensued he trailed a humiliating fourth to Herschel V. Johnson, garnering only 14 of 189 votes cast.[74] The embarrassing defeat only confirmed Toombs's disgust with Georgia's legislature, which seemed slavishly to back the Davis administration. Still, he resolved to return to state politics again the next summer, very possibly to run to succeed Brown as governor if he did not seek reelection, though this was months into the future.[75]

Meanwhile, people in Richmond began to wonder when or if Toombs would return to his command. "What has become of Brigdr. Genl. Robert Toombs?" wrote Gilmer on Christmas. "Is he still rusticating at his plantation and counting the bales of cotton he raised in opposition to public opinion." Commenting that "his ambition to be a big General seems to be 'played out,' " Gilmer wondered if Toombs any longer had much of a following either in the army or at home in Georgia.[76] While he was absent Toombs also missed the dreadful battle at Fredericksburg, Virginia, that December, and apparently he did not actually rejoin his command until as late as January or even February 1863. It was certainly a happy reunion with the men of his brigade when he did arrive, but as the winter wore on it became all too evident to Toombs that there would be no promotion forthcoming, nor would Lee probably ever recommend him for one.

In fact, Toombs may have spent most of his time in Richmond rather than in the camps, for Benning seems actually to have exercised command of the old brigade throughout that period.[77] And by mid-February Toombs had come to a decision. He would resign. "I am fully satisfied that I cannot remain in the service with any advantage to the public or honor to myself," he wrote Stephens, who was back in Crawfordville. "I know the President has much desired my resignation; but I waited my own time and points, and got them as well as was possible from so false and hypocritical a wretch."[78] What those "points" were, he did not say, but it is evident in the main that Toombs finally realized that there would be no promotion coming. Even his admirers admitted that he was accustomed to being in the forefront, "to priority" said one, and he found it all but impossible to be a subordinate. Colonel Thomas W. Thomas of Georgia, who had known him well for years, remarked once that "Toombs has always been the big frog in the pond."[79] Now, however, he saw tadpoles like Pickett moving ahead of him, and it was intolerable.

Typically, Toombs made something of a production of his resignation, staying in Richmond for several days to make maximum political capital—such as it was—from his action. He sent it to Davis at the beginning of March, then waited for the president's formal notification of acceptance, which arrived on March 3. Then, rather than saying farewell to his brigade in person, he drafted a letter to them from the capital and sent it out to the army. "Under existing circumstances," he told them, "in my judgment, I could no longer hold my commission under President Davis with advantage to my country, or to you, or with honor to myself." He refrained from giving them his reasons, but almost everyone knew of his antipathy toward the administration and the army high command. "Nothing less potent than the requirements of a soldier's honor could, with my consent, wrench us asunder," he said. And yet what brought about this parting, in fact, was nothing less than his thwarted ambition, which spoke volumes about Toombs's egotism and selfishness but not at all well about anything connected with honor. Presented the choice between what he all along proclaimed as his sense of duty and desire to fight for his country, and a perceived personal slight, he opted in the end to make his first loyalty himself.[80]

If Toombs thought his decision, so well publicized in advance during his days in Richmond, would work to his advantage by raising an outcry of opposition to Davis over the loss of such an indispensable general, he was disappointed. There was some brief discussion in the capital for a few days, but everyone seemed to know already that he acted out of pique at not being promoted. Also, there were rumors of his seeking the governorship in Georgia, and even talk of treasonous designs to make a separate peace for Georgia with the Yankees. Few people really believed that, but it indicated how widespread was the realization of the extremity of his disaffection. Knowing that, few were surprised at his resignation.[81] One Richmond paper suggested, "There will be a general feeling of regret that this distinguished statesman and soldier has resigned his command," but it was a sentiment not shared in the army's high command.[82] On March 3, before Davis formally accepted the resignation, the adjutant general sent a telegram to Lee to ask if he wished to oppose its acceptance. Lee's almost chilly reply was the eloquently brief statement, "I make no objection to the resignation of Genl Toombs."[83]

Nor would Jefferson Davis be sorry to see him leave the army, to which he never wanted to appoint him in the first place. In justification of having done so, he remarked a few months later, "I could not but feel a hope of his displaying on the field qualities to justify my giving him the post he solicited," but in the end, "this hope was not realized." Throughout 1862, while Lee and his high commanders were free in recommending many of their subordinates for promotion in reward for good service, Davis saw also the eloquent absence of any recommendation to promote Toombs to fill any vacancy at all. Once only, in Lee's report of Antietam, were Toombs's actions commended, and even then Lee recommended others for elevation, but not him. "Having in the first instance appointed General Toombs to a high military grade before his capacity to command had been tested, I had gone so far as my sense of duty permitted, and can only regret that he failed to secure from his superiors that appreciation of his ability which would warrant his promotion."[84] In the polite language of a statesman, Davis rendered perhaps the most damning condemnation of Toombs as a soldier. The Georgian's commanders had no confidence in his ability to give their endorsements to his ambition, and the president had insufficient faith in him to act without them.

Yet to Toombs himself, what could it be but more evidence, as if any were needed, of the venal corruption of the president and his generals in their unholy cabal to keep him down? Worse, in his growing monomania over Davis's war policy, he perhaps began to suspect, if he had not for some time, that Davis and the West Pointers' true aim was not to win the war at all but to drag it out as long as possible for their own benefit, the free exercise of their "science" of war at the expense of Southern blood and the steady usurpation of more and more power by a nascent dictator in Richmond. In his self-obsessed thinking, Toombs could easily see Davis forcing him out of the field as one way of prolonging the war, for surely if the Georgian and his ideas of strategy were given high command, he would defeat the North in short order. The evidence suggested that there was more than one war to fight. Removing himself from the battle against the Yankees enabled Toombs to devote himself fully to an even more important contest, one for the soul of the Confederacy as well as its very life: the war against its president, a war already being fought by his only true ally, Little Aleck.

Uncivil War

Vice President Stephens, so different from so many of his associates, certainly stood apart from almost all of them in one respect. He never evidenced the least inclination to trade the broadcloth of a politician for the uniform of a general. No doubt in the main it was because he knew his own physical limitations well enough to know that he was not suited for such an active life. No doubt, too, unlike Toombs, he realized that soldiering was best left to real soldiers, not to dilettantes. He even opposed his much more robust brother Linton's entering the military and rejoiced when he resigned after a few months' service. He did not want his brother to risk his life for the cause, and it is not hard to interpolate even by 1862 that his own commitment to that cause was not yet at such a temper that he felt it worth risking personal loss. The old accusations of reconstructionist still echoed occasionally in Richmond and in Georgia, and ironically, the radicals like Rhett did not come to accept Stephens as a truly dedicated Confederate until he joined their chorus against Davis. In their eyes, attacking and undermining the president was ample evidence of patriotism.

Stephens never felt any enthusiasm for his position as vice president, regarding it as no more significant in this new concern than it had been in the Union, and his personal distance from Davis even before they left Montgomery ensured that he would have no influence with that very private man, who jealously guarded the prerogatives of his office. The Georgian's differences with the president's policy he had not tried to conceal, though he was far more temperate and circumspect in their expression than his friend Toombs. And when the Confederacy suffered its first major setback in the losses of Forts Henry and Donelson in February 1862, costing them Nashville, west Tennessee, and control of the vital Tennessee and Cumberland Rivers, he gave way easily to his old despondency. "The Confederacy is lost," he tearfully told his friend Martin Crawford a few days later.[1]

The events of the next few months hardly changed his mood. Jealous, like Toombs, of personal liberty, he always feared the effects of revolutionary necessity on individual freedoms, yet when Congress authorized Davis to suspend the privilege of the writ of habeas corpus just days after his inauguration, Stephens said nothing publicly or privately in opposition. The writ empowered the president, through his agents, to arrest and imprison anyone without charge, thus making any conduct, even merely disagreeing with the administration, an act subject to imprisonment for an indefinite period. After barely six weeks of the session of the new Congress, the vice president simply left Richmond and went home, disgusted at being a political shadow with no influence in the administration and no forum before the public for his own views. It was typical of the attitude he had shown several times before when Davis tried to entrust him with missions that Little Aleck did not find either interesting or to the point. Bored or unchallenged by a responsibility, he simply turned his back on it.

But he did not turn his back on the news of Davis's actions, and immediately after getting home he was first aroused by the passage of a national conscription act. Stephens had been in favor of Toombs's failed bill to call out hundreds of thousands of militia, through the agency of the governors. That did not violate state sovereignty, for a governor could conscript the men of his own state. But for the president to be given authority to do so directly over the heads of the governors seemed to him and to Davis's opposition a clear usurpation. Moreover, in theory Davis could cripple state governments and the existing state militia by drafting men away from state and local offices. Governor Brown immediately protested on behalf of his state and himself, and he soon learned that the vice president supported him, politics once more making peculiar bedfellows. Though Stephens differed over some details with Brown, they were in accord that the central government lacked the constitutional power to raise troops directly and could only call on the governors for them to raise regiments and turn them over to Richmond. Brown himself commenced a lengthy and tedious correspondence with Davis in which each sought to counter the points of the other, and after two months of it, with no resolution, Davis simply broke it off. Somehow these exchanges also found their way into the press, and Brown blamed Davis, thinking it improper for him to release the letters without Brown's permission. Davis, who had little regard for or interest in the press, probably had nothing to do with their publication, the secretary of war's office being the more likely source, but Brown thought he saw in the act an attempt to mold public opinion in favor of the president. "If so it was more the trick of the politician than the act of the statesman," he told Stephens. Toombs was not the only one who saw conspiracy in Davis's heart, and with his encouragement and Brown's as well, Stephens might one day see it, too.[2]

By June, his alliance with Brown growing, Stephens himself began to speak privately of the threat to constitutional liberty posed by Davis, who once had been a strict constructionist of the Constitution but had clearly been seduced by the power of his office into seeking to aggrandize that power. At the same time, Stephens continued to vacillate between utter despair over the fate of the Confederacy and a faint but always guarded optimism. He did not like the caliber of the men in the new Congress, thinking them not up to those who had sat with him in the Provisional Congress, and at one point told Linton, "The country must work out its own deliverance." In February he had expected the war to be decided by May one way or another, but in April he was seeing some signs for hope, though admitting, "I do not, however, permit myself to be much elated by successes, just as I do not permit myself to be much depressed by reverses."

Stephens stood firmly in accord with his friend Toombs when it came to Davis's preference for appointing West Point graduates to high command, and given his own utter lack of study or experience in military affairs, it is likely that Little Aleck simply borrowed his opinions wholesale from his friend. Somehow Stephens believed Toombs had great military sagacity and was one of those who had favored his appointment as secretary of war during that brief abortive movement. "If the West Point policy should prevail fully," he told a friend, "we shall be beaten." Since they could never match the North man for man, the South could only hope to win because of the independent spirit of Southern men as "gentlemen," but professional military policy was to discourage individualism in the interest of discipline. Perversely, Stephens and Toombs believed that it was those very qualities that made Southern men bad soldiers that gave them the moral strength to win over greater odds.[3]

Little Aleck stayed at home month after month, nursing his resentment at being left an outsider and his growing discouragement that "it is too late for anything." He really hoped not to have to return to Richmond at all. "I can do no good there," he complained to a friend, and it embarrassed him to be a part of an administration whose measures he could not support.[4] Not until August did he return to the capital when Congress convened a new session, and if he felt an outsider, nothing confirmed it more than the fact that he could not immediately see Davis on his arrival because the president was in a cabinet meeting, and Stephens was not invited to join them. Neither could he gain an immediate audience with any of the cabinet members, a clear message that no one wanted his views or even to keep him informed. Had he known that the recently replaced attorney general Thomas Bragg actually thought Stephens's views "puerile," Little Aleck would have felt even more rejected.[5] Thus, he turned to the individuals with whom he could hope to have some influence, friendly members of Congress. As the session commenced and wore on, Stephens began trying to persuade certain receptive members to support opposition to what he saw as a growing menace of a military despotism, especially after some of

Davis's generals overstepped the authority granted by the writ suspension and were declaring martial law in their commands, including in Georgia itself. Here, at least, he had some success, in-
ducing members to speak out and pass legislation to curb the
generals' excesses, though he could do nothing to repeal the temporary suspension of habeas corpus. Adamantly, he told all who
would listen that it were better that their countryside be ravaged
and Richmond itself fall to the enemy than that the people should
submit to the erosion of their constitutional liberties, a much
greater and inevitably fatal calamity. "It is the principle involved,"
he protested in September, and no plea of military necessity of the
moment could justify even temporary infringement of rights.
Otherwise, they were no better than their enemies, whose denial of
their constitutional rights with their property had set this whole
movement in train in the first place.[6]

Stephens finally came out publicly for the first time in an unsigned letter opposing conscription in September to the *Atlanta
Constitutionalist*, though everyone soon knew he was its author. The
next day he went further, sending a letter over his signature to the
civil governor appointed under martial law in Atlanta by General
Braxton Bragg. He did so only after consulting with Brown, and
finding their views in accord, he released the letter to the local press
and saw it widely republished. It left no doubt where the vice president stood; he had made little effort to be diplomatic. Generals had
no more power over civilians than a common prostitute, he declared, and Congress itself had no power to declare or authorize
martial law unless it chose to set aside or abrogate their Constitution. If the people acquiesced in the act of creating this civil governor under military authority, then they opened the door to tyranny
and despotism.[7] Stephens went home again a few weeks after writing the letter, hoping that he had accomplished something, but
within short order Congress passed a new conscription act and another writ suspension that, though temporary like the last one and
devoid of any authorization for martial law, still incensed Stephens.
It seemed a blatant repetition of the most recent usurpations just as
he had some hope of their being successfully resisted.

Brown came out openly against both actions, but the legislature

refused to rise to the occasion, earning Toombs's enmity and his determination to try to change the complexion of Georgia politics and
the legislature at the next election. Stephens, claiming that his opinions were on record, did not come out publicly to support Brown,
but did make several speeches in his neighborhood to promote enlistment and renewed spirit. On November 1 he spoke in Crawfordville, ostensibly to help raise contributions of money and clothing for Georgia soldiers, and though he stayed away from discussing
divisive issues like conscription, he could not keep his jaundiced
feelings entirely submerged. He was raising contributions, he said,
because "ample provision is not made by the government." That
said, he tried to impress on his audience an answer to the question,
"What is all this for?" His answer was that they suffered and fought
to preserve constitutional liberty and personal freedom. He did not
need to mention recent legislation out of Richmond to make the
point that their rights were being threatened by their own leaders.
He did, however, go over again his old adherence to the policy of
exporting and selling overseas all the cotton possible to raise money
to buy ships to break the blockade and to meet their other expenses.
Though he did not overtly criticize Davis for not adopting such a
policy, he made it clear that, though now more difficult, it still was
not too late.[8]

When Congress reconvened in January 1863, the vice president
was not there, being more and more content to allow the president
pro tem to preside over the Senate as he felt himself increasingly
unnecessary. It was a season of political reassessment for Little
Aleck. He still thought he had good personal relations with Davis
but felt the president's want of confidence in him, lamenting that
in the past eighteen months Davis had actually sent for him to consult only once. He even denied that Toombs and Davis were outright enemies, evidence if any were needed that in the year and
more that Toombs had been with the army and away from
Stephens's direct influence and observation, his friend had
changed more dramatically than Stephens realized. In the direct
face of the general's repeated declarations of animosity toward the
president, Little Aleck told a friend that winter, "Toombs treasures
resentment against no one," an absurd statement, considering just

what Toombs had been writing in his letters for months. Arguing that Toombs and Davis were on good terms personally, Stephens showed the extent of his own unfamiliarity with the president's opinions by declaring, "The President thinks very highly of General Toombs's ability."[9]

In fact, however, Stephens may already have been in the act of subtly molding the perception of relations, for in denying any hostility on Toombs's part, he did suggest that there might be some old resentment from Davis, setting up the proposition that the hostility that he knew existed between them was really the president's fault. At the same time he also began to alter his own record with Davis. In telling friends that winter that he had always thought Lee the greatest general in the land—something Stephens had certainly never said in 1861—he added that in November 1861, the last time Davis had asked his opinion, he had suggested appointing Lee to command in Charleston, and Lee was sent. It was an outright lie, for Stephens had actually suggested either Beauregard or Joseph E. Johnston and still conceded that he thought Johnston the better tactician. Little Aleck was subtly trying to put himself on the right side of the question after the fact, and as well to remove any responsibility on his own part for Davis's loss of confidence in him.[10] His motive may as yet have been clouded, but at this same time he was in correspondence with Brown, who did not at the moment intend to seek reelection and was talking about either Linton or Toombs as a successor. The chances of either would be greatly enhanced if Stephens could downplay the impression that Toombs's vocal antipathy for Davis was causing among loyal administration Georgians, and softening his own disaffection would keep it from working against Linton's chances.[11]

In the end, Linton backed out of contention, and Brown asked Stephens to approach Toombs immediately after he resigned his commission. Little Aleck went in person to see Toombs in March, as soon as his friend reached home from Richmond, but found him very ill, and while he tended Toombs he also heard his emphatic refusal to entertain being nominated. Indeed, Toombs protested that he wanted to do nothing for the rest of the year but recuperate, read in literature and the law, and pursue what he called "my neglected political studies." Indeed, he intended to run for Congress in the fall to take his war with Davis to a new battlefield.[12]

Eventually, Brown decided to run again, and Stephens encouraged and did support him, though Brown, who was almost as adversarial toward Davis by then as Toombs, professed that he would not allow himself to be presented as an antiadministration candidate or a party to any anti-Davis organization, though only because he knew how popular Davis was with Georgians at large. Stephens, too, deluded himself that he was not a part of the small but growing Davis opposition, and deluded himself even more when he denied that Toombs was one of its most vocal and bitter proponents. Yet his awareness of where he really stood was evidenced by his reluctance to serve at his post in Congress and his seizure of any pretext to leave Richmond, as if his mere presence would make him a party to policies he opposed. It put him in a very embarrassing position. Absenting himself invited widespread criticism and concerns about his patriotism, whereas actually performing his functions as vice president made him a part of the administration from which he was all but estranged personally. He might have resigned, but unlike Toombs he seems not to have considered seriously that alternative, and ultimately it would probably have called down just as much criticism as he already received for his absence, if not more.

In fact, in April, after yet another visit to the ailing Toombs, Stephens gave in to repeated entreaties and returned to Richmond, though only for two weeks and to find Congress only a few days from adjournment. He resumed his chair in the Senate on April 27 and saw the session close on May 1, his only real business during this brief visit being an audience with Davis in which the two spoke more openly and cordially than they had for some time. It was a puzzling visit, seemingly pointless on the face of it, and yet Stephens's motive for the trip probably lay in his growing suspicion of Davis. "I am beginning to think that our President is aiming at the obtainment of power inconsistent with public liberty," he said on April 7. Significantly, this was just after his second visit to the ailing Toombs, from whom Little Aleck naturally heard much of the supposed conspiracy and usurpation that Toombs imagined. Thanks to that species of hero worship that always played a role in Stephens's attachment to Toombs, he now, as before, allowed himself to be influenced far more than the genuine wisdom and intelligence of his friend warranted.[13] Yet the result of his visit with Davis seemingly left the vice president temporarily better disposed toward the president, and scarcely a month after returning to Crawfordville, he actually went back to Richmond to see Davis again.

Furthermore, probably as a result of the thawing of relations between them in their recent meeting and perhaps as a result of some preliminary discussion then, Stephens wrote to Davis on June 12 with a proposition. Recent events gave him hopes that the Union might be amenable to a loosening of its rigid policy on the exchange of prisoners of war. Sensing this, he offered his services as a mediator with Washington if Davis thought he could help. That was merely a pretext, however, for the real substance of Stephens's proposal came next in his suggestion that once meeting with Yankee representatives, he was "not without hope" that he could turn the discussion to a general adjustment of the hostilities themselves, at least an armistice, and perhaps actual peace. "I am not without *some* hopes of success," he reiterated, and then stated somewhat equivocally that he would only entertain such discussions on the basis of "the recognition of the sovereignty of the States and the right of each in its sovereign capacity to determine its own destiny."

Though his words could be read to conform with an aspiration for Confederate independence, nowhere, in fact, did he suggest such a thing, and his expression literally addressed only the same demand for states' rights that he and others had made before secession. In short, though Davis might have thought Stephens was proposing to work for independence, Little Aleck might just as well have had reconstruction in mind, as his critics had accused all along. Earlier in the year he repeatedly asserted that the outlook for victory and independence seemed bleak, and such a sentiment could well have lain behind his proposal. At the same time, Lee had just won a smashing victory at Chancellorsville early in May, and the North might be receptive to a peace proposal with constitutional guarantees in return for reunion, especially after nearly two years of almost unrelenting defeat in the east. It might just be possible

to achieve what he had wanted in 1860, one nation with a constitutional acknowledgment and protection of Southern slave rights.
Once again, it may be no coincidence that Stephens made his proposal not long after meeting with Toombs, perhaps lending some
credence after all to those rumors that Toombs himself had in mind
seeking some kind of negotiated peace with the North.[14]

Davis immediately responded to the letter with a telegram asking
the vice president to come to Richmond, and there they held several conferences late in June. To Stephens's chagrin, however,
Davis's wishes and Little Aleck's ideas were not the same. The Georgian had hoped to capitalize on the recent victory and low spirits in
the North, but he had learned that Lee was embarked on an invasion of Pennsylvania, and hoping that Lee would gain another victory on enemy soil, Davis proposed to send Stephens along with the
army to go to Washington under truce flag, assuming that he would
be bargaining from an even greater position of strength as an emis-
sary from a victorious invader. Stephens thought it undercut his
whole idea, however. "I have but little hope of being able to effect
anything," he wrote Linton on June 28, but when Davis and the
cabinet insisted, he agreed to try.[15]

Stephens left aboard a steamer on July 3, unaware that Lee was
that same day being decisively turned back at Gettysburg. He got
as far as the Union enclave at Newport News, Virginia, where the
next day under flag of truce he made his mission known. Waiting
two days, he received word from Washington that the Federals
would not enter into any negotiations with him, and that effectively
closed the matter, for which he had lost all heart in any event. News
of the defeat at Gettysburg and the July 4 surrender of the enormously important army at Vicksburg, Mississippi, presented a dramatic turn of events and gave the enemy the upper hand once
more. He could only return to Richmond, and as usual when dispir-
ited, settle into musings of gloom and hasten to return to Liberty
Hall.[16] Along the way he made a few speeches appealing to the
people not to lose heart in the face of the recent disasters. At the
same time he also told them that reconstruction was impossible and
that "such an idea must not be tolerated for an instant." The Con-

federacy must have final and complete separation or annihilation. He said it as an admonition to his audiences, but it might well have been an admission to himself. Reconstruction was dead.[17]

It is surprising that despite the influence Toombs could exert on his friend, Little Aleck may not have fully accepted the impossibility of reconstruction much earlier. With the exception of a single rumor, nothing connected the resigned general's name with anything other than resolute resistance. Indeed, there lay much of his reason for so adamantly opposing the Davis administration, which Toombs himself charged in some of his wilder moments with wishing to bring North and South together again and thus not prosecuting a vigorous and victorious military policy. His health recovered that spring, Toombs wasted little time in declining to run for governor and instead happily supported Brown's successful reelection campaign. Candidly, Toombs declared that in the current state of Davis's accumulation of centralized power, no governorship had much authority, and the only venue in which to meet and defeat Davis was in Congress, which made that the place for him. He almost hoped that the administration would try to oppose him, for if it did so, "I shall be justified in any extremity to which the public interest would allow me to go in hostility to his illegal and unconstitutional course."[18]

That declaration suggested that Toombs was anxious for a fight, and yet, typically, he wavered on where to make his battle. He announced his candidacy for Congress on June 17 and purposely restrained his invective against Davis in order not to put off voters, though still laying out his whole program of issues on which he opposed the administration, conscription, the impressment of foodstuffs and materials from civilians by military authority, Memminger's whole fiscal policy, and of course the suspension of the privilege of the writ of habeas corpus and any extension of martial law authority to the military. Every one of these measures represented governmental or military usurpation and potent threats to the liberties for which they were fighting.[19]

Less than a month later, however, Toombs told Stephens that he felt little taste for staying in civil life, said nothing at all about his campaign for Congress, and confessed that he really wanted to get back into the army. He would take the colonelcy of a new Georgia regiment to be raised if he could get it, and if not, then he would join the state militia, even though his injured hand was still not fully useful. He told Linton, meanwhile, that he feared he could accomplish little even in Congress and felt that only the army was the proper arena for him. Toombs was reeling back and forth between decisions, in the span of a few weeks going from glowing confidence of his future power in Congress to a conviction of impotence. Worse, he was clearly unable to read the verdict on his military capabilities so eloquently attested by his problems in the army and its disinclination to recognize even his meritorious services at Antietam.

Besides his now erratic thinking, he must also somehow have persuaded himself that there would be a better climate for him in the army following Lee's defeat at Gettysburg. "An army in a defensive position needs but little talent in its commander & Lee has scarcely enough even for that," he declared, apparently overlooking the fact that he had been in a defensive position at the Rorhbach Bridge and that therefore his condemnation might just as easily be applied to himself. When it came to leading an invasion, however, he asserted that Lee lacked "sufficient genius to command an invading army."[20] He may have expected Lee to be relieved—the Virginian did attempt to resign—and that his replacement, most likely the senior-ranking Longstreet, with whom he was on much better terms, would give Toombs more opportunity to distinguish himself. Meanwhile, in the interests of state defense, he even defended the government against false charges that discouraged militia enlistment, though assuring Little Aleck, "I owe them no favors." It may also have been Toombs's way of trying to pave his way back into an army command by softening his formerly harsh opposition.[21]

On August 8 Brown sent Toombs a commission as colonel of a militia regiment of cavalry, but almost immediately the new colonel deprecated his command as nothing but "a body guard to protect us when we have all to flee to the mountains," an extremity to which Davis's policy must soon bring them.[22] He was wavering back to politics again. Since his speech in June, Toombs had done little or nothing to advance his candidacy for Congress except to publish a lengthy letter regarding Confederate finance, criticizing the administration for trying to finance the war on credit and without resort to tax, and for flooding the country with depreciating paper currency. The only solution was taxation and foreign loans, he said, and yet it was a singularly antiseptic paper for Toombs, devoid of bombast and saying not a syllable about his seeking office.[23] A few days later, however, he told a friend that the only hope for the country lay in "opposition." Davis and his West Pointers were steadily accumulating all power unto themselves, and if that continued their cause must fail. "They have neither the ability nor the honesty to manage the revolution," he declared, and they must be brought down or controlled. "I do not see how anything else is left to me," he said on August 29. "The only question for a patriot is, will resistance or acquiescence do most harm to the public cause?" he concluded. "I think the latter and must act accordingly."[24] On the stump, he denounced every administration measure and in private conversation attacked Davis personally, saying that the president's adherence to his "West Point Jannisaries" was the means by which he expected to seize absolute power. "Toombs has done great injury," a friend in Georgia warned Davis. Some feared that if Toombs won the congressional seat he would become a rallying point for the disloyal and disaffected. But then in mid-August Toombs suddenly dropped out of the race without giving a reason.[25] Knowing that there would be an election in the legislature in December to fill one of Georgia's seats in the Senate, Toombs apparently decided that this would be a more fitting arena for his talents.

For the next two months Toombs trained his new six months' militia regiment and by late October had them in Atlanta. Late that month, when Davis came through Atlanta on a visit to his western armies and commanders, Toombs left town as soon as the president arrived and perhaps in order not to have to see him. He went home to Washington to prepare himself for a trip to the capital in Milledgeville. Having abandoned interest in a seat in the House of Representatives, or perhaps realizing that he had dallied too long to wage an effective campaign, he decided to put himself forward for election to the Senate, a selection made by the legislature and not the voters at large. Even if he could not find support to win, he still could make the fight "to rally and embody those who agree with me in principle, in order to offer whatever resistance I can to the ruin of the revolution and the destruction of public liberty." Revealingly, Toombs told Stephens that he came to his decision to seek the seat "after long and earnest if not deliberate consideration." In fact, Toombs had done little or nothing "deliberate" since the previous fall, vacillating from one intention to another, guided throughout by the varying pitches of his hatred of Davis, his genuine concern for the fate of Confederate fortunes, and the frustration of his own thwarted ambition.[26]

Toombs should have remembered the legislature's reluctance to send him to Richmond twice before. Putting himself forth as an avowed opponent of Davis, he found they had no interest in him at all. Even with Brown's support—Toombs considerately did not call on Stephens to support him, since his being an antiadministration candidate would have put Stephens, as vice president, in an awkward position—he was easily defeated by the incumbent Herschel Johnson on the third ballot, Toombs's support never rising above 51 of 166 members voting.[27] It was not the sort of rebuff that Robert A. Toombs took lightly. Rather, it only incensed him further at the craven manner in which the legislature cowed before the authority of Jefferson Davis. Did no one see the dangers he saw? Could no one see that he was the one to lead them from the shadow of Davis's tyranny and inevitable defeat?

Not surprisingly, Little Aleck Stephens did share Toombs's vision, if not his vehemence or intemperance, but understandably he did stay quiet during the senatorial contest, though no one doubted where his sympathies lay. No wonder he was furious when Howell Cobb sent him a bizarre suggestion in September that the Confederacy needed a dictator. Davis was getting close enough to autocracy as it was, and yet Cobb's plea was understandable. By late fall 1863 a Yankee army was in Chattanooga, on Georgia's doorstep, while other forces threatened its Atlantic shores, especially Savannah. The Mississippi River was lost to them, and Lee was at bay in Virginia, too battered after Gettysburg to take the offensive again. Their currency was deflating, there was no sign that recognition would ever come from European powers, desertion was mounting in the armies, and people at home were feeling the pinch of hunger and deprivation. If he could not quite share Toombs's radicalism, still Stephens heard similar sentiments from other close sources, including Linton, who hinted in October that Davis might have to be removed by assassination if more democratic means failed.[28]

There Little Aleck confronted a terrifying prospect, one that probably undergirded much of his attitude toward Davis. Actually asked what he would do if Davis died in office and he had to take power, Stephens recoiled from the thought. While offering some few rather ineffectual suggestions that he thought might improve morale, Stephens was at pains to say that he hoped such an eventuality would never occur. Indeed, he declined even to speak of it again and confided his severe doubts that he could do the job well. In short, happy as he was to carp at the administration from the safety of his own meaningless office, he recoiled from the responsibility of the presidency itself. Ironically, Stephens needed Davis in the executive chair, not only so he could indulge his disapproval of anyone who did not conform to his own ideas but also as a protective barrier against his ever having to try to implement his ideas himself and thus risk incurring the criticism from others in which he so freely indulged.[29]

Stephens went to ground for the rest of the year. He did not come out for Brown in his reelection bid, and he said nothing public on behalf of Toombs in November. When the new session of Congress opened in December, the vice president did not go, and no amount of cajoling and persuasion from others could seem to convince him that he was needed there, or that in shirking his own elected responsibility, he was, in his way, injuring the cause he seemed otherwise so anxious to save. In fact, by the new year the vice president no longer believed that he could do anything to halt the coming disaster, and that being the case, he might as well stay at home. Where Toombs had always been mercurial, up one minute and despairing the next, Stephens's prevailing mood was pessimism, interrupted by brief spells of expressed hope. "You have given up the contest in your *judgment*," Herschel Johnson complained to Stephens on December 29, "whilst your patriotic *heart* bleeds over our fate." Johnson, Howell Cobb, and a chorus of others agreed that the fact that their case was dire actually demanded Stephens in Richmond, where his wisdom and prudence might do some good.[30]

Stephens indeed changed his mind and decided to go to Richmond in January, but bad weather and Linton's serious illness kept him from going, and then he fell seriously ill himself, too ill to travel. While he convalesced, new disturbing news came from Richmond. The conscription laws were strengthened, their reach extended by cutting back the list of occupations that provided exemption, and there was talk of yet another suspension of the writ. On January 22 Stephens wrote to the president emphatically urging him not to sign such a bill, to relax conscription, and to halt impressment. It was perhaps the first time that he had taken it on himself to volunteer advice on national policy to Davis. Aside from the fact that Stephens's ideas, though theoretically sound, were impractical for a budding nation in the throes of war against a superior foe, the letter also betrayed the vice president's own woeful grasp of human frailty. Jefferson Davis did not take advice well. To him it smacked of an attempt to dictate to him in matters that were his responsibility alone and carried as well the scent of criticism, which he took no better than advice. Coming as it did from his vice president, it was evidence, if any were needed, that Stephens was fundamentally disloyal to him and not fully committed to independence, perhaps a reconstructionist after all. Davis dealt with the letter by ignoring it, and a few days after receiving it sent a message to Congress asking for a new suspension of the writ.[31] If Stephens needed final confirmation that his views were not welcome, here he had it.

Thus coincidence, and the timing of Davis's latest affronts to personal liberty, gave renewed impetus to Toombs's near-vendetta and finally shoved Stephens toward the front rank of the opposition with him. Bristling over his rejection by the legislature, Toombs took his regiment to the defenses of Savannah and made no effort to conceal his irritation, even taking his anger out on civilians. But then he went too far, as only he could. Privately, he declared that Davis must be either killed or deposed or their cause was lost, and in his tent in Savannah he spoke freely in front of his staff and even a reporter, Henry Cleveland, of his ideas for a counterrevolution. As if that were not enough, he assembled his regiment and other militia on January 24 and gave them a harangue that almost begged for the administration to take action against him.

"We are in a revolution, grand, powerful, dangerous, terrific," he yelled. They were past the point of emollients curing the ills of dissension and dissatisfaction that plagued the cause. He feared civil war within the Confederacy itself if the government did not respect the rights of the people. Reminding his men that he had been a revolutionary against the Union, he declared, "*I will be one till I get liberty.*" The Yankees were a barrier to that freedom and he fought them, and "if domestic traitors stand in the way, I am their enemy." Only tyrants would wish to take away habeas corpus. Only tyrants would take the farmer's produce by impressment. Only tyrants would make white men carry passports like Negro slaves when they traveled in and out of military lines. And as for the conscription law that would put almost every man in the army, when that happened the whole population would be, by military law, subject to the commander in chief, one man. In effect, Davis would have become dictator. When that happened, he said, "It will be time to draw the bayonet."

General Jeremy Gilmer, chief engineer of the department, was there listening, and when Toombs uttered this last, Gilmer went to his horse and rode away to Savannah to report what Toombs was saying to his superior, Beauregard, who commanded the department. Toombs continued unmindfully and became even more intemperate. "Better die than bear such oppressions," he told his troops; "die and leave a glorious name like Brutus . . . or Cromwell." The implication of revolt or even assassination was inescapable, and even if it were nothing but Toombs's usual hyperbole, it matched his private expressions of late. "Save your country, your family; above all, save liberty," he excoriated them. "Defend liberty against Congress, against the President, against whoever assails it." They were free before Jefferson Davis was born, he told them, "and I trust you will have it after he is dead." He did not ask them to mutiny, he went on, "*unless it be necessary in defense of constitutional rights.*"

His feeble protestation that he spoke theoretically, and with "no disrespect" to Davis the man, was transparent, and so was his un-

derlying motive of pique and disappointment about his personal
ambitions. Hundreds of professional officers had left the U.S. Army
to join the Confederacy in 1861, he said, yet not one was a true soldier. Citing that General Braxton Bragg, recently replaced after the
loss of Chattanooga and most of Tennessee and north Georgia, had
once protested that he did not want politicians made into generals
for his army, Toombs pointed out that Bragg, a professional and a
West Pointer, had "lost an empire." Instead, Toombs asserted, "wherever we had victories, politicians were among the commanders,"
then repeated his frequent boast that while he commanded his
Georgia brigade, there was not one desertion. The message was
clear enough. Denying Toombs promotion and high command was
just more evidence of Davis's tyranny. Worse was the administration's plea that these infringements of liberty were imposed out of
"necessity" and would be only temporary. "Do not listen to the miserable plea of necessity," he warned. "Treachery and robbery are
never necessary to a good cause." The militia enlistments of the
men before him would expire in February. When the men returned
to their homes, he enjoined them to sustain the revolution against
every enemy, "foreign and domestic."

To Cleveland, as to many others present, it sounded as if Toombs
were inciting them to revolt against the administration. In private,
and most likely in his cups, Toombs had spoken of several state governors, Stephens, and a number of generals, including Beauregard,
Johnston, John C. Breckinridge, and possibly even Lee, as being in
sympathy with him. In fact, none would have countenanced such
ideas, and Stephens for one never heard Toombs make such a proposal. In his obsession, and probably fueled by drink, he simply assumed that others who expressed opposition to Davis or to aspects
of the administration's policy would naturally share his extreme
views.[32]

But Toombs did get a response to his speech. When he put his
regiment on the Central Railroad cars in Augusta for the trip to Savannah, he lost his temper at a railroad employee who protested the
militia's mistreatment of company property. Again most likely
driven by alcohol to overreaction, Toombs had the civilian arrested
and then publicly berated and insulted him and threatened his life

if he tried to interfere again. The agent later protested to his employers, and the Central Railroad lodged a complaint with Beauregard not only for damage to its property but also for the unlawful—Toombs would have said dictatorial had Davis so behaved—arrest of a civilian by a militia officer.[33] It may only have been coincidental that Beauregard acted on the complaint at the same time that Toombs made his incendiary speech, but a report of what he was saying, brought by Gilmer, must surely have convinced the commander that it was time to curb both Toombs's irresponsible words and behavior. Once again, on January 28, Toombs found himself under arrest.

Beauregard ordered a court-martial and preferred charges relating to Toombs's conduct with the railroad official, though many people in the country soon believed it was because of his speech before the militia. When Toombs appeared in court, he immediately reverted to being a lawyer and challenged the authority of the court to preside over him, citing violations of the articles of war in that the court's officers were not his peers, not being militia officers. Further, he accused the court of favoritism, since one of its members was related to the president of the railroad, and implied that the whole affair was being directed by Jefferson Davis to silence him. Moreover, since Toombs's militia commission had expired on January 31, the court meeting in February had no jurisdiction over him, he being by then a civilian. Having lodged those objections in person, Toombs left the court and wrote to Beauregard directly, repeating his stance and then informing the general that he refused to attend the sitting of the court thereafter. For two weeks Toombs gathered documents for his defense and carried on a bitter correspondence with Beauregard's chief of staff, but he never again set foot in the court, which considered trying him in absentia for a while before the general simply dropped the charges. It was enough to have Toombs out of the military once more. Trying him would only give him a forum for further fulminations. For his part, Toombs, who once thought well of the general, even including him in his imaginary cabal, now damned him privately as "that snivelling Frenchman Beauregard." By then Toombs had already returned home under parole, and ironically, soon thereafter a local judge secured his release from nominal arrest by a writ of habeas corpus.[34]

Just as Stephens saw Davis's directive to expand conscription as a rebuff to his letter of suggestions, so Toombs's friends saw it as the president's response to the challenge issued in the Georgian's militia speech.[35] While Toombs returned home and remained unaccustomedly quiet for awhile, with neither military position nor political forum to proclaim his views, Stephens at last became actively involved in the movement to thwart Davis. In late February he met with Brown, an insurgent too as a result of conscription, impressment, habeas corpus, and other issues; and as a response to their discussions Brown called the legislature into session in March, intending to have it send a memorial to Richmond stating Georgia's protest over injustices and a petition for redress and reform. It was what Southern states had done with Washington for a generation before the war. It never achieved anything then, and there was no reason to suppose that the tactic would fare better now, but it was the only means available. Had there been an organized second party in the Confederacy, dissidents like Toombs and Stephens could have expressed their opposition in that forum, but in the absence of such a body, the memorial seemed the only option that could give their individual dissent the authority and dignity of something more than the mere barking of malcontents.

Linton Stephens undertook to get the memorial through the legislature, while his brother tried to enlist the help of Georgia's delegates in Congress and urged that public sentiment be mobilized. Always a believer in the power of mass opinion, Stephens felt that if the people spoke out, not only through their representatives but also in mass meetings and in their courts, Davis would have to hear them. Brown had an uphill fight in Milledgeville with his condemnation of the suspension of the privilege of the writ and also with the other part of their plan, a proposal to call on the Union for peace negotiations after any and every Confederate victory in the field. Little Aleck himself came to the capital to speak in behalf of the resolutions. "I am for no counterrevolution," he told them, but once they lost liberty, in any form, for any cause, it was lost for good.

Even should they achieve their independence, if it came at the cost of loss of their rights and the accumulation of tyrannical power in Richmond, then they would have lost after all. He was out of the closet at last. The vice president had called on the legislature of his state to rise and challenge the policy of his president.[36]

The memorial narrowly passed, and not without heated debate, and caused just the sort of uproar in Georgia at large that Stephens wanted. While the public discussion raged in the press, the reactions to Stephens's role personally were just as extreme. "You have allowed your antipathy to Davis to mislead your judgment," Hershel Johnson scolded him. Cries of "traitor" rang all across the South. In Richmond itself reports of the speech were exaggerated into assertions that he had denounced the government as tyrannical and, as one War Department official said, "not less worthy of resistance than the Yankees." Finally, he was lumped with Toombs and Brown as one of the leading malcontents. "These people," said the head of the Bureau of War, "are the most pestilent set of demagogues in the land."[37] The vice president denied animosity toward Davis, though few would believe that, but he did confess to "suspicion and jealousy" of the president, calling him "weak and vacillating, timid, petulant, peevish, obstinate, but not firm."[38] He also denied wanting to form an anti-Davis party, but in fact he had placed himself almost right behind Toombs at the opposition's forefront. If Toombs's loud invective made him a prominent leader, the mere fact of Stephens being vice president and breaking with the administration put him in the same rank.

Perhaps in order to quieten the outcry against himself, Stephens actually decided to attend the opening of the next session of Congress in May. It would be a show of devotion to duty and a fulfillment of his constitutional duty as a member of the administration. It might also give him a chance to mend fences, perhaps even with Davis. But he was delayed when he became involved in yet another scheme that he hoped might stop the fighting and lead to a negotiated peace. Lincoln would be up for reelection in November, and it had been proposed to Little Aleck that the president's opposition was so strong in the northwestern states that a Confederate promise to observe an armistice and enter negotiations in the event of a

Republican defeat might be enough to sway the election. Stephens always believed that if ever the fighting stopped and discussions began, the Yankees would never return to the battlefield and Confederate independence would be inevitable. Little Aleck wrote to Davis once more outlining the proposition, and though disinclined to have anything to do with his vice president, Davis did at least respond, though he all but ignored the Georgian's intent in bringing it before him. The affair came to nothing, and Stephens finally started for Richmond, hoping at least that he and other opponents of the habeas corpus suspension could engineer a repeal that would survive any Davis veto. Before he could reach the capital he learned that backers of the repeal plan had given up without trying, and that was discouraging enough for him simply to turn around and go home to Crawfordville.[39]

Within weeks, events virtually propelled Stephens toward an antipathy to Davis that virtually matched Toombs's. Davis published a letter relating to the abortive July 1863 peace mission that Stephens found almost entirely out of line with his own recollection of events, and soon afterward he discovered he that Davis had apparently lied to him in another matter connected with the more recent proposal for armistice feelers. He could only conclude that Davis did not want the war to end except by military conquest, and only after it had gone on long enough for his aggrandizement of power to be complete. At the same time, the vice president regarded Davis as a mean liar, "as much a knave as fool."[40] Knowing that, what reason was there to maintain any longer a pretense of standing apart from the opposition? In fact, since Toombs had no public forum and was not likely to gain any, why should Little Aleck not take his place as a leader of the anti-Davis forces?

Meanwhile, Toombs became strangely quiet politically. Early in April he had complimented Little Aleck on the passage of the Georgia memorial, once more condemning the suspension of the privilege of the writ. It was a red flag to Toombs, who promised his friend, "I shall certainly give Mr. Davis an early opportunity to make me a victim by advising resistance, resistance to the death, to his law."[41] Certainly Toombs never softened, and it was costing him friends, including an old companion, General A. R. Lawton and his family. Lawton's daughter missed Toombs's companionship. "I make great allowances for him," she said, but they simply could not stomach his increasingly apparent inclination to promote dissent and revolt under the guise of disinterested patriotism. "He has gone too far, but the same luxuriance of mind & feeling, which when rightly directed shone as talent & glory, now drives him on & in the wrong direction," she continued. "It is violence & rebellion. *The man is the same*, & . . . the same feelings which have led him astray, have often swelled in my heart, & if I mistake not, in yours also, but in him, stronger than the restraints of wisdom & prudence." Nevertheless, she said, "that he truly loves his country *I could never doubt*."[42]

But before Toombs could challenge Davis again, or speak out more, or lose more friends, military affairs diverted his attention. When William T. Sherman began his advance on Atlanta in May, Toombs left his home and took a place on the staff of his old friend General Gustavus W. Smith, commander of the Georgia militia and serving with the Army of Tennessee led by Joseph E. Johnston. At last the war had come to Georgia, and for the next four months Toombs was in the thick of the resistance. Smith assigned him to raising recruits for the militia and training them, and Toombs threw himself into the task with his old energy renewed, happy to be once more in uniform and with a prospect of action. Through May and June he was almost constantly in the saddle with his militia, even as Sherman slowly pushed Johnston back until, by July, they were in the environs of Atlanta itself. "The militia are coming up finely," Toombs told his wife, but they turned out green, ill-disciplined, and with inadequate officers. "It keeps us at work day and night to bring order out of this confused mass." Worse, they had to be thrown into the defensive works as soon as they arrived, experiencing their first enemy fire before they had suffered a single day's drill.

No doubt, Johnston's policy of withdrawing without giving battle only confirmed Toombs's prejudice against West Pointers, but when Davis finally relieved Johnston and appointed General John Bell Hood in his place, Toombs's spirits lifted. He liked Hood's spirit and energy. "He is a most excellent man, and undoubtedly of great military talent," Toombs concluded, despite his being one of Davis's pets. It helped that Hood had but one instinct and that was to attack, however unwise it might be. Just three days after taking command, Hood launched a daring attack at Peachtree Creek, trying to drive Sherman back from the city, and on July 22 he used Toombs's militia in a general battle for Atlanta. Though unsuccessful, Toombs and his men fought well, and thereafter for the balance of the siege he acted with a spirit of subordination and discipline that would have amazed his old commanders in Virginia. He was often seen with Hood inspecting the city's defenses, his militia devoted to him. Hood himself, an unsophisticated but earnest officer whose judgment of men was not much better than his strategy, seemed won over by Toombs and entrusted considerable responsibility to the Georgian.[43]

Still, the lengthening siege began to wear him down. By the end of August he confessed to Stephens that Atlanta was doomed. The Army of Tennessee was in a deplorable state, and even though Hood was rearranging the high command it was still riddled with Davis's "pets." Toombs meanwhile was even critical of Hood, whom he thought "the very best of the generals of his school; but like all the rest of them he knows no more of business than a ten year old boy."[44] He would rather have abandoned Atlanta, or even seen it destroyed, especially since the citizens were not turning out in numbers for their own defense. In fact, on September 1, the day after Toombs wrote to Stephens his dire prediction, Hood began the evacuation. Shortly afterward Governor Brown disbanded the militia, since the state could not support it and the state government itself was virtually on the run. Having no command, Toombs himself simply went back to Washington. With Georgia invaded and about to be cut in two, and with the Confederacy in crisis everywhere, he returned to his law practice.[45]

Though Toombs seemingly had taken himself out of the political forum, Stephens, once thrust to the forefront of the dissidents, stayed there. He spent some of spring 1864 trying unsuccessfully with Brown to place an anti-Davis editor in charge of one of Georgia's most influential newspapers, and then fell ill again and spent most of the course of the Atlanta campaign sick at Liberty Hall. He still held hope for Lincoln's defeat in November and for the prospect of peace if the Confederacy could withstand Davis's criminal management long enough for a Democrat to take office in Washington. Even the fall of Atlanta, discouraging as that was, did not completely dispel his optimism, and when the Northern Democrats nominated McClellan to challenge Lincoln, Little Aleck actually felt encouraged. He believed McClellan could beat Lincoln, and that was what the Confederacy needed.

It was in that belief that Stephens remained ever receptive to suggestions for means of negotiated peace. Before McClellan's nomination Little Aleck ignored a suggestion that he publicly propose a cease-fire with the North, leading toward a convention of all the states, North and South, to adjust their difficulties constitutionally. But the choice of McClellan seemed to augur for a more receptive mood among the Yankees. Then two weeks later it was proposed to him that he and Herschel Johnson combine to try to promote peace by negotiation. Of course, it was Davis's prerogative alone to inaugurate such policy, and Stephens wisely declined to try to lead any such movement, but still he spoke strongly in favor of cooperating with the peace faction in the North and of the proposed convention. It was not quite a direct challenge to Davis's war policy, but it came close and aroused even more criticism and charges of reconstructionism. After all, who could control what such a convention might decide, and would the Southern states be bound by such a decision?[46]

Coincidentally, Stephens received a note from, of all people, General Sherman. He had heard enough of Stephens's sentiments to suspect that he might use him to his own ends. He asked Little Aleck and Governor Brown to meet with him in Atlanta, his aim to offer them an opportunity for Georgia to make a separate peace with the North and separate itself from the Confederacy. Brown declined, but Stephens considered the suggestion, asking Toombs for his thoughts. For a change, it was Toombs who spoke for caution. "Do not by any means go to see Sherman," he advised. "It will place you in a wrong, *very wrong* position." Better that they be defeated than that Georgia abandon her sister states. The question of making terms for peace lay exclusively with the president, and amazingly Toombs argued against challenging Davis on this. "Nothing could be of more evil tendency," he said, than for anyone else to try to interfere with the president's prerogative in the matter.[47]

Stephens finally rejected Sherman's invitation but still clung to any hope for a negotiated peace that would stop the fighting. Unfortunately, Davis refused to countenance any attempt to interfere with the election in the North or to offer any overt encouragement to the peace movement in the Union, which infuriated his vice president. "His whole policy has been to weaken, cripple and annihilate them," he complained.[48] Even after Lincoln actually defeated McClellan in November, and by a margin handsome enough to make it evident that the peace party in the North never had the strength seriously to challenge the incumbent, Stephens remained resentful of Davis's policy. Worse, the mere association of Stephens's name with such peace feelers only kept alive the old charges of reconstructionism, and on November 10 he actually felt compelled to explain himself by an open letter to the public challenging the "insinuations and *flings,* if not direct charges," being hurled at him. He reiterated his belief that the Confederate States in their combined and "absolute sovereignty" were alone empowered to make peace with the North, rejecting entirely the idea of individual states making their own separate peace. As he said elsewhere, any convention held with the Northern states would have to confirm individual state sovereignty or there would be no basis for peace. He wanted independence, not surrender. The old Union was dead and could never be resurrected, he said. That should make his position clear enough for all.[49]

Unfortunately, it did not satisfy Davis, especially when Stephens complained that the president had not encouraged McClellan's cause and even preferred that Lincoln win so that there would be no chance of a negotiated peace—which might lead to reconstruction—and that the Confederates thus would be invigorated to renewed determination for victory, knowing there would be no alternative. Davis did not care for that, and almost immediately launched an acrimonious correspondence with Stephens that soon became notorious. Though Richmond circles generally thought Davis got the better of it, neither of them looked good as they devoted far too much time to a seemingly endless contest for the last word on pettifogging points while there was so much better use for their time in the Confederacy's crisis. It only revealed what so many others could have told them, that much of the reason that Stephens and

Toombs and Davis could not get along was that they were constitutionally so much alike, self-important, convinced of their own rec-
titude, and intolerant of disagreement. Toombs and Stephens had
themselves both said that there was no point in Confederate victory
if they gave up principles along the way. The fact was, in their insistence on the moral certainty of their views, they would rather win
an argument than independence.[50]

Perhaps in order to explain himself more fully, as well as to oppose yet another anticipated bill for a new suspension of habeas corpus, Stephens went to Richmond in December for the next sitting
of Congress, the first time he had taken his constitutional post in
more than a year. Even at that, he arrived a month after the session
opened. The vice president found Congress in a mood that actually
served his purpose, for a change. The war was going disastrously
everywhere. Lee's army was bottled up and besieged in and around
Richmond and Petersburg. Sherman was marching across Georgia
and in imminent reach of taking Savannah. Mobile had fallen. The
Yankees marched almost where they chose in the South at will. With
Lincoln reelected on a mandate for another four years of prosecution of the war, Davis's policy of trying to win independence by victory seemed more illusory than ever. Stephens could see easily
enough that the only hope for them was some negotiated peace before they were utterly defeated, and the more ground they lost, the
less they had to take to the bargaining table, if indeed they even had
anything. Congress, too, saw this, and at last the dissident elements
found allies in many of the moderates. They soon enlisted the vice
president in their plans for introducing a new resolution calling for
peace feelers.

If more evidence were needed of Stephens's temperamental
need to have his own way or nothing at all, it came when the bill to
suspend the writ came to a vote and tied in the Senate on December 20. That gave the vice president the deciding vote, his chance
at last to kill this measure. Intending to use the moment as a forum
for his already widely known views, he announced that he would
make some remarks before voting. But few wanted to hear what they
had been hearing for years, and when a senator tried to change his
vote to kill the suspension bill, Stephens—who would have had what

he wanted in the defeat—actually protested at being denied his say and his vote. The Senate overwhelmingly sided against him in a rebuke to its absentee presiding officer that Stephens felt to the quick. He declared to friends that he would resign at once, and only a conciliatory gesture from the Senate asking him to address them on the current state of affairs mollified him somewhat. When he spoke two weeks later on January 6, it was nothing new. They must change their policy on all the old outrages, from conscription to impressment, while in the field they must avoid pitched battles as Johnston had and simply keep the cause alive by maintaining their armies and holding their standards aloft, even if it meant abandoning Richmond to save Lee's army. Eventually they must wear down the enemy's resolve to carry on, and if they continually held out the offer of an armistice and negotiations, he believed that once the guns were silenced, they would never start again, and the Confederacy would by default gain its freedom. In the face of the facts of the current situation, it was a policy bordering on the delirious.[51]

The speech revived his hopes, aided no doubt by someone important finally wanting his views. But the fact was that the disillusioned and the dissident were growing so strong that, though they could not stop Davis, they could at least use every means to try to embarrass him, and in this instance they used the vice president. Still, Stephens strove toward his ultimate goal of a convention of all the states to advise Washington and Richmond on an acceptable mode for peace. Resolutions embodying this end almost got to the floor of the House, with his assistance, and though they failed, other expressions in Congress gave him hope that the opposition to Davis's measures was gelling and that Congress might actually take over and reverse the evil policies of the past. By the end of the month, with the Confederacy militarily on the verge of complete collapse, he suddenly felt almost ebullient.[52]

Then came what he had been hoping for all along. Davis had agreed to send emissaries to a conference with Lincoln and others to discuss bringing about peace. Lincoln's terms were well known by Davis, and just as unacceptable, for the Union would agree only to complete reconstruction and the abandonment of slavery. Davis, of course, could accept nothing less than Confederate independence. Knowing that their separate aims were mutually exclusive, Davis nonetheless cynically agreed to the conference, knowing it would be doomed. His hope was that such a failure would reinvigorate Confederates into renewed commitment and sacrifice, realizing there was no alternative short of utter defeat. But he did not say this to Stephens. Instead, aware of the vice president's longtime devotion to negotiations, Davis set aside his antipathy for Stephens and asked him to discuss the matter privately. Accepting the irreconcilability of the two governments' aims, still Stephens approved the meeting, as always hoping that once any kind of talks began, they could be guided in the right direction. He suggested that Davis himself should go, but the president almost cruelly asked him to represent the Confederacy, setting him up to confront the impossibility of his long-cherished ideas. Stephens resisted, not wanting to be removed even briefly from the Senate, where he felt he was making headway in getting legislators to change administration policy. He also had reason to suspect that his mission would be doomed to failure and did not want that stigma attached to himself. In the end, Davis outmaneuvered him, and Stephens accepted the assignment.

He should have known better. Indeed, he felt some optimism after all in the hours before he left for Hampton Roads to meet with Lincoln, but when he received his actual instructions from Davis as he was leaving, he saw anew that unless Lincoln would give way on independence, there was no basis for discussion. The peace conference that ensued on February 3, 1865, was a charade, both Lincoln and Davis using it as a show to their people that the other side would never give up and would have to be beaten by renewed commitment. Stephens returned to Richmond in a foul mood, perhaps realizing how he had been used, and even tried to avoid writing a report of the affair. But Davis insisted and then widely publicized the failure of the mission, which worked exactly as he had hoped, by stimulating a sudden renewal of patriotic feeling. Instead of weakening the administration, Stephens had unwittingly made it stronger among the people than it had been for months. Even the Senate no longer entertained his suggestions for some means to a convention and peace.[53]

Stephens made his last public appearance in Richmond at a rally on February 9, though he refused to speak, and in a day or two afterward left for good. On his way home, as he passed through South Carolina, he sent his parting counsel to Wigfall, then still carrying the banner in Richmond for those opposed to Davis, by arguing for trying to unite Confederate sympathy with the masses in the North who were tired of the war. "We should show them that we are fighting their battle as well as our own," Stephens said. "If we go down— if our liberties are lost in this contest—theirs will be too." They must not let Davis deter them by raising the specter of reconstruction to prevent a convention. The Congress must pass resolutions appealing to the people of the North and its Congress to shift "from the arbitration of armies to the forum of reason—upon the great principles of self government on which all American institutions are founded." If they could but achieve the beginning of talks, and if they could drag them out for two years, then there still might be independence. If they could not wear the Yankees out on the battlefield, Stephens knew that he and others could beat them at the conference table. It was their only hope, for "the only peace that the sword alone will bring us in fighting the united North will be the peace of death & subjugation."[54] When he reached Crawfordville on February 20, he settled in to watch the last days of the Confederacy from his drawing room. Whatever happened, he washed his hands of any further involvement.[55] His critics rejoiced that at last "his failure has at least *silenced his* pernicious tongue."[56]

Indeed, Stephens and Toombs were both silenced, at least publicly, though Toombs continued to grumble in his letters to his friend and to others. Unlike Little Aleck, Toombs had something useful to occupy his days in those last months. When Sherman approached Savannah, Brown called out the militia again, and Toombs went back into uniform, marching with his command to shadow the Yankee army's right wing. By November Toombs was in Macon, but soon after the authorities ordered the militia to Savannah. Along the way Toombs managed to impress at least one general, and ironically it was Davis's brother-in-law Richard Taylor. Repeating his performance of the year before when he bullied and threatened a railroad agent, he overwhelmed officials who stood in the way of acquiring adequate transportation to move Taylor and his own militia to Savannah. "A man of extraordinary energy, this same Toombs," Taylor concluded.[57]

But neither Toombs nor any other reinforcements could save Savannah, which fell to Sherman December 21. In the evacuation, Toombs removed his militia to Augusta for the winter, and there he made one last speech on February 16, urging the people to strengthen their resolve. "On with the Revolution," he declared, even if it were to last another twenty years. For a change, he somewhat softened his criticism of Davis, but there was still enough to bring jeers from the largely loyal audience. One onlooker wondered if Toombs ever approved of anything that anyone other than himself thought or did. [58] Like Stephens, he was discovering that there was no longer a constituency who wanted to hear him.

During the winter Toombs, too, went home and watched from afar. He simply poured out his venom to his friend Little Aleck, who no doubt responded in kind. They were beaten men, defeated not by the enemy but by Davis and the unwillingness of the Confederate people to follow their lead. A bright spot for Stephens, at least, came on February 22, 1865, when Davis gave in to congressional pressure and restored Joseph E. Johnston to command the remnants of his old army. It was militarily pointless by then, but at least it represented a victory for Wigfall and the others with whom Stephens had made strange alliance against the president. Little Aleck later maintained that Johnston's policy of avoiding battle with Sherman in 1864 had been the right one, so presumably he approved the general's reinstatement.[59] As for Toombs, who had applauded Johnston's relief the year before, he, too, probably approved, solely because of the rebuff to the president.

By mid-March Toombs confidently expected the imminent fall of Richmond and carped about Davis getting through Congress a bill to enlist slaves as soldiers. By then Congress, in his eyes, was no more than a "Junto," slavishly following the president's whim. "There is but one remedy," he told his friend. "It is begone Davis." Significantly, he wanted more than ever for Stephens and his family to come to Washington for a visit. In the times about to befall them, they would need one another.[60] Months before, when it was learned

that Toombs was with the army in Atlanta resisting Sherman, someone asked what he was doing. A wag responded, "Talking."[61] By
April Toombs seemed to understand, as did Little Aleck, that there
was nothing more to say. It was time for friends to stand by each
other for the uncertainty that lay ahead.

Exultations, Agonies, and Love

A poet would have had them meet the end together,
as they had been side by side for so much of the
drama of the decades that had gone before. Indeed,
they were still together in spirit and act, each having
abandoned any personal participation in the events
of the last days, leaving to its own fate a Confederacy
that would not dance to their tune. Yet each in his
separate way met the news of defeat and surrender in
most appropriate circumstances. Stephens, morose
and fatalistic, gathered his family around him at Liberty Hall to await the end, morbidly visiting the family graveyard, giving way to the old depression that
had so long been his comfortable refuge from involvement and responsibility. Just as typically, news of
Lee's surrender on April 9 found Toombs engaged in
a convivial dinner with an old enemy, Governor
Brown, whom mutual hatred of Davis had made into
an ally.[1]

Unlike his fatalistic friend, Toombs had no intention of being captured and put on parade as a trophy
by the victorious Yankees. Yet before he sought to escape the spreading Federal tentacles in Georgia, fate

gave him one more chance to strike a symbolic blow at the foe he hated even more, Jefferson Davis. Following the fall of Richmond on April 2, the Confederate cabinet and its archives and functionaries made a steady retreat through Virginia and the Carolinas, fleeing pursuing Yankees even while the president tried unrealistically to organize some continued resistance. By May 3 their flight brought them, of all places, to Washington, Georgia, where they found Toombs at home. Postmaster General John H. Reagan came to Toombs's house and was invited to stay the night. More than that, his host offered him money if he needed any. Surprisingly, he even offered to extend money to Davis if needed, though it was most likely far more from concern over the Confederacy being humiliated by the capture and prosecution of its president than from any real concern for Davis the man. He also offered to send his own carriage for Davis's use in his flight, if needed. But that was as far as he would go, and it was only official courtesy due to the office. He adamantly refused to invite Davis into his home or to see him. Reagan and later Secretary of War John C. Breckinridge had the hospitality of his house, but not the president.[2]

Davis and most of his entourage left the next day, and Toombs was out in the street to watch them go, refusing to acknowledge Davis to the last, and very likely intentionally placing himself where he could snub any gesture of recognition or greeting as the president rode by. Instead, he stood there beside his carriage, wearing a shabby hat and a dirty coat, and roundly cursed the enemy in a string of oaths that all but shocked Davis's private secretary. That done, he got in his buggy to drive to Liberty Hall to see Stephens, but not before Breckinridge came to him. The secretary of war was overseeing not only the flight of the government but also its remaining treasury and was already disbursing most of it to remaining soldiers. The rest went into a local bank vault or was handed to trustworthy citizens so that the Yankees would not find all of it. Breckinridge himself handed Toombs a sack with $6,000 and asked him to look after it.[3]

With a wonderful irony, Robert Toombs, present at the creation of the Confederacy in Montgomery, witnessed its final organized acts there in Washington. The fortunes of the war and his own char-

acter had turned him from a dynamic participant and founding father into nothing more than an idle observer, his force reduced in
the end to futile blasphemies. He was still with Stephens a day later,
May 5, when the Yankees arrived and occupied Washington. News
of their coming prompted caution at first, and instead of going
home Toombs met his son-in-law and former staff member Major
William Felix Alexander and set out, probably for Milledgeville.
They had traveled about twenty miles when they passed through
Sparta, Alexander driving an old military ambulance while Toombs
rode inside out of sight. Passing through the town Alexander saw
Sutton S. Scott, whom Toombs had known in Richmond. The ambulance slowed, and as it passed Scott, Toombs drew back the can-
vas curtain. "What are you doing here?" Toombs asked. Scott said
he was heading for Richmond. "To Richmond?" exclained the Georgian. "Great Heavens! Haven't you heard the news? Richmond has
fallen; our armies are scattered; and the Confederacy is gone—
gone—gone! I am on my way to the coast. I do not expect to stop
until I shall have put the Atlantic between me and this unfortunate
country!" That said, Alexander put the horses at a gallop and the
ambulance rolled off in a whirl of dust, carrying with it, as Scott believed, "the biggest minded, and I had almost said, the biggest
hearted man of the South."[4]

Toombs, however, soon decided there was less immediate danger
than he thought and returned home a few days later, coming so qui-
etly that the Federals did not notice or know of his arrival, though
they had already visited his house in his absence and removed almost all his private and official papers from his Confederate years,
and not a few of his other personal and household possessions.[5] It
seemed as if they might leave him unmolested, and Toombs himself
almost dared them to come for him by remaining at home. In fact,
as soon as he returned he apparently approached a Yankee officer
and handed over the $6,000 left with him by Breckinridge, since it
could do the Confederacy no good, and he was not a man to keep
something that was not his own.[6]

He and Julia were taking an inventory of what was missing from
their house on May 11 when, shortly after noon, a squad of Federal
cavalry pulled up in front. Hearing the commotion, Toombs peered

out from his office, saw that at last the Yankees had come for him, and calmly walked out his back door and into the fields beyond while Julia stalled the callers at the front door. With help from a friend he got Gray Alice from his stable and rode east to the Savannah River, then north along the stream to the safety of Elbert County, one of his old political strongholds. There he remained, idling away more than a month in hunting and fishing, before setting out southward as Federal vigilance slackened in the wake of the complete collapse of resistance. Hoping somehow to reach the coast and a passage abroad, he rode within a few miles of Washington itself, but did not dare to try to see Julia, and then discovered that the Yankees still had all avenues of escape closed.

With no alternative, he returned again to the north Georgia mountains and stayed there for nearly four months, living on the kindness and loyalty of old friends in a region little penetrated by the Yankees. So confused were the Yankees as to his whereabouts that one report said he had escaped to Cuba with Breckinridge early in June, and another declared that Toombs had committed suicide.[7] In August he got word to Julia to inquire of the Federal commander in Georgia if he could return home in safety if he gave his parole, but the response was that Toombs was to be arrested and sent north to prison if taken.[8] With no choice but to leave the country, at last in October he tried again and this time turned west. Fortunately for him, the Federals seemed to believe that he had in fact already left the country and thus relaxed their vigilance. Toombs rode into Alabama without incident and simply traveled to Mobile by public transport. He then took a steamer to New Orleans, where, under the assumed name of Luther Martin, he boarded a ship November 4, bound for Havana and exile. Not surprisingly, he immediately began to entertain his fellow passengers with accounts of all that had been wrong with the Confederacy.[9]

Had Toombs but known fully the fate of his friend Stephens, he might not have put himself to all the trouble of those months of uncertainty, for Little Aleck's ordeal at the hands of the Yankees ended some weeks before Toombs left the country, and the vice president was a great deal more important to the victors than a mere onetime cabinet minister and general. The bluecoats came up the drive to

Liberty Hall on the morning of May 11, responding to the same orders that sent them to Toombs's house a few hours later. Stephens
had heard the cavalry were in Crawfordville and immediately realized they had come for him. He went to his room and began to
pack, and then awaited the callers in his library. It was almost chill-
ingly civil; Stephens had a polite conversation with the officer in
charge, then was allowed more time to finish packing and even to
take a servant with him. They boarded a waiting train in Crawfordville and then traveled to within a few miles of Washington,
where the cavalry remounted and went to arrest Toombs. The only
joy for Stephens this day came when the commander returned and
told him that his friend had escaped.

Stephens reached Atlanta the next day, for the first time the true
reality of his condition as a prisoner really hitting him. He was allowed to go abroad in the city, but only under guard until he gave
his parole not to attempt to escape. At the same time, he learned
that on May 10 Davis had been captured with Reagan and several
other followers and that the president was also being brought to Atlanta. Actually given his choice of the route by which he was to be
conveyed north, Stephens simply asked that he not go the same way
as Davis, not wanting to have to face him or travel in his company.
Each was taken on a separate train toward the coast, but even when
they were both in the same station and Stephens learned that the
passenger car on Davis's train was more comfortable, he declined
to switch, to avoid confronting Davis. Even when they reached Augusta for the steamboat trip down the Savannah River to the coast,
the two Confederates rode in separate carriages. When they
boarded the little tug for the ride to Savannah, Davis rode below
deck, Stephens stayed above. Still they had neither seen nor spoken
to one another. Not until the next morning when Davis came up on
deck did they finally meet, their first encounter since the abortive
Hampton Roads conference in February. "His salutation was not un-
friendly," Stephens noted, "but it was far from cordial." They spoke
only a few words of meaningless conversation, then kept apart. During the voyage north up the coast from Savannah, they spoke again
occasionally, and with somewhat more cordiality, and Stephens even
took a few meals with Davis and his wife and some of the other cap-

tives. On May 19 they reached Hampton Roads, where Stephens learned that he was to be taken to Fort Warren in Boston for incarceration while Davis would remain, to be kept in Fort Monroe. On May 21 Little Aleck said his farewells to his companions and had a last encounter with Davis, who said nothing other than farewell but took his hand with some considerable emotion. They never saw each other again.[10]

While Davis went to the fort that was his prison for the next two years, Stephens soon boarded another vessel for the passage to Boston, and there on May 25 he was shown into his room, or cell. Even with a coal fire burning and furnishings that provided more comfort than most prisoners enjoyed, it was still a shock. "For the first time in my life I had the full realization of being a prisoner," he remembered. "I was alone." Nevertheless, his jailers were not unmindful of his fragile health. Davis was actually manacled for a time, and his movement severely restricted for several months, but the vice president suffered no such humiliation or privation. For two months he was not allowed out of his room, but then they permitted him much wider freedom, including the privilege of going anywhere in the fort at will. Authorities allowed friends to send him packages of fruit and vegetables and other niceties to supplement his diet, and in late August they moved him to a better room for the remainder of his stay.[11]

While he languished in his prison, thinking, conversing with his guards, writing his endless letters, Stephens wondered at his fate. He would have been amused to know just how much his captors wondered, too. Lincoln had been assassinated on April 14, and but for that Stephens might never have been arrested at all, for Lincoln had hoped at the end that Davis and the other high officials of the Confederacy might just escape. It would save the Federals the trouble of deciding what to do with them and prevent especially the danger of making them martyrs if they went to trial for the treason indictments outstanding against most of them. Such a spectacle must inevitably work against efforts to keep the recently conquered Southern states quiescent and to prepare them for reconstruction. Lincoln's murder, however, raised immediate questions about who was responsible, and in the vengeful tenor of the moment, many people wanted Davis and his leaders to pay, whether they had been involved or not. After the conviction and execution of four conspirators in July, and the complete failure of the government to establish any connection between Confederate leaders and the crime, the passion of the North toward men like Stephens quickly subsided. By fall their continued incarceration proved an embarrassment, as the government showed an ever-dwindling inclination to bring them to trial. In June Stephens wrote to President Andrew Johnson to inquire after his eligibility to be covered under an amnesty proclamation of May 29, providing he applied for an executive pardon. When that produced no satisfactory reply, he demanded an end to his imprisonment without benefit of habeas corpus and a trial under the Constitution. That got no response either, but Johnson was playing his own game, and on October 11 he ordered the release on parole of Stephens, Reagan, and almost all other imprisoned Confederate leaders except Davis. With Reconstruction inaugurated, Johnson needed moderates like these men back in their home states speaking for reconciliation. Within two years even Davis was released, denied the trial that he wanted. It was a course of wisdom that no one would have expected either from the lightweight Johnson or the victorious Union, but it went far toward defusing sectional animosities by denying the diehards the trials that could provide focal points for protest.

Little Aleck returned to Liberty Hall on October 26, unwell but neither broken nor subdued. There was a new order confronting him in the country. Emancipation had freed 4 million slaves, and though he never abandoned his conviction that the black man was inferior to the white, he accepted the inevitability of abolition, recognized that blacks should be allowed to own property, and even argued that they might be granted voting rights and the opportunity to hold elective office, though always under a system of control that virtually ensured the continuation of white supremacy. It was the best that could be made of a bad situation for the South after the war. More to the point, it called for men like him to take the lead in building a new political South to ensure and protect that supremacy. Incredibly, after abandoning his elective office instead of working actively to save the Confederacy from the evils he saw killing it,

Stephens determined that it would now be his duty to seek public office in order to fight to shape a new order that the verdict of the war had forced upon his section. Within days of reaching home, Stephens learned that Brown and others were suggesting him for the governorship, and he did not discourage them. They did not organize in time to effect their result, but others were already working toward another goal, as support grew to elect him to the Senate when the state legislature assembled in December. In January 1866 they overwhelmingly elected him, even though there was doubt that he would be allowed to take his seat since he was still on parole from his treason indictment and could hardly take the required oath of office denying that he had ever abetted the Confederate cause. Yet he wanted office, despite all his demurrals of years past. In peace he strove to achieve the goals of white over black and strict construction of the Constitution that in war he had so petulantly abandoned.[12]

His friend Toombs's abandonment was even greater for the moment, in that he had left the country entirely. No sooner did Stephens get home than he wrote to Toombs to notify him of his release and to urge him to apply to Johnson for parole and pardon. The letter found his friend still in Havana and in no mood to be contrite. Exaggerating his own importance as usual, he was convinced that he was well advised to flee the country; and despite the fact that Confederate figures much higher and more prominent than he had been freed, he believed that if captured he would have been imprisoned perhaps indefinitely. Nor did he have any inclination to return to live in a conquered country. He had no use for Johnson's conciliatory reconstruction and condemned Southern leaders who spoke of cooperation and putting the past behind them. In a rare break with his friend, he also advised Stephens against accepting the Senate seat. The only proper course for them was to do nothing at all, to take no part whatever in government, and to let the Yankees run their own government to ruin as they tried to deal with the social and economic problems created by emancipation. "That it will end in ruin is clear," he told his friend. "That such a government may end in blood I earnestly pray for."

For himself, he liked Cuba, where slavery made the planters

prosper, but he anticipated that before long emancipation would be forced upon the island. He thus turned his eyes toward Mexico, where already thousands of expatriate Confederates had gone to set up new communities. Though Mexico was currently in revolt, its native Spanish leaders fighting against an imposed French administration, Toombs expected either European rulers to take it eventually or else what he called an "Anglo-Saxon" regime, which could mean the English or perhaps even his fellow former Confederates. In either case, he told Stephens, "I shall stand a better chance than in an old established society." Always prudent with his money, he managed to keep enough hard currency with him during the war that he could live comfortably abroad while choosing his next move. It is not hard to imagine that already he saw himself as a potential great force in such a new society.[13]

Toombs, having been joined by Julia, remained in Havana until spring 1866, by which time circumstances dramatically changed his plans. In Mexico, the French gave up their dreams of empire and announced that they were pulling out, virtually ensuring that the native insurgents would come to power. That ended Toombs's hopes of starting over under a conducive regime. Then he learned that his only remaining child, Sallie DuBose, was fatally ill and had perhaps only months to live. Suddenly, returning to the United States did not look so unthinkable after all. Still under indictment, and still too proud to apply for pardon or parole, Toombs went to Paris in May, while Julia went back to Georgia briefly to see their daughter. Significantly, she also brought with her a public message from her husband in which he asked Georgians to apply themselves to the resurrection of their state and section. He still did not counsel actively working with their conquerors, but his bitterness was notably absent. It may have been a first effort at establishing himself as reasonable and responsible enough to be allowed to return.[14]

Not surprisingly, Paris suited Toombs. He spent considerable time at a health resort near the city, and when in Paris was often seen at the theater, occupying a seat in the orchestra and viewing the frequently risqué performances with an immobile expression of affected boredom.[15] He watched events at home as best he could but felt in the dark as to what was going to happen, especially as

Johnson and the Radical wing of the Republican Party went to war with each other and it appeared that Johnson might be impeached. He regarded Johnson as a tyrant who would give power to moderates like Herschel Johnson, whom Toombs thought hardly better than traitors for their support of Davis, expecting they would do nothing to protect Southern rights and Southerners from enfranchisement of the blacks. Johnson's Radical opponents would achieve the same result, but by different means. "He is already lost," Toombs declared of Johnson in October. "Nothing can save him but physical force." He expected General Grant, commanding the army, to step into the fray and use the military if necessary. It was a poor prophecy, but out of it Toombs extracted the hope that by the end of the year the various authorities in the North would be so distracted fighting one another that he would be "too inconsequential, to attract the attention of the combatants" and could simply slip home to Washington unnoticed. Toombs felt no confidence that the several amnesty proclamations that had come out by then would do him any good, for they had exclusions or exceptions that he felt left him outside their provisions. He counted instead on simply being overlooked, something he had never allowed to happen before.[16]

His desire to return home was sharpened, however, when word came of his daughter's death in late October. The news all but prostrated Toombs, who poured out his grief to Stephens. "It has crushed my heart and buried my hopes in the grave," he declared. Julia returned to Georgia immediately, but her husband remained in Paris, suffering a bleak and lonely Christmas. "God knows I cannot regret that 1866 is gone," he wrote at the New Year. He turned increasingly morose and even thought of braving arrest by going directly to New York, in spite of promising Julia that he would take no such risk. Life looked ever more gloomy, and yet it could hardly be worse, even if he were arrested, especially as he had seen by then that almost everyone but Davis was released. "Is this state of things to last forever?" he complained. "To me it is becoming intolerable." He even began to realize self-doubts that hardly had characterized his deportment before. "Pray for me that I may be a better man in the new year than in all the old ones before in my time," he wrote Julia.[17]

When he could wait no longer, he boarded a ship for New Orleans on January 17, 1867. "The worst that can happen to me is prison," he wrote his wife before leaving, "and I don't see much to choose between my present condition and any decent fort."[18] He spent several days in Havana along the way and arrived in Louisiana just as the news came in that Congress had passed the first of the Reconstruction Acts, providing for division of the South into districts to be administered by military occupation. Many former Confederates were to be disenfranchised, and the federal government would seek to revolutionize Southern politics as well as forcing black suffrage. "It took all by surprise," Toombs remarked, "& made me wish myself back in Paris again." But he foresaw that there would be weeks of further debate in Congress before the act could go into effect and decided to go to his home in Washington. In New Orleans he learned that his private finances were in much worse shape than he had believed from what Julia and his friends had told him while abroad, and he had to see to them personally.

Spending just two days in New Orleans, he left for a brief business visit to Mobile and then went directly home. What he found as he traveled through the South dismayed him greatly. "Every thing looked much worse than I expected," he said a few weeks later. "Changes had been rapid & radical, the spirit of the great body of the people utterly broken, bankruptcy & ruin wide spread throughout the land, the pressure of physical wants absorbing all the time & thoughts of all the people, & the best & truest people in utter despair at the prospect before them." Indeed, things looked so bad that he did not think the military bill would make them any worse, but he did see resentment growing, and in that he found hope. Clearly, the Radical Republicans in Washington intended never to allow the Southern states back into the Union until all political power was in the hands of Republicans and their scalawag fellow travelers and the state constitutions so altered as to preserve Republican rule for the remainder of their generation.[19]

Toombs was hardly surprised to see his old enemy Joe Brown working with the Radicals in order to put himself in power again and condemned the "political bucaneers" working with him, accusing most of being little more than hirelings, nothing but "the great body of the negroes, Yankee refugees & such other waifs & floats as can be alarmed by the cry of confiscation, or bribed by the expectation of place or plunder." The very thought of Negro suffrage outraged him, and he fully expected that unscrupulous Northern politicians and traitorous Southern men like Brown would use and manipulate the votes of ignorant blacks to their own ends. Moreover, on reaching home he traveled around his old professional circuit, and in the courthouses and barrooms he heard mutterings that the military authorities intended to make life difficult for "the old incorrigible traitors, such as myself." Hearing that, of course, Toombs's instinct was only to speak his mind more stridently. "I have not minded my words," he said in April, almost challenging the Yankees to arrest him. "Therefore you may not be surprised any day to hear of me, in some of those sanctuaries of liberty now vulgarly called forts," he sarcastically told a friend in April.

Toombs was probably disappointed that no one wanted to arrest him, yet another sign that even the old enemy did not think him important enough to bother about. Still, he did not expect to remain at home long, just in case, especially since he had hopes that there might be another uprising in the South against Yankee military rule. He wanted to get his family safely out of the way and secure from want "against the coming storm or far worse, the dead calm of african despotism." For several weeks he did what legal and financial business he could, saw good crops come in on his property, and made plans to take Julia and his grandchildren to a safe haven in Toronto in July. A small Confederate colony perched there on the other side of the New York border, with men like General Jubal Early, Confederate diplomat James Mason, and eventually Breckinridge, and there Toombs could hope to be among friends and convivial company. Beyond Canada, however, Toombs began to think of a permanent relocation in Brazil. Thousands of other Confederates were talking of relocating there, with active emigration societies forming, and the Brazilian government eagerly encouraging them, promising that with slavery still in place, the country would be not only politically but also socially agreeable to Southerners. Always ambitious, always the politician, Toombs thought that if enough old Confederates went to Brazil—or anywhere else—they could become "an important element in any govt." All depended on what happened under Reconstruction, of course, but at the moment he expected that the next two years would either see a renewed war between North and South "or the greatest exodus that has ever been witnessed in modern times." Hyperbolic as always, he declared to his friends that rather than see permanent dislocation, he "would much prefer to see the whole population perish in defense of their native land."[20]

Once in Canada, he remained only a short time before he decided that his predictions of another upheaval were ill-founded. Finally, in fall 1867 he went straight to Washington, DC, to meet with President Johnson himself, who chose simply to ignore the issue raised by Toombs's return to U.S. jurisdiction. There would be no arrest, nor would there be any oaths of allegiance or contrition.[21] Toombs could simply go home, and that was all he wanted for the moment. And so at last both Toombs and Stephens were once more in their own households. Indeed, it was almost as if the war had never happened, for all the effect it had on them. Neither lost any property to confiscation, though Toombs had had to sell some of his Texas land to support himself abroad. Both still had their substantial Georgia plantations, and though emancipation had freed their slaves, in fact almost all of their blacks remained on their properties working the fields in return for shares of the crops. Just as each had enjoyed the freedom to absent himself from participation in the war and the government during the recent conflict, so now they could safely stand aside, enjoying their relatively substantial fortunes while the state and the South endured the throes of Reconstruction. But of course they did not.

Toombs before long placed himself in the thick of state politics and economic recovery and remained there for the next decade. Stephens was a prominent figure even longer, both of them struggling to save something of the old prewar regime against the assaults of the Republicans, carpetbag rule, and enfranchised blacks. And once more they were together on almost every issue, united in opinion and aspiration, especially when the time came to spare some of their attention from current events to reconsider their personal and sectional past. It was not enough to stand on the right side as they

faced the challenges ahead. They could not do so with the authority to lead unless they could convince their people—and themselves
—that they had always stood on the right side, even if it meant
rewriting history in the process.

Toombs immediately returned to the practice of law and almost
at once regained his place at the head of the Georgia bar. Despite
the losses of the war, within three years of coming home Toombs
built his personal estate to $200,000, nearly half what it had been
before the war. He still held large acreage in Texas, and this he skillfully built by substantial acquisition, even borrowing large sums to
add more land. By 1872 an investigator for a loan backer reported
that Toombs was a very wealthy man, worth at least $50,000 more
than any other man in his county and good for any amount he
should seek to borrow. Whatever else his performance during the
war revealed about his abilities, no one doubted that he was as acute
as ever when it came to money.[22] A few years later, when Georgia's
finances virtually collapsed, Toombs twice lent the state money from
his own fortune to meet its immediate needs, until tax revenues
could reimburse him.

It did not need his becoming one of the state's creditors to make
Toombs feel entitled to a loud voice in its political counsels, despite
the disabilities that meant he could never vote or hold office himself unless he sued for pardon, which he would never do. "Popular
wrongs never were and never will be redressed by silence and inac-
tion," he told Stephens in November 1867. Naturally, he and other
former leaders must speak out. But then, his last three years in the
Confederacy had been days of constant vocal opposition without an
office for a pulpit, so he was used to his position, perhaps even comfortable with it, for no one could ever expect him to put his ideas to
the test, especially as the grip of the uncompromising radical that
squeezed the moderate out of him during the war still had its hold.
He was thus destined to discover almost at once that in a Georgia
anxious to get through and beyond Reconstruction as quickly and
easily as possible, few people were interested in his message of confrontation and resistance.[23]

He made his first public appearance at an Atlanta rally in July
1868 supporting Democratic nominee Horatio Seymour against the

presidential candidacy of General Grant, a speech in which he sounded the old bells of alarm and called all Georgians to rally, this time to the polls to elect Seymour, who pledged an end to Reconstruction and the immediate withdrawal of occupying army forces from the South. Seymour won the state, but controversy kept Georgia's electoral vote from being counted, not that it would have mattered. Seymour lost handily, but Toombs felt he had scored another triumph a month later when the legislature defeated Joseph Brown's bid for a Senate seat. As governor, Brown had yielded to Yankee rule too quickly and easily to suit Toombs, who despised the moderates with whom he once was numbered. "There was political justice in making the earliest traitor defeat the worst one," Toombs crowed. He almost equally despised Joshua Hill, whom Toombs had supported in spite of Hill's having been a Unionist. Perversely, he wanted nothing in return for his favor except for Hill not to speak to him, for Toombs had backed him not out of preference but merely because Hill was running against Brown.[24]

Toombs spoke several times during the campaign in support of Seymour and was gratified in November to see Georgia one of the few states in the country carried by the Democratic ticket. Perhaps that persuaded him that he could again exert his influence in state affairs as of old, but if so he was soon disillusioned. Like Stephens, he was fighting against history and trying to turn it back. In the governorship race that same year he supported General John B. Gordon against his opponent, the Radical cooperationist Rufus Bullock, and damned the existing regime in the state as a mass of floating filth, "which rises as it rots and rots as it rises." Decrying the several congressional acts that imposed Reconstruction and damning the recent Thirteenth and Fourteenth Amendments to the Constitution—eliminating slavery and granting the start of civil rights to blacks while prohibiting former officials of the Confederacy from holding public office without pardon—the Gordon forces were well beaten by Bullock. Toombs had yet to accept that what the war had done could not be undone. Indeed, he never accepted it.[25]

On taking office, Bullock requested Federal troops to preserve order in Georgia, just as they were going into other former Confederate states that balked at ratifying the new amendments and recognizing the result of the war. Toombs regarded Bullock's measures as nothing less than a "coup d'etat" and went to the new capital in Atlanta to try to fight it, but to no avail. He charged with only slim foundation that men were won over by bribes of money and office, with the military prepared to back Bullock completely. The conservative forces could only try to win enough seats in the legislature to curb Bullock, and Toombs actually joined forces with Joseph Brown in an effort to bring about the election of a speaker of the statehouse who could lead the assembly in resistance. "Rather a strange conjunction is it not?" he told Stephens. "But you know my rule is to use the devil if I can do better to save the country." Toombs thought he did some good in the end, but in fact Bullock's hold remained secure, and Georgia was in for a year of controversial rule, even if not as corrupt and arbitrary as Toombs believed.[26] It was a time in which Toombs's uncompromising animosity only increased. Better thirty years of war than to have to suffer Negroes voting, he told his friend. Better that blacks should all be dead, and in his usual hyperbole, he expressed the hope that he could do something to send them all to the next life quickly and before they could pollute the ballot box and help their Radical masters tyrannize white Southerners.[27]

Bullock's regime lasted only a year, fortunately, and thanks in part to strenuous efforts by Toombs, the Democrats regained the state in 1870. He made a speech repeatedly around the state that called on Georgians to stand firm and to make no compromise. In the face of their recent experience with Bullock, for a change they listened. Sadly for Toombs, however, it was to be almost the last time. All across the South rising new Democratic leaders could see that the only future for them lay in abandoning romantic dreams of the past and of a South that perhaps never was. They must capitalize, industrialize, and modernize in order to compete for an equal place in the Union and a share of its wealth. Without abandoning respect for their elders and the sacrifices of the Confederacy, they saw clearly that the Old South was the dead past, and a New South must be built. They must make their peace with Congress and the Radicals, accept the amendments to the Constitution, get the troops out of their states, and move on.

It was a stance that Toombs could neither understand nor countenance. He had been an uncompromising opponent of all that was new for so long that he could not change. As a result, 1870 saw the last of the glory for him. For years more he spoke out at every opportunity, but while his voice had to be heard, listeners heeded less and less. When he argued that the South ought to remain an agricultural economy and railed against the new gods of wealth and industry—neatly overlooking his own lifelong acquisition of wealth through business and investing as well as through planting—his was a voice from the outmoded past. "Toombs is a ponderous, inappeasable old blatherskite, as malignant as Jeff Davis, but lacking discretion sufficient to go under shelter from a rainstorm," one Georgia paper claimed. "The South needs more than anything else at this time about a hundred first class funerals, and her own sensible people would gladly give nuisances like Toombs and Davis the precedence in ordering their coffins."[28] It would be hard to say which hurt Toombs more, seeing Georgians themselves start to look on him as a dangerous anachronism or being lumped together with Jefferson Davis. It was only made worse when the unstoppable Joseph Brown made a comeback in state politics and by 1872 was once more a potent force. Toombs denounced him for corruption and collaboration with the Republicans during his last term in office, and Brown responded by calling Toombs a liar. Talk of a duel naturally followed, and Brown apparently took it quite seriously, but Toombs did not. As a result, since no meeting took place, Brown gained in stature by being willing to fight, and Toombs lost more of his public following by seeming to have provoked the confrontation in the first place and then by failing to take action.[29]

In 1872 he and Stephens both stood aloof from the New Departure movement of Southern Democrats to join with an emerging liberal wing of the Republicans that repudiated the harsh policy of the Radicals to nominate Horace Greeley to run against Grant for the presidency. At the state party convention that year Toombs fought against its delegates being pledged to Greeley; but when he saw how they were leaning, he gave up and spitefully—and typically—proclaimed to the convention that the delegation had been packed. It was almost pathetic. He was sixty-two, his eyesight going, his health no longer vigorous, drink and disappointment and extremism increasingly clouding his judgment and soon even his lucidity. He could only sit on the sidelines and watch as other New South leaders like Gordon became the darlings of Georgia's body politic. It was a repeat of Montgomery and the Confederate presidency. He responded as he always did, intemperately, bitterly, and loudly. Toombs sarcastically remarked that without the scar on his cheek from a famous wound at Antietam, Gordon would have been a failure in politics. Toombs had his Antietam scar, too, but on his hand, and his reward was oblivion. His envy and jealousy of Gordon in particular were such that in a few years when Gordon ran for the governorship, Toombs exclaimed, "John B. Gordon, governor, Hell! You could put Gordon in a hermetically sealed glass jar, give him twenty gold pieces to count, and he would lose half in the enumeration!"[30]

Only once more did Toombs feel briefly the old adulation of Georgians as he led them, this time in the often bitter debate over revising the 1868 constitution under which the state had applied for readmission. It had several defects to his mind, chiefly the enfranchisement of blacks and its provision allowing the state to invest its funds to support railroad and industrial interests. In private practice Toombs did a great deal of railroad and corporation work in the 1870s and consistently supported state regulation of the railroads and their sharing a proper portion of the tax burden in keeping with their profits. Too often they had sought charters and state investment or tax favors, then failed and left Georgia holding their debt. In 1870 the legislature even provided to lease the major state railroad to private investors, thinking that the payments from the lease would at least generate some revenue. Stephens at first went along as a partner in the new company but backed out immediately after Toombs advised him against it, and meanwhile Toombs denounced the sale of bonds by the state to raise funds for investing in new lines.

As a result, Toombs quickly became the leading attorney in the state for suing railroads and other corporations against monopoly and unfair advantages from government. It culminated in 1877 when, after vigorous calls on his part for more than a year, a convention was summoned to draft a new constitution. Indeed, Toombs's adamancy and intemperance in his demands for reform almost killed the convention movement, especially his repeated denunciations of the 1868 "nigger constitution." The rest of the South and the North were watching Georgia. The Democratic Party was gaining in strength, and 1876 looked like a year when it might regain the presidency, and with it, power to end Reconstruction and to encourage Southern progress. Black suffrage was, for the moment, a fact of life, and if Georgians wanted to move on in the new world, they had to accept that fact. Toombs did not, further marginalizing the old warrior. Still, when the convention met, he was there as a delegate, though his friend Little Aleck was not, and Toombs managed to dominate much of the proceeding from the first. Ultimately, it produced a constitution that did not incorporate several reforms in the judiciary and apportionment that he wanted, but he pushed through his provision banning state aid to railroads and exemption from taxation, outlawing monopolies, and providing state regulation of railroad rates. Not content to stop there, he canvassed the state that fall, arousing support for the new constitution, and when it went before the people in February 1878, it passed overwhelmingly.[31]

Like a setting sun, Toombs flashed briefly with the acceptance of the constitution, but his further positive influence in state affairs was virtually ended. By contrast, during his friend's mostly futile decade of kicking against the bricks of Reconstruction and New South rule, Stephens found his voice as welcome as ever, no doubt because he was less inclined to use it in condemning any and all with whom he disagreed. Despite being elected to the Senate early in 1866, he never presented his credentials or attempted to take his seat simply because Georgia had not yet applied for readmission and could not until after the constitution of 1868 was framed. But by his election, Georgians had decreed that they wanted him, unlike Toombs, in their councils, and his first public remarks after that indicated that he was going to stand for his old moderation, unabated by the ravages of war, a result that he accepted with far more equanimity than his friend Toombs. Georgia soon passed laws offering to blacks protection of their rights and property, at Little

Aleck's urging, helping to pave the way for a Reconstruction experience that would be less harsh and onerous than that suffered by most other former Confederate states. Only on granting the vote to blacks by congressional or constitutional act did he balk. The right to do that remained only with the states, and despite the result of the war, somehow Stephens still believed that states' rights arguments had some force in the new order. He was disappointed, and when presented with the Fourteenth Amendment, enacting black suffrage and effectively reducing the congressional representation from any state refusing them the vote, he was outraged. He was a moderate only to a point, and this was it. Though never as intemperate as Toombs, he was in his friend's camp from then on when it came to opposition to the inevitable. The difference was that Stephens tried to make the best of a situation he could not change; Toombs preferred making a futile effort to hold back the waves rather than ride on them.

Not surprisingly, Georgia rejected the Fourteenth Amendment, and though Stephens did not openly campaign for such a result, it did not displease him. He saw the logical absurdity of Georgia presumably having the right to accept an amendment but not having been granted the right to participate in the debate over its drafting, which took place during the war. And if it were not a readmitted state that could send him to the Senate yet, then how could it vote for ratification, which was by definition the act of a full-fledged state? The trouble was, in the power structure of the moment, such niceties were meaningless. It was the Radicals' game at the moment, and they made the rules. Stephens responded by simply bowing out of the political debate altogether for the next two years. Besides, he had something else to occupy him.

Both Stephens and Toombs were quite familiar with the works of Shakespeare, especially the tragedies, those timeless dramas in which men destroyed themselves and sometimes nations. They knew, too, of those recurring elements of ambition, weakness, and ultimately revenge that drove Macbeth and the other great tragic heroes. But it is hardly likely that Stephens or his closest friend ever recognized those fatal elements in themselves or their careers. The great tragedy of their lifetimes was the rise and fall of the Confederacy. Each, especially Toombs, allowed ambition to play its role in giving birth to the new nation. Both felt the full sway of their ambition to lead, whether in the highest office or by oracular dictation. When they failed, it was the weakness of their disappointed ambition and hurt pride that primarily turned them into deadly enemies of Davis. Lacking the inner awareness to see how their own weaknesses had helped crush their cause, yet perhaps driven by an unacknowledged fear of their own degree of responsibility, they naturally looked to the only alternative. The true story of the Confederacy must be known, their version of the truth, the one in which if only people had listened to them, the South would have won its freedom. That version required villains other than themselves, of course, and that meant Jefferson Davis. The time had come for revenge.

While in prison, Stephens received more than one inquiry from publishers suggesting that his memoirs of his Confederate career could be highly salable should he write them. By fall 1866 he decided to do it, but what his publisher did not know was that he had no intention of producing the exciting and dramatic inside account of Montgomery and Richmond. For one thing, there were so many details that he simply did not know, since he had absented himself from the capital for most of the war. Rather, he saw this work as an opportunity to present a vindication of his political beliefs and course throughout his career, a point-by-point statement of the validity of limited republican government as he had envisioned it, and a justification of secession itself. The old arguments about state sovereignty and the nature of the Union would be there, presented as any good lawyer would make his case, with a lot of supporting evidence and a limited recognition of the existence of any ideas to the contrary.

It took Stephens two years to produce his first volume, writing it in the form of a dialogue between himself and a number of fictional characters who fed him questions carefully framed to set up his unassailable answers. When the first volume of *A Constitutional View of the Late War Between the States; Its Causes, Character, Conduct and Results* appeared in 1868, his readers were much disappointed, for it contained not a word about his Confederate career, but presented instead 647 pages of the background for his conception of the nature of the Union and the Constitution, the wrongs suffered by the slave states, and the construction of the argument for the legality of secession. Worse, it was hopelessly boring and legalistic. Nevertheless, it enjoyed a wonderful sale, over 64,000 copies in a few months. But once subscribers saw what they were getting, they refused to take the second volume when it appeared two years later, for they knew what it would contain, and barely 20,000 copies were purchased, especially after critics savaged the first volume. At least he dealt with the war years in five chapters of volume two, but there was precious little of the personal reminiscence that publisher and readers wanted and instead a great deal of criticism of Davis, second-guessing, and seemingly endless appendixes.

Not surprisingly, Stephens could not handle the criticism from reviewers and public. Obsessed with having the last word, he wrote lengthy responses to almost every critical review and in 1872 published them in book form to stand beside his *Constitutional View*.[32] It was pointless, for his arguments were just as obscure and obsolete in his responses as in the original set of books, convincing few but himself. He thought he would be producing the great justification of himself and his section, but in the end his work had only two real influences. By its title, it virtually began the movement to call the recent conflict the War Between the States, whose subtle difference from "civil war" suggested a contest between independent equals rather than a mere internal separatist movement. And it was also the first major salvo in what became a quarter-century's war of words between Jefferson Davis and his critics. Stephens's work was the earliest memoir from any prominent Confederate leader, civil or military, and the first public bill of particulars against the Confederate president. In its way, it cast the mold for all that would follow, harping repeatedly on the themes of executive usurpation, inflexibility, blindness to the use of cotton, refusal to make proper preparations financial and military at the outset of the conflict, obstinate refusal to try negotiations with the North, and inept interference with the military conduct of the war, especially relieving Joseph E. Johnston from command before Atlanta. These charges were the mantra of Davis's critics for the next generation, all of whom borrowed from Stephens and enlarged upon his arguments, as he did himself in the years to come. Ironically, the tone of his writings was remarkably similar to a memoir that appeared in 1881, when Jefferson Davis published his own. As so often before, the two men were more alike than either ever cared to admit.

Despite the criticism of his work, Stephens found that he liked rewriting history, and no sooner did he finish his second volume than he began work on a *Compendium of History of the United States,* published in 1872. He envisioned a school text as a means of getting the proper story of the development of the Union and American democracy before the young, "to keep our children from further imposition as well as dependence upon Northern primary books."[33] After it appeared, this first attempt to put a Southern viewpoint before Southern students went through three editions, and in a few years Stephens went to work on another expanded version, *Comprehensive and Popular History of the United States,* which when it appeared in the first of three editions in 1882, continued his arguments before an ever wider audience. In fact, his school histories, far more than the largely unread and unreadable *Constitutional View,* influenced future generations in viewing secession as a constitutional right and the Southern effort as one motivated by principle and prompted by injustice and aggression from Washington. They also neatly and sophistically all but removed slavery entirely from the equation of secession and civil war. The man who declared in 1861 that slavery was the "cornerstone" of the movement, in his book maintained that though of course it was important to the South, it was quite peripheral to the South's true and heroic stand on constitutional issues and "state rights." Future generations were much persuaded by the states' rights arguments that Stephens put forward, overlooking, as he chose to do, that the only states' "rights" being debated in 1860 were those connected with slavery.

Stephens continued his writing, including numerous essays and reviews, even while his political career resumed. After the Senate fiasco, he stayed out of overt politics for a time, though always a careful and interested observer of Georgia's shifting fortunes during Reconstruction. He tentatively spoke out against the rise of the violence-prone Ku Klux Klan, privately advised President Johnson to mount a determined fight to defend himself against impeachment, and in 1868 met informally with organizers looking to pit Seymour against Grant. Though he somewhat liked Grant personally, Stephens predicted that if elected president, the general would stage a coup and make himself a dictator backed by the army. He changed his mind after the election, typically, and even expressed some hope that Grant might in fact be lenient with the South. But then Bullock brought the Federal troops into Georgia, and Reconstruction for the next year took a dramatically more severe course before Bullock himself was turned out. In 1870 the political turmoil finally settled down, Georgia grudgingly accepted the Thirteenth, Fourteenth, and the new Fifteenth Amendment that ensured Negro suffrage, and its elected delegates to Congress were at last seated.

Stephens was finishing work on his second volume of *Constitutional View* and the first of his textbooks during most of this period and thus had no time to take a more active part in politics, and no real forum. But in 1871 he bought a partnership in the *Atlanta Sun* and began to use its pages to espouse his ancient message of constitutionalism, shortly after acquiring the sole proprietorship. However, just as increasingly few readers of the first volume of his book wanted to keep hearing the same old song in the second volume, so readers turned away from the *Sun*. By early 1873 Stephens had almost bankrupted himself with it, and he sold it at a loss to the *Atlanta Constitution*. One day soon afterward Toombs came for a visit. Unexpectedly, he placed in Little Aleck's lap a stack of the notes Stephens had spread around Atlanta in return for loans to keep the *Sun* going. His old friend had been round to the creditors and bought every one of them to present as a gift to him.[34]

During the 1872 campaign, Stephens, like Toombs, refused to side with their Democratic friends backing Greeley and the liberal Republicans, even though it was in their best interest in the situation. Besides, he had no stomach for politics that year after his brother Linton died in July. It was said that when the news reached Liberty Hall, Stephens let out one anguished scream and then fell completely and inconsolably quiet.[35] "My God, what can I do but mingle my tears with yours?" Toombs wrote in his own bereavement, while Little Aleck himself could not even attend the funeral because of his own illness.[36] "The light of my life is extinguished," Stephens lamented, "and everything is gloomy cheerless and almost hope-less."[37]

Yet he rallied, as he always did, though this loss could never be repaired. At first he took refuge in attacking Greeley in the *Sun,* and though that failed, still his stand reinforced his popularity in many quarters of the state, even though a large faction resented his stub-born refusal to embrace the New South. Unlike Toombs, however, Stephens had not made his opposition so vitriolic and personal as to alienate the moderates entirely, and after Grant's reelection when Greeley was no longer important, some individuals began to speak again of placing Little Aleck in the Senate. In the event, Gordon won the seat, with Stephens coming in second and some observers believing that only his bull-headed opposition to the fusion of Democrats with the liberal Republicans had prevented his election. No sooner was the result known than some supporters began to plan putting him forward for a special election to fill a vacant seat in the House of Representatives. It was a mark of esteem for him personally rather than an endorsement of his outmoded views, but Stephens won the seat all the same and held it for the next nine years. While often controversial, and usually outspoken, Stephens did little more in his new congressional tenure than represent his own views, occasionally exciting some response, but in the main only attracting grudging admiration from his constituents for his often "peculiar" views. All the while he tenaciously clung to things as they had been rather than acknowledging what they had become. By 1882 he was almost an anachronism.

It might have been expected that Toombs would be at least a little jealous of his friend's return to office, if not influence, yet he seems only to have been pleased that Little Aleck had something to do and that at least he could continue to champion the death grip on the past that meant so much to both of them. Besides, Toombs's health was deteriorating badly, his eyes clouding with cataracts, and Julia was not at all well, either. And Toombs was still lionized as a lead-ing member of the bar, consulted and lauded, while his always care-ful management of his private fortunes occupied him much, and even took him into the hotel business in Atlanta. For Stephens he had only encouragement and frequent advice. There was a brief and painful break between them in 1874 over a misunderstanding on Stephens's ill-advised share in the railroad lease business, which he had Toombs handle for him. Once again Toombs's habitual salutation "Dear Stephens" in his letters became "Dear Sir," and the hurt was palpable. "I very deeply regret that any thing should have occurred to break our long and, certainly on my part, sincere friendship," Toombs told Stephens. Happily the rift was soon repaired, just as it had been years before. The love between them was simply too great for misunderstanding or the prickly temperaments of either to sever the bond.[38]

Toombs himself looked on national politics only from afar, and with general contempt. "I have no interest in men or parties who recognize the 14th and 15th amendments," he complained, and as for the Civil Rights bill passed in early 1875, he expected it would result only in civil disturbance, giving President Grant an excuse to call out more troops to impose Yankee law on the South. During the election of 1876, despite the good chance that Democrat Samuel J. Tilden had to defeat the Republican Rutherford Hayes for the presidency, with all that might mean to the South, Toombs refused to endorse Tilden because years before he had been a supporter of Van Buren, a Free-Soiler. The modern Democratic Party members were "mongrels" bent on plunder, just like the Republicans, and in any case he expected the Republicans to cheat in the electoral ballot count if they saw themselves heading for defeat, which is virtually what happened. "We are in the midst of a revolution," he told Stephens just after the election. The North had overthrown the Constitution before the war and was still trying to defy it in order to maintain power. The backroom machinations by which the popular result in favor of Tilden was going to be reversed to put Hayes in the White House were likely to be carried out by force of arms, he expected, and the Democrats needed to decide if their victory was worth fighting for. He believed they only had to stand their ground in Congress, reject all compromise, and insist on the full operation of the constitutional process in the electoral college. Tilden would be declared the winner, "a peaceful consummation of an accomplished revolution." If the Democrats submitted to the machinations the Republicans were to try in the electoral count, then they would be slaves for a generation.[39]

When Hayes took office and honored the bargain to end the military Reconstruction that put him there, Toombs at least rejoiced at the withdrawal of occupying troops from the South. "The day of military [rule] has passed," he told Stephens, but added ominously, "until another war comes." Indeed, his bitterness only grew with the advancing years. He railed at every act of Congress, especially when Democrats sometimes supported Republican measures like a pension bill for Union veterans, whom he regarded as being "alien and domestic hirelings for overturning the government and plundering the pepole [sic]."[40] Toombs saw corruption and venality everywhere, in state politics as well as national. He agreed with almost no one but Stephens, and occasionally mused on what he would accomplish if only he could take the floor of Congress for half an hour.

With his friend's example before him, Toombs did finally contemplate writing instead of talking. He had no interest in conventional autobiography or in having his biography composed by another, for that matter. "I prefer that mine should not be written until I am dead," he had said in 1858, and his attitude did not change.[41] Over the years some friends had suggested that he compile his state letters and speeches for publication, but he always dismissed them with typical bombast, declaring that he had written his life "on the pages of his country's history."[42] But by 1879, as his failing eyesight—he was all but blind in one eye—and declining health forced him gradually to reduce his practice, he turned his still active mind to a forum greater than Congress and a pulpit from which he could hold forth inestimably longer than thirty minutes. He would write a book on what he called "the true science of government," his ideas as radical as always and seasoned at this point by increasing signs of something like temporary irrationality. He would argue for the abolition of corporate property, which he regarded as gained by theft. Since slavery, the source of Southern wealth, had been abolished, then so too should all Southern debt be abolished, since Southerners had seen the means of producing money to pay their debts forcibly emancipated. "We need a year of Jubilee with amendments suited to our special condition," he told Stephens, including the abolition of public debt, for that was inevitably theft, too. "Let the world take a new start," he would proclaim in his book, though he expected that bad government could not be eradicated peacefully. "It may be bloodless, tho' I fear it will not be, but come it must and will."[43]

Toombs, of course, did not have the temperament of the scholar and never got beyond the talking stage with his book, nor would his health have allowed him to accomplish the task except with an application and diligence that conflicted with his essentially spontaneous and intuitive nature. Yet if he could do nothing else, he would still essay to teach the next generation to hate those people of the past and present who had betrayed Georgia and the South.[44] His motto had become his refusal to apply for a pardon or take the oath of allegiance, declaring that he could hardly do so when he had not yet pardoned the Yankees. Instead, he liked to say, "I am making money for my grandchild, and to buy guns in the next revolution."[45] Basking in the attention of the press, for whom he always made good copy, he gave innumerable interviews that provided him a pulpit to excoriate the Yankees and to damn Jefferson Davis and all who had disagreed with him over the years. "The trouble with Davis was and is, that he has an exalted idea of his own importance," Toombs delighted in saying in 1881, entirely oblivious that his remark applied equally to himself, if not more so. When Davis published his own memoir of the Confederacy, Toombs took pleasure in saying that he would not read it and had even refused Davis permission for his picture to appear in it with those of other cabinet members. Davis responded coolly that Toombs was "an erratic man, and not always accurate."[46] Indeed, Davis was right, for an engraving of Toombs sat atop a grouping of the first cabinet in Montgomery in the first volume of his memoir.[47] Choosing not to see it, Toombs simply declared that it was not there. In 1886, a year after both Toombs and Stephens were gone, Davis was asked to name three men whom he thought "fair types of Georgians." He named three, including their old enemy Benjamin Hill, but neither the names of Stephens nor Toombs escaped his lips.[48]

Toombs's truth had always been flexible, and in old age he in-

creasingly lost the ability to distinguish between fact and his own exaggerations and inventions. Toombs happily corresponded with
anyone who bent his efforts to attack Davis, especially with Rhett
until he died in 1876, and then with Rhett's son as he continued
fighting his father's battles with the Confederate president. As time
went on, Toombs's once great grasp of figures lost all proportion
as he strengthened his arguments against Davis's fiscal, cotton, and
diplomatic policy by rank invention.[49] By 1879 he was declaring that
in Montgomery, the delegation from Mississippi—which actually
put Davis forward—opposed his election. Georgia, Mississippi, and
Louisiana really preferred Toombs, he claimed. Davis had only
Florida and South Carolina, the latter because of Rhett's support of
Davis—another wild fancy—and then Davis gained the support of
Alabama "by one vote—by means of what trickery I will not discuss."
There was the old conviction of conspiracy to hold him down again.
It was all nonsense, as he well knew, or should have known, if his rea-
son had not been clouded by age, failing memory, and undimin-
ished hatred of Davis.[50]

Nor would he ever be forgiving of his enemies in blue. When
Chicago almost disappeared in a disastrous fire in October 1871,
Toombs cheered the news and wished for a good wind to fan the
flames. As late as 1880 he was still complaining that he had outlived
the Constitution, arguing that Southern Democrats should break
from their national party as in 1860 and run their own candidates,
perhaps in the hope of achieving the same result, and frankly declaring that he still hoped to see the complete destruction of the
Union.[51] Without being aware of it himself, he had become a curiosity, a novelty, a remembrance of past times that reporters could
always turn to for interesting, if outrageous, commentary. Only
Stephens's admiration remained undimmed. "Toombs is one of the
most extraordinary men I have ever known," he said. Confessing
that Toombs was usually his own worst enemy, still Little Aleck could
not but admire his friend's open and frank manner. Toombs lacked
only self-control to achieve the greatest heights. "He has brain
enough, if its energy had been properly directed, to govern an empire," said Stephens. "As there is enough waste of water at Niagara
to turn the machinery of the world if it were controlled and applied,

so with Toombs, there is and has been waste enough of mental power for want of system and discipline to control the destinies not only of this continent, but of all the nations." There spoke more than just love, and certainly more than a balanced or reasoned judgment of the real Robert Toombs. There spoke worship of a hero.[52]

It was the sort of encomium that might have graced a eulogy, but Stephens did not get to eulogize Toombs. Rather, it was to be the other way round. Little Aleck was not really the same after the mid-1870s. His several ailments, and then the death of Linton, reduced him to a heavy dependency on morphine to kill pain, and alcohol perhaps to help him forget, and in the grip of those two, combined with advancing age, he, too, lost his grasp on reality from time to time. Once the most dedicated of Whigs, then later an adherent of the Union, and finally of the Democratic Parties before the war, he now proclaimed that he never belonged to any political party in his life but had always been an independent. Then in spring 1882 his name was bandied about as a candidate for governor on both the Democratic ticket and for that of an Independent faction. One day he said he would not run, the next he said he would. In May, he received visitors while he lay abed with a sprained ankle, unable to walk and dosing himself with drugs, and though he appeared the least likely person to elevate to the governor's mansion, he approved a telegram announcing himself as an Independent candidate. But just when the news hit the papers, he denied that he had ever seen or agreed to such a telegram. The Independents felt betrayed, and even Toombs feared for his friend's mental health. Stephens himself most likely was not certain from one day to the next of what he had said or done. But the Democrats knew what they were doing, and they immediately enlisted him as their candidate. He might be frail, addicted, and moving through the stages of senility, but he could still be a powerful vote-getter. Easily nominated, he was almost as easily elected in October.

A month later he was inaugurated. He worked hard from the first, but it was all too much for him. After just less than four months in office, that small, half-finished body could go on no longer, and the incredible spirit that so often sustained him could not keep him alive by itself. By January he was so weak his signature was unrecognizable. By the end of February 1883, just turned seventy-one, he was desperately ill. In the predawn hours of March 4, after occasional delusional ramblings about his past political contests, he died.[53]

Though many would speak over the dead governor, there could only be one voice at the official state funeral that Georgians really wanted to hear. "I come only to bring my tears," Toombs said before the throng in Atlanta.[54] For a while it appeared that tears were all he could give them. Standing beside the coffin of his closest friend and companion of the past half-century, Toombs could not control himself. The breaking of his heart, the sentimentality of age, and very likely the ravages of drink simply reduced him to incomprehensible mumbling and blubbering. Twice he started to speak, then broke down. He struggled for five minutes to regain his composure, for the first time in his public life unable to control himself. Holding his handkerchief to his eyes, he wept openly, his sobbing shaking his heavy frame. "There stood the great secessionist above the clay of the great unionist of the South," said Henry Cleveland, who was in the audience. "To me the most eloquent things in our history are those falling tears of old Robert Toombs." Finally, when he did speak, it was largely garbled and inaudible until he finally rallied and delivered a tender and affectionate address to a crowd that had to realize that in honoring the passing of one of the great friends, they were really witnessing the end of both.[55]

Exactly six months later to the day, Julia died, after years of ill health. The twin blows were all but crippling. Those at her funeral wondered if Toombs himself could outlive the trauma of her passing. Thereafter he seldom left Washington but stayed in his spacious old home with his memories. "I have withdrawn from all of the active duties of life," he wrote a friend at the end of 1884. "I find Moses was a wise man. My experience vindicates his wisdom when [he] said 'The days of the years of man's life are three score years & ten & if by strenth [sic] they be four score, yet their strength is weakness.' " He was seventy-four then, all too aware that his own strength was waning as he found himself on the road to fourscore, and with little desire to complete the journey.[56]

Until he could join Julia and Stephens where he knew they would be waiting, he took refuge and solace from a late-life conversion and baptism into the Southern Methodist Church, and in his old friend the bottle.[57] They were the actions of a man waiting to die. He was all too aware of what his friends like John Reed could see when they visited. "Of course his powers were declining," said Reed. "Near the end he deliberately chose to drain full cups of purpose to sweeten bitter memories." Indeed, Toombs even cared so little about living that for the first time in his life he became careless in his financial affairs. When his hotel in Atlanta burned in 1883, it was discovered that he had neglected to keep the fire insurance up to date and had to pay largely out of his own pocket to finance the rebuilding. Reed even speculated that Toombs's drinking shortened his life. "It was a pitiable sight to see him," he said. "During all this time he was dying by inches."[58] Unfortunately, his disappearance into the bottle became so generally known, though forgiven by friends like Reed who knew him and his sadness at the end, that well into posterity he was largely known not for his dramatic stand at Antietam but for his intemperance.[59]

But he still had one last surprise in him, one last flash of the old warrior, an echo even of the onetime Unionist who, with his insepa-rable partner Little Aleck Stephens, stood up for moderation. After the brokered election of Hayes in 1876, the Republicans held the White House for another eight years. But then in 1884 the country, weary of corruption and longing for a change after almost a quarter-century of Republican presidents, turned to Grover Cleve-land, a reformer and a new kind of Democrat, who presaged the di-rection the party would take in the next century. Toombs was so pleased by the result that when a crowd in Washington gathered in front of his house and chanted his name to get him to come out and give his reaction, he addressed them, though almost too weak to stand or be heard. It was a glorious result, he said. At last the good people of America had thrown off the Republican yoke that bore on them for so long. He actually felt hopeful for the future of the nation, and even told friends that he regretted not having applied for pardon so that he could have taken office again after all, to help speed this result.[60] Typically, he assumed that he could have had an office for the asking, oblivious, like Stephens, of how the times had passed him by and how his old constituency had moved away from him. Stephens only gained office again in spite of his archaic ideas, thanks to the kindly personal feelings that so many supporters held. Toombs, a lifelong bridge burner, probably would have received no such blandishments, for he had alienated too many people in high places during and after the war.

He held on for another year, almost never leaving his house. Then on September 30, 1885, he suffered a collapse and was confined to his bed. During the remaining weeks he was often distracted, alternately lucid and delirious. When conscious he still took some pleasure in hearing the daily news, and still amused his friends with those famous bon mots that had so marked him as a social lion in bygone days. Often toward the end, when his mind wandered and the delirium took over, he spoke to his friend Stephens, only to be reminded by his doctor that "Mr. Stephens, you know, has crossed over the river." When he regained his faculties, the old man admitted that yes, he knew that Little Aleck was gone, but when the reverie returned, Stephens was there again. Finally, on the evening of December 15, just as the sun was setting, he embarked on those same waters himself, on the brief yet endless journey to the other side where his friend was waiting.[61]

In their better parts and their worse, they were the finest Georgians of their time, embodying in themselves all the strengths and weaknesses and contradictions that had so deeply upset their state prior to secession. Further, within them were mixed the passions, ambitions, convictions, and more that split not just one nation, but two, the Union and the Confederacy. Nature made them as opposite as men could be, chance made them friends, and trial and adversity made them inseparable. No other friendship of their time brought to bear such a concentration of mental and emotional power, and no other placed such a combination of personal foibles and destructive jealousies in the way of achieving the goal that both so earnestly desired. They loved the South as once it was, the Union as they thought it ought to have been, and a Confederacy of their dreams that never came to be. They lost all three in the end, but through it all their friendship survived. Despite their failings, their pettiness, self-indulgence, short-sightedness, and frequent hypocrisy, still until the very end they revealed one transcendent gift. They knew how to love.

Both of them liked the English poet William Wordsworth, Toombs especially. Both of them would have been familiar with his verses "To Toussaint L'Ouverture."

> There's not a breathing of the common wind
> That will forget thee; thou hast great allies;
> Thy friends are exultations, agonies,
> And love, and man's unconquerable mind.

NOTES

Biographical materials for the lives of these two Georgians are abundant, especially for Stephens, whose incessant pen and habit of saving everything left behind thousands of letters sent and received. The most important and useful collections are the Alexander H. Stephens Papers at the Emory University Library, Atlanta; Duke University, Durham, North Carolina; the Library of Congress; and especially at Manhattanville College of the Sacred Heart in Purchase, New York. Unfortunately, much of Toombs's personal collection of papers either disappeared or was scattered at the end of the Civil War when Federal soldiers temporarily occupied and looted his home; still, several small but useful collections survive, particularly the Robert A. Toombs Papers at Duke University; the University of Georgia, Athens; the Georgia Department of Archives and History in Atlanta; the Library of Congress; the Robert Toombs Letterbook in the South Caroliniana Library, University of South Carolina, Columbia; and his Compiled Service Record in Record Group 109, National Archives, Washington, DC. An indispensable collection of the letters of the two men is Ulrich B. Phillips, ed., *The Correspondence of Robert Toombs, Alexander H. Stephens, and Howell Cobb*, in the Annual Report of the American Historical Association for the Year 1911, vol. 2 (Washington, DC, 1913).

Although Toombs left behind no published memoirs, Stephens wrote extensively. Most notable, though of limited value as a personal narrative, is his *Constitutional View of the Late War Between the States: Its Causes, Character, Conduct and Results,* in two volumes published in Philadelphia, 1868–1870. His prison memoir, along with some important general reminiscences, is in Myrta Lockett Avary, ed., *Recollections of Alexander H. Stephens: His Diary Kept When a Prisoner at Fort Warren, Boston Harbor, 1865* (New York, 1910).

Both men have been the subject of numerous biographies, though Stephens has been better served. Outstanding is Thomas E. Schott, *Alexan-*

der H. Stephens of Georgia, A Biography (Baton Rouge, LA, 1988). Excellently researched and trenchantly presented, it is as definitive as any Stephens biography is likely to be and I have relied on it heavily in writing this book. E. Ramsay Richardson's *Little Aleck: A Life of Alexander H. Stephens, the Fighting Vice President of the Confederacy* (New York, 1937) is valuable chiefly for recollections gleaned from later generations of Stephens's family and for a few sources available to Richardson that have since disappeared. Among biographies by Stephens's contemporaries, the best is Richard M. Johnston and William H. Browne, *Life of Alexander H. Stephens* (Philadelphia, 1878), which benefits from first-person recollections of the authors and extensive extracts from Stephens's letters to Johnston over the span of many years. Henry Cleveland's *Alexander H. Stephens in Public and Private: With Letters and Speeches, Before, During, and Since the War* was the first biography, published in 1866 in Philadelphia, and again has useful personal reminiscences from one well acquainted with his subject. Rudolph Von Abele, *Alexander H. Stephens, A Biography* (New York, 1946), chiefly attempts a psychological portrait of its subject and offers some good insights though little in the way of new information. Of considerable interest are the reminiscences of Stephens in James C. Derby, *Fifty Years Among Authors, Books and Publishers* (New York, 1884).

Toombs, thanks no doubt to the relative paucity of personal papers, has been less studied in print. Most important, and still probably the best guide to the man, is Pleasant A. Stovall's *Robert Toombs: Statesman, Speaker, Soldier, Sage* (New York, 1892). Stovall had the benefit of actually knowing Toombs in his later years, as well as many people who were acquainted with him, and also had access to many of Toombs's personal papers that are now scattered or missing. Clearly sympathetic to his subject, still Stovall is not uncritical, nor does he avoid dealing with Toombs's weaknesses. Less useful because of its brevity, but still important, thanks to personal intimacy with Toombs and also the inclusion of a few lost letters, is Henry W. Cleveland's article "Robert Toombs," in *Southern Bivouac*, New Series 1 (January 1886): 449–59. Also somewhat useful is James U. Vincent's *A Pen-Picture of General Robert Toombs, with a Glimpse of the Mental Characteristics of Hons. A. H. Stephens and Benj. H. Hill*, published in 1886 in Louisville, Kentucky, the year after Toombs's death.

Only two scholarly biographies of Toombs have appeared, the first being Ulrich B. Phillips's *The Life of Robert Toombs*, published in New York in 1913. It relies heavily on Stovall and on Phillips's own edition of the Toombs-Stephens-Cobb correspondence but is an excellent work for its time. William Y. Thompson's *Robert Toombs of Georgia* (Baton Rouge, LA, 1966) is the most recent work. Marred by numerous careless errors, and limited by the author's failure to use a number of important sources that may not have been available at the time of writing, it is still the most complete and certainly the most balanced assessment of the subject's life, though it supplements rather than supplants Stovall. A full-scale and definitive biography of Toombs yet remains to be done, if such is possible, given the nature of the sources.

Full citation for all other sources used in this work will be found in the notes.

1. DISUNION AND REUNION

1. Unidentified newspaper clipping, 1889, in Scrapbook CC 70, vol. 1, pp. 29–30, Chickamauga and Chattanooga National Military Park Library, Chattanooga, Tennessee.
2. Robert A. Toombs to Alexander H. Stephens, October 22, 1860, Alexander H. Stephens Papers, Woodruff Library, Emory University, Atlanta, Georgia.
3. Stephens to Linton Stephens, November 8, 9, 1860, Alexander H. Stephens Papers, Manhattanville College of the Sacred Heart, Purchase, New York.
4. John C. Reed, *The Brothers' War* (Boston: Houghton Mifflin, 1906), p. 267.
5. Ulrich B. Phillips, *The Life of Robert Toombs* (New York: Macmillan, 1913), pp. 200–201.
6. Reed, *Brothers' War*, p. 267.
7. Quoted in Michael P. Johnson, *Toward a Patriarchal Republic: The Secession of Georgia* (Baton Rouge: Louisiana State University Press, 1977), p. 38 n.
8. Henry Cleveland, *Alexander H. Stephens in Public and Private: With Letters and Speeches, Before, During, and Since the War* (Philadelphia, 1866), pp. 694–713.
9. Reed, *Brothers' War*, p. 268.
10. Myrta Lockett Avary, ed., *Recollections of Alexander H. Stephens* (New York: Doubleday, 1910), p. 58. This incident appears in Avary's introduction, and she gives no source for the quote, though it is typical of Toombs.
11. U.S. War Department, *War of the Rebellion: Official Records of the Union and Confederate Armies* (Washington, DC, 1880–1901), ser. 2, vol. 2, pp. 608–9 (hereinafter *OR*).
12. Ibid., p. 609.
13. Cobb to Marion Cobb, February 9, 1961, Thomas R. R. Cobb Papers, University of Georgia, Athens.
14. Thomas E. Schott, *Alexander H. Stephens of Georgia* (Baton Rouge: Louisiana State University Press, 1988), p. 20.

15. Toombs to E. B. Pullin et al., December 13, 1860, in *The Correspondence of Robert Toombs, Alexander H. Stephens, and Howell Cobb*, ed. Ulrich B. Phillips (Washington, DC: American Historical Association, 1913), pp. 520–22.

16. Stephens to Richard M. Johnston, December 22, 1860, in Richard M. Johnston and William H. Browne, *Life of Alexander H. Stephens* (Philadelphia, 1878), p. 370.

17. Milledge L. Bonham to William Gist, December 3, 1860, Milledge L. Bonham Papers, South Caroliniana Library, University of South Carolina, Columbia.

18. Toombs to the People of Georgia, December 23, 1860, in Phillips, ed., *Correspondence*, p. 525.

19. Ibid., Stephens to J. Henly Smith, December 31, 1860, p. 527.

20. Ibid., Toombs to the *Augusta True Democrat*, January 1, 1861, p. 528.

21. Ibid., Julia Toombs to Stephens, January 1, 1861, p. 528.

22. U.S. Congress, *Congressional Globe* (Washington, DC, 1861), 36th Cong., 2d sess., p. 271 (hereinafter *Cong. Globe*).

23. William Y. Thompson, *Robert Toombs of Georgia* (Baton Rouge: Louisiana State University Press, 1966), p. 154.

24. Henry W. Cleveland, "Robert Toombs," *Southern Bivouac*, new series 1 (January 1886): 459.

25. Johnson, *Patriarchal Republic*, pp. 63–64.

26. Johnston and Browne, *Stephens*, pp. 378–79.

27. Stephens to Linton Stephens, January 10, 1861, Stephens Papers, Manhattanville College.

28. Toombs to Francis W. Pickens, January 11, 1861, Francis W. Pickens Papers, Duke University, Durham, North Carolina.

29. Alexander H. Stephens, *A Constitutional View of the Late War Between the States*, 2 vols. (Philadelphia, 1868–1870), 2: 315–16, 321.

30. Ibid., 2: 322; Stephens to Johnston, February 2, 1861, Johnston and Browne, *Stephens*, p. 384.

31. Stephens, *Constitutional View*, 2: 322–23.

32. Johnson, *Patriarchal Republic*, p. 153.

33. Thompson, *Toombs*, p. 159.

34. Stephens to Johnston, February 2, 1861, Johnston and Browne, *Stephens*, p. 384.

35. Reed, *Brothers' War*, p. 272–73; Cobb to Marion Cobb, February 11, 1861, Cobb Papers, University of Georgia.

36. Thomas R. R. Cobb to Joseph Brown, January 28, 1861, Governors' Papers, Joseph Brown, Georgia Department of Archives and History, Atlanta.

2. THE MAKING OF A FRIENDSHIP

1. Avary, ed., *Recollections,* pp. 11–12.
2. Johnston and Browne, *Stephens,* p. 89.
3. Schott, *Stephens,* provides the best physical and temperamental description of Stephens (pp. 20 ff.), but see also William C. Davis, *"A Government of Our Own": The Making of the Confederacy* (New York: Free Press, 1994), pp. 51–52.
4. Schott, *Stephens,* pp. 16–23; Johnston and Browne, *Stephens,* p. 69.
5. Thompson, *Toombs,* pp. 5–6.
6. Pleasant A. Stovall, *Robert Toombs, Statesman, Speaker, Soldier, Sage* (New York, 1892), pp. 4–7.
7. Ibid., pp. 8–9.
8. Thompson, *Toombs,* pp. 8–11; statement attached to C. M. Waldron to Robert S. Pelletreau, September 28, 1931, Robert A. Toombs file, Georgia Department of Archives and History, Atlanta.
9. Thompson, *Toombs,* p. 12; Stovall, *Toombs,* p. 13.
10. Stovall, *Toombs,* pp. 14–15; Avary, ed., *Recollections,* pp. 426–27.
11. Stovall, *Toombs,* pp. 5, 15.
12. Schott, *Stephens,* pp. 22–23.
13. Johnston and Browne, *Stephens,* p. 88.
14. Schott, *Stephens,* p. 29; Stovall, *Toombs,* pp. 16–17, 90, 94; John McAnerney Memoir, Virginia Historical Society, Richmond.
15. Cleveland, *Stephens,* pp. 49–50; Avary, ed., *Recollections,* p. 16.
16. Stovall, *Toombs,* p. 30; Phillips, *Toombs,* p. 18. Thompson, *Toombs,* p. 16, mistakenly says that Toombs was elected in 1836.
17. Stovall, *Toombs,* p. 32.
18. Schott, *Stephens,* pp. 39–40.
19. Stovall, *Toombs,* pp. 32–33.
20. Thompson, *Toombs,* p. 18.
21. Stovall, *Toombs,* pp. 36–41.
22. Thompson, *Toombs,* pp. 18–19, 21.
23. Schott, *Stephens,* pp. 43–45.
24. See Michael F. Holt, *The Rise and Fall of the American Whig Party* (New York: Oxford University Press, 1999), pp. 823–24, 956 ff.
25. Schott, *Stephens,* p. 46; Stovall, *Toombs,* p. 39.
26. Stovall, *Toombs,* p. 18.
27. Ibid., pp. 46–47.
28. Stephens to George W. Crawford, January 8, 1845, Charles Hamilton auction catalog no. 11, New York, January 31, 1966, item 207.
29. Toombs to Stephens, January 24, 1845, in Phillips, ed., *Correspondence,* pp. 61–62.
30. Schott, *Stephens,* pp. 60–63.

31. Toombs to Stephens, February 16, 1845, in Phillips, ed., *Correspondence*, pp. 63–65.

32. Johnston and Browne, *Stephens*, pp. 169, 194–95; Thompson, *Toombs*, p. 31.

33. Toombs to George W. Crawford, February 6, 1846, in Phillips, ed., *Correspondence*, p. 74.

34. Schott, *Stephens*, p. 73.

35. Johnston and Browne, *Stephens*, p. 207.

36. Ibid., pp. 208, 210.

37. Schott, *Stephens*, pp. 77–78.

38. Johnston and Browne, *Stephens*, pp. 218–19; Thompson, *Toombs*, p. 41.

39. Phillips, *Toombs*, p. 57.

40. Varina Howell Davis, *Jefferson Davis, Ex-President of the Confederate States of America, A Memoir by His Wife*, 2 vols. (New York, 1890), 1: 409–11.

41. Johnston and Browne, *Stephens*, p. 226.

42. Ibid., pp. 227–28; Avary, ed., *Recollections*, pp. 21–22.

43. Johnston and Browne, *Stephens*, pp. 232–34; Schott, *Stephens*, p. 92.

44. Toombs to John J. Crittenden, September 28, 1848, in Phillips, ed., *Correspondence*, p. 127, and George S. Houston to Howell Cobb, September 23, 1848, p. 126, and October 23, 1848, p. 131.

45. Cleveland, *Stephens*, pp. 90–93 and note, quoting the *Augusta Chronicle and Sentinel*, September 18, 1848.

46. Stovall, *Toombs*, pp. 62–63.

47. Stephens to John J. Crittenden, September 26, 1848, in Phillips, ed., *Correspondence*, p. 127, and Toombs to Crittenden, September 27, pp. 127–29, and November 9, 1848, p. 136.

48. Ibid., Toombs to Crittenden, January 3, 1849, pp. 139–40, and January 22, 1849, pp. 141–42.

49. Ibid., Toombs to Crittenden, January 22, 1849, pp. 140–42, and February 9, 1849, p. 147.

50. Ibid., Stephens to Crittenden, February 6, 1849, p. 146.

51. Ibid., Toombs to Mrs. Chapman Coleman, June 22, 1849, p. 165.

52. Quoted in Schott, *Stephens*, p. 105.

53. Ibid., pp. 106–7.

54. Stovall, *Toombs*, pp. 64–65.

55. Johnston and Browne, *Stephens*, pp. 237, 241.

3. THE BREAKING OF A FRIENDSHIP

1. Stovall, *Toombs*, p. 70.

2. Johnston and Brown, *Stephens*, pp. 240–41.

3. Stephens to James Thomas, February 13, 1850, in Phillips, ed., *Correspondence*, p. 184.

4. Johnston and Browne, *Stephens*, pp. 243–44.

5. Toombs to Linton Stephens, March 22, 1850, in Phillips, ed., *Correspondence*, p. 188.

6. Stovall, *Toombs*, pp. 80–82; Stephens, *Constitutional View*, 2: 201–4.

7. Stovall, *Toombs*, pp. 64–65; Schott, *Stephens*, pp. 114–15; Thompson, *Toombs*, pp. 61–62.

8. *Cong. Globe*, 31st Cong., 1st sess., p. 1216.

9. V. Davis, *Jefferson Davis*, 1: 411–12.

10. Toombs to Young L. G. Harris, April 20, 1850, Robert Toombs File, Georgia Department of Archives and History, Atlanta.

11. Ibid.

12. *Charleston Mercury*, July 18, 1850; Stephens to the editor of the *Baltimore Clipper*, July 13, 1850, in Phillips, ed., *Correspondence*, p. 195; Stovall, *Toombs*, pp. 64–65.

13. Phillips, *Toombs*, p. 88; Schott, *Stephens*, p. 123.

14. Richard H. Shryock, *Georgia and the Union in 1850* (Durham, NC: Duke University Press, 1926), pp. 295–96.

15. Stovall, *Toombs*, p. 83.

16. Schott, *Stephens*, p. 127; Thompson, *Toombs*, p. 73.

17. Shryock, *Georgia*, pp. 319 ff.

18. Ibid., p. 332.

19. Stephens to Linton Stephens, February 3, 1851, Stephens Papers, Manhattanville College.

20. Quoted in Thompson, *Toombs*, p. 81.

21. Augustus Kenan to Stephens, July 3, 1851, in Phillips, ed., *Correspondence*, p. 241; Phillips, *Toombs*, p. 105.

22. Schott, *Stephens*, pp. 147–52.

23. Jefferson Davis to V. A. Gaskill, September 21, 1853, in *Jefferson Davis, Constitutionalist: His Letters, Papers and Speeches*, comp. Dunbar Rowland, 10 vols. (Jackson: Mississippi Department of Archives and History, 1923), 2: 277–78; Thompson, *Toombs*, p. 92.

24. Johnston and Browne, *Stephens*, p. 277.

25. Quoted in Thompson, *Toombs*, p. 104.

26. Ibid., p. 109; Stovall, *Toombs*, pp, 152–54.

27. Toombs to George W. Crawford, May 30, 1856, in Phillips, ed., *Correspondence*, p. 365.

28. E. Merton Coulter, "Alexander H. Stephens Challenges Benjamin H. Hill to a Duel," *Georgia Historical Quarterly* 56 (summer 1972): 175–92.

29. Johnston and Browne, *Stephens*, p. 316.

30. Ibid., pp. 329–30.

31. Thompson, *Toombs,* pp. 121–22; Stovall, *Toombs,* pp. 164–65.
32. Robert Barnwell Rhett Jr. to William Porcher Miles, April 7, 1858, William Porcher Miles Papers, Southern Historical Collection, University of North Carolina, Chapel Hill; Schott, *Stephens,* pp. 250–51; Toombs to Buchanan, April 18, 1858, in Phillips, ed., *Correspondence,* p. 433.
33. Schott, *Stephens,* pp. 258–59.
34. Johnston and Browne, *Stephens,* p. 348.
35. Cleveland, *Stephens,* pp. 637–51 passim; Stephens to J. Henly Smith, July 29, 1859, in Phillips, ed., *Correspondence,* pp. 446–47.
36. Thompson, *Toombs,* pp. 130–31; Toombs to Stephens, December 26, 1859, in Phillips, ed., *Correspondence,* p. 452, and January 11, 1860, p. 455.
37. Toombs to Thomas W. Thomas, December 4, 1859, in Phillips, ed., *Correspondence,* p. 450, and Toombs to Stephens, December 26, 1859, p. 452, and December 28, 1859, p. 453.
38. Stovall, *Toombs,* pp. 170 ff.
39. Thompson, *Toombs,* p. 135.
40. Toombs to Stephens, February 10, 1860, in Phillips, ed., *Correspondence,* p. 461.
41. Toombs to James Madison Spurlock, March 17, 1860, James Madison Spurlock Collection, Georgia Department of Archives and History.
42. Stephens to J. Henly Smith, May 8, 1860, in Phillips, ed., *Correspondence,* p. 470; Stephens to Thirteen Gentlemen of Macon, May 9, 1860, Johnston and Browne, *Stephens,* pp. 357 ff.
43. Toombs to Stephens, May 12, 1860, in Phillips, ed., *Correspondence,* p. 477.
44. Frequent letters from Toombs to Stephens during spring 1860 are in Phillips, ed., *Correspondence,* commencing on p. 478.
45. Schott, *Stephens,* pp. 291–92.

4. FOUNDING FATHERS

1. Johnston and Browne, *Stephens,* pp. 383–84.
2. Stephens to Linton Stephens, March 5, 1861, Stephens Papers, Manhattanville College; James Chesnut to William T. Walthall, January 24, 1880, William T. Walthall Papers, Mississippi Department of Archives and History, Jackson; Stephens to the editor, January 12, 1880, *Atlanta Daily Constitution,* January 16, 1880; Johnston and Browne, *Stephens,* p. 389.
3. See Davis, *"A Government of Our Own,"* pp. 431–32 n, for a discussion of this conversation and its sources.
4. Cobb to Marion Cobb, February 3, 1861, Cobb Papers, University of

Georgia; Stephens to Linton Stephens, February 4, 1861, Stephens Papers, Manhattanville College.

5. Isaac Moore to Stephens, February 1, 1861, and J. Seymour to Stephens, February 1, 1861, Alexander H. Stephens Papers, Library of Congress, Washington, DC.

6. *Charleston Mercury,* February 5, 1861; Reed, *Brothers' War,* p. 236; Martin Crawford to the editor, June 25, 1870, Walthall Papers, Jackson.

7. Stephens to Linton Stephens, February 5, 1861, Stephens Papers, Manhattanville College.

8. U.S. Congress, *Journal of the Congress of the Confederate States of America,* 7 vols. (Washington, DC: Government Printing Office, 1904–1905), 1: 17; Davis, *"A Government of Our Own,"* pp. 65–77.

9. Stephens, *Constitutional View,* 2: 326–27, 710–12.

10. Stephens to Linton Stephens, February 5, 1861, Stephens Papers, Manhattanville College.

11. *New York Herald,* March 4, 1861; *Daily Columbus (GA) Enquirer,* March 23, 1861; *Montgomery Weekly Advertiser,* February 13, 1861.

12. *Montgomery Weekly Advertiser,* February 13, 1861; U.S. Congress, *Journal,* 1: 20–22.

13. Lawrence Keitt to James Henry Hammond, February 13, 1861, James Henry Hammond Papers, Library of Congress; Stephens to Linton Stephens, February 6, 1861, Stephens Papers, Manhattanville College; Stephens to Cotting, February 6, 1861, Joseph F. Burke Papers, Emory University.

14. Robert Barnwell to James L. Orr, February 9, 1861, Orr and Patterson Family Papers, Southern Historical Collection, University of North Carolina, Chapel Hill.

15. Stephens to Linton Stephens, February 9, 1861, Stephens Papers, Manhattanville College; U.S. Congress, *Journal,* 1: 26–30.

16. *New York Citizen,* April 20, 27, 1867.

17. Johnston and Browne, *Stephens,* p. 391; Reed, *Brothers' War,* pp. 272–73.

18. Stephens to Linton Stephens, February 23, 1861, Stephens Papers, Manhattanville College.

19. Thomas R. R. Cobb to Marion Cobb, February 16, 1861, Cobb Papers, University of Georgia.

20. Cleveland, "Toombs," p. 452; Reed, *Brothers' War,* pp. 284–85; Stephens to Linton Stephens, February 23, 1861, Stephens Papers, Manhattanville College.

21. *Mobile (AL) Daily Advertiser,* February 9, 1861.

22. U.S. Congress, *Journal,* 1: 30–31.

23. *New York Herald,* January 31, February 5, 1861; *New York Daily Tribune,* February 5, 1861; *Montgomery Weekly Confederation,* February 15, 1861; *Macon (GA) Daily Telegraph,* February 9, 1861.

24. Cobb to Marion Cobb, February 8, 1861, Cobb Papers, University of Georgia; U.S. Congress, *Journal,* 1: 33.

25. C. Vann Woodward, ed., *Mary Chesnut's Civil War* (New Haven: Yale University Press, 1981), p. 786.

26. The offer of the presidency to Stephens is most thoroughly discussed in Davis, *"A Government of Our Own,"* pp. 106–8, 444 n.

27. Johnston and Browne, *Stephens,* p. 390.

28. Martin J. Crawford to the editors, June 25, 1870, Walthall Papers, Mississippi Department of Archives and History, Jackson; Cobb to Marion Cobb, February 8, 1861, Cobb Papers, University of Georgia.

29. U.S. Congress, *Journal,* 1: 39.

30. The fullest account of the election is in Davis, *"A Government of Our Own,"* pp. 110–20.

31. Stephens, *Constitutional View,* 2: 331.

32. Davis, *"A Government of Our Own,"* pp. 120–21, 451 n. Rhett several times in later years said that Cobb got Georgia's initial vote, and one of Tom Cobb's letters seems to indicate the same, but no one else present ever mentioned it. The session being secret, unfortunately no reporters or other spectators were there to leave accounts that might settle the issue.

5. DISILLUSIONMENT

1. Stephens to James P. Hambleton, February 22, 1861, James P. Hambleton Papers, Emory University; Johnston and Browne, *Stephens,* pp. 62–63; Jefferson Davis, *Rise and Fall of the Confederate Government,* 2 vols. (New York, 1881), 1: 241–42.

2. Stephens to Linton Stephens, February 19, 25, 1861, Stephens Papers, Manhattanville College; Cobb to Marion Cobb, February 19, 1861, Cobb Papers, University of Georgia; Toombs to Robert Barnwell Rhett Jr., December 20, 1882, Robert Barnwell Rhett Sr. Papers, South Caroliniana Library; Toombs to Jefferson Davis, February 20, 1861, Charles Colcock Jones Jr., comp., Autograph Letters and Portraits of the Signers of the Constitution of the Confederate States of America, Duke University.

3. Cobb to Marion Cobb, February 21, 1861, Cobb Papers, University of Georgia; A. W. Redding to S. W. Anderson, March 15, 1861, *OR,* ser. 2, vol. 2, p. 613.

4. *Rome (GA) Tri-Weekly Courier,* March 3, 12, 1861; L. Q. Washington, "The Confederate State Department," *Independent* 53 (September 19, 1901): 2222.

5. Thomas C. DeLeon, *Four Years in Rebel Capitals* (Mobile, AL, 1890), p. 33.

6. Davis, *"A Government of Our Own,"* p. 190; Schott, *Stephens,* p. 340.

7. Richard M. Johnston, *Autobiography of Colonel Richard Malcolm Johnston* (Washington, DC: D. Appleton, 1909), p. 126; *New York Citizen,* July 6, 1867.

8. Cobb to Marion Cobb, February 16, 1861, Cobb Papers, University of Georgia.

9. Robert Barnwell Rhett, Memoir, Aiken Rhett Collection, Charleston Museum, Charleston, South Carolina.

10. Stephens to Linton Stephens, February 22, 25, 26, 1861, Stephens Papers, Manhattanville College.

11. *Charleston Mercury,* March 9, 1861.

12. Toombs to Davis, February 20, 1861, Jones, Autographs, Duke University.

13. Thomas R. R. Cobb, notes on the Constitutional Committee, in A. L. Hull, "The Making of the Confederate Constitution," *Publications of the Southern History Association* 9 (September 1905): 286–87; Stephens to Linton Stephens, February 17, 1861, Stephens Papers, Manhattanville College.

14. Stephens to Linton Stephens, March 1, 3, 1861, Stephens Papers, Manhattanville College; U.S. Congress, *Journal,* 1: 862.

15. Stephens to Linton Stephens, March 3, 4, 1861, Stephens Papers, Manhattanville College; U.S. Congress, *Journal,* 1: 863.

16. Alexander H. Stephens, *A Comprehensive and Popular History of the United States* (Raleigh, NC, 1884), p. 600

17. Thompson, *Toombs,* pp. 104–7; Schott, *Stephens,* pp. 78, 117.

18. U.S. Congress, *Journal,* 1: 868–69.

19. Stephens to Linton Stephens, March 8, 1861, Stephens Papers, Manhattanville College.

20. Jabez L. M. Curry, *Civil History of the Government of the Confederate States, with Some Personal Reminiscences* (Richmond, VA: B. F. Johnson, 1901), p. 63.

21. Stephens to Linton Stephens, March 8, 1861, Stephens Papers, Manhattanville College; U.S. Congress, *Journal,* 1: 881–84, 885–86.

22. Stephens to Linton Stephens, March 9, 1861, Stephens Papers, Manhattanville College; Curry, *Civil History,* p. 74; U.S. Congress, *Journal,* 1: 893.

23. Stephens to Linton Stephens, March 10, 1861, Stephens Papers, Manhattanville College.

24. *Atlanta Daily Intelligencer,* March 12, 13, 1861.

25. *New Orleans Daily Delta,* March 10, 1861.

26. *Montgomery Weekly Advertiser,* March 6, 1861; *Charleston Mercury,* March 6, 1861; Cobb to Marion Cobb, February 16, 1861, Cobb Papers, University of Georgia.

27. Toombs to Stephens, April 6, 1861, Stephens Papers, Emory University; *Harper's Weekly,* March 9, 1861; *Montgomery Daily Post,* February 22, 1861; Stephens to Linton Stephens, March 10, 1861, Stephens Papers, Manhattanville College.

28. Stephens to Linton Stephens, March 1, 1861, Stephens Papers, Manhattanville College.

29. *Charleston Mercury,* March 18, 1861.

30. The full address is in Cleveland, *Stephens,* pp. 717–29.

31. Thomas DeLeon, *Belles, Beaux and Brains of the 60s* (New York: G. W. Dillingham, 1907), pp. 83–84.

32. *New York Citizen,* April 20, 1867.

33. Toombs to Stephens, April 6, 1861, in Phillips, ed., *Correspondence,* p. 558.

34. Martin Crawford, John Forsyth, and A. B. Roman to Toombs, April 8, 1861, Robert Toombs Letterbook, South Caroliniana Library.

35. Stovall, *Toombs,* p. 226. For a discussion of Toombs in this meeting, see Davis, *"A Government of Our Own,"* pp. 309–10.

36. *Montgomery Weekly Advertiser,* April 17, 1861.

37. Stephens to Linton Stephens, April 16, 17, 1861, Stephens Papers, Manhattanville College.

38. Toombs to Rhett Jr., December 20, 1882, Rhett Papers, South Caroliniana Library.

39. Stephens to Linton Stephens, April 18, 1861, Stephens Papers, Manhattanville College.

40. Ibid., April 19, 1861.

41. Ibid., April 29, 1861; Woodward, ed., *Mary Chesnut,* p. 56.

42. *Montgomery Weekly Advertiser,* May 1, 1861.

43. Toombs to Stephens, July 5, 1861, Robert Toombs Papers, Duke University; Stephens to Linton Stephens, May 14, 1861, Stephens Papers, Manhattanville College.

44. Toombs to Stephens, July 5, 1861, Toombs Papers, Duke University. Years later, with badly failing memory, Toombs said that this Cotton Loan came too late in the war to do any good, when of course it came at the very outset. Toombs to Rhett Jr., December 20, 1882, Rhett Papers, South Caroliniana Library.

45. Rhett, Memoir, Rhett Collection, Charleston Museum.

46. Stephens to Linton Stephens, May 14, 1861, Stephens Papers, Manhattanville College; Cobb to Marion Cobb, May 4, 1861, Cobb Papers, University of Georgia; Augustus Kenan to Martin Crawford, May 9, 1861, and Crawford to Stephens et al., May 9, 1861, Stephens Papers, Library of Congress; John B. Jones, *A Rebel War Clerk's Diary at the Confederate States Capital,* 2 vols. (Philadelphia, 1866), 1: 39.

47. Johnston and Browne, *Stephens,* p. 405.

48. Quoted in unidentified clipping, 1881, Toombs Papers, Duke University.

49. Johnston, *Autobiography,* p. 164.
50. Johnston and Browne, *Stephens,* p. 403; Stephens to William H. Hidell, May 14, 1861, William H. Hidell Papers, Historical Society of Pennsylvania, Philadelphia.
51. Stephens to Linton Stephens, May 4, 10, 1861, Stephens Papers, Manhattanville College; Toombs to Stephens, May 1861, Stephens Papers, Emory University; Woodward, ed., *Chesnut,* p. 56; *Montgomery Daily Post,* June 6, 1861.
52. William Howard Russell, *My Diary North and South,* 2 vols. (London, 1863), 1: 179.
53. *New York Citizen,* May 25, 1867.
54. Stephens to Linton Stephens, May 9, 1861, Stephens Papers, Manhattanville College.
55. Ibid., May 22, 1861.
56. Toombs to Joseph Brown, July 12, 1861, Telemon Cuyler Collection, University of Georgia.

6. LOYAL OPPOSITION?

1. Thompson, *Toombs,* p. 172.
2. Toombs to Stephens, July 5, 1861, Toombs Papers, Duke University; Toombs to Brown, July 12, 1861, Cuyler Collection, University of Georgia; Toombs to Stephens, June 8, 1861, in Phillips, ed., *Correspondence,* pp. 568–69.
3. Toombs to Stephens, June 8, 1861, in Phillips, ed., *Correspondence,* pp. 568–70; Toombs to Stephens, July 5, 1861, Toombs Papers, Duke University; Toombs to Stephens, June 21, 1861, in Avary, ed., *Recollections,* p. 67.
4. Toombs to Stephens, June 21, 1861, in Avary, ed., *Recollections,* p. 67; Toombs to Rhett Jr., December 20, 1882, Rhett Papers, South Caroliniana Library.
5. Toombs to Crawford, February 20, 1861, Robert Toombs Papers, Miscellaneous Manuscript Collection, Library of Congress.
6. Toombs to Stephens, June 8, 1861, in Phillips, ed., *Correspondence,* pp. 568–70; Toombs to Stephens, June 21, 1861, in Avary, ed., *Recollections,* pp. 67–68; Stephen R. Mallory diary, August 11, 1861, Stephen R. Mallory Papers, Southern Historical Collection; Jones, *Diary,* 1: 39–40.
7. Toombs to Stephens, July 5, 1861, Toombs Papers, Duke University.
8. Toombs to Brown, July 12, 1861, Cuyler Collection, Duke University.
9. Johnston and Browne, *Stephens,* p. 403.
10. Brown to Stephens, July 8, 1861, in Phillips, ed., *Correspondence,* p. 572.
11. Johnston and Browne, *Stephens,* p. 467.

12. Cobb to Marion Cobb, May 8, 1861, Cobb Papers, University of Georgia.

13. Jefferson Davis to David W. Lewis, September 21, 1863, in Rowland, comp., *Davis,* 6: 43–44.

14. Robert Toombs Combined Service Record, Record Group 109, National Archives, Washington, DC.

15. U.S. Congress, *Journal,* 1: 271.

16. Toombs to Davis, July 24, 1861, in *The Papers of Jefferson Davis,* ed. Lynda Lasswell Crist and Mary Seaton Dix, 10 vols. to date (Baton Rouge: Louisiana State University Press, 1992), 7: 266, and Davis to Toombs, July 24, 1861, 7: 266. Cobb to Marion Cobb, July 22, 1861, Cobb Papers, University of Georgia, says, "Toombs will resign as Secretary of State today and goes immediately into the field." Toombs himself, in his letter to Rhett Jr., December 20, 1882, Rhett Papers, South Caroliniana Library, says that he resigned "a few days before the first battle of Manassas was fought," but his memory was almost always faulty by that time.

17. Cobb to Marion Cobb, July 25, 27, 1861, Cobb Papers, University of Georgia.

18. Ibid., July 30, 31, 1861.

19. Thompson, *Toombs,* p. 179.

20. Gabriel Toombs to Stephens, July 31, 1861, in Phillips, ed., *Correspondence,* p. 573.

21. Schott, *Stephens,* p. 341.

22. Woodward, ed., *Chesnut,* p. 124.

23. Ibid., pp. 128, 129, 132; Cobb to Marion Cobb, August 1, 4, 1861, Cobb Papers, University of Georgia.

24. U.S. Congress, *Journal,* 1: 307, 326–27, 353, 359.

25. Johnston and Browne, *Stephens,* p. 410; Schott, *Stephens,* pp. 344–45.

26. Toombs to Stephens, September 22, 1861, in Phillips, ed., *Correspondence,* pp. 576–77.

27. Ibid., pp. 575–76, and September 30, 1861, p. 577; A. C. Myers to William Porcher Miles, November 20, 1861, Miles Papers, Southern Historical Collection.

28. Toombs to Davis, September 1, 1861, in Crist and Dix, eds., *Papers,* 7: 316.

29. Toombs to Howell Cobb, April 23, 1861, Howell Cobb Papers, University of Georgia.

30. Toombs to Stephens, September 30, 1861, in Phillips, ed., *Correspondence,* pp. 577–78.

31. Cobb to Marion Cobb, August 31, September 10, 11, 1861, Cobb Papers, University of Georgia.

32. Toombs to Davis, September 1, 1861, in Crist and Dix, eds., *Papers,* 7: 316–17.

33. Ibid., p. 316.

34. Quoted in Thompson, *Toombs,* p. 178 n.

NOTES {271}

35. Ibid., pp. 179–80.

36. Stovall, *Toombs,* pp. 238–39.

37. Toombs to Stephens, September 22, 1861, in Phillips, ed., *Correspondence,* p. 576, September 30, 1861, p. 578, and October 3, 1861, p. 579.

38. Cobb to Marion Cobb, November 26, 1861, Cobb Papers, University of Georgia.

39. Ibid., October 16, 1861.

40. Littleton Washington journal, August 3, 1861, transcript in possession of Douglas Gibboney, Carlisle, PA; Woodward, ed., *Chesnut,* p. 204; Toombs to Stephens, September 22, 1861, in Phillips, ed., *Correspondence,* p. 576.

41. Schott, *Stephens,* p. 347.

42. U.S. Congress, *Journal,* 1: 652, 672, 846.

43. Cobb to Marion Cobb, January 14, 1862, Cobb Papers, University of Georgia.

44. U.S. Congress, *Journal,* 1: 693, 736, 747.

45. Ibid., p. 757; Rhett, Memoir, Rhett Collection, Charleston Museum.

46. U.S. Congress, *Journal,* 1: 693, 749–50, 781–82.

47. Thompson, *Toombs,* p. 180.

48. Cobb to Marion Cobb, November 26, 1861, and January 18, 19, 24, 28, February 2, 1862, Cobb Papers, University of Georgia.

49. Thompson, *Toombs,* p. 180. Stovall, *Toombs,* p. 241, erroneously says he was elected in January 1862.

50. Cobb to Marion Cobb, February 1, 1862, Cobb Papers, University of Georgia.

51. Stovall, *Toombs,* p. 241.

52. Myers to Miles, November 20, 1861, Miles Papers, Southern Historical Collection; Stovall, *Toombs,* p. 243.

53. Toombs to Stephens, March 4, 1862, in Phillips, ed., *Correspondence,* p. 590; Stovall, *Toombs,* p. 242.

54. Cobb to Marion Cobb, February 16, 1862, Cobb Papers, University of Georgia.

55. Stovall, *Toombs,* p. 242.

56. Cobb to Marion Cobb, March 16, 1862, Cobb Papers, University of Georgia.

7. ENEMIES FRONT AND REAR

1. Stovall, *Toombs,* pp. 239–40.

2. Toombs to Stephens, March 4, 1862, in Phillips, ed., *Correspondence,* p. 590, and March 24, 1862, p. 592.

3. Ibid., March 28, 1862, p. 593.

4. Toombs to George W. Crawford, March 31, 1862, James Cross Collection, Florida Atlantic University, Boca Raton.

5. Stovall, *Toombs*, p. 243.

6. Cobb to Marion Cobb, April 3, 1862, Cobb Papers, University of Georgia.

7. G. Moxley Sorrell, *Recollections of a Confederate Staff Officer* (New York: Neale Publishing Company, 1905), p. 59.

8. Stovall, *Toombs*, p. 241.

9. Ibid., p. 244.

10. Cobb to Marion Cobb, April 16, 1862, Cobb Papers, University of Georgia.

11. Ibid., April 19, 1862.

12. Halsey Wigfall to Louly Wigfall, April 30, 1862, Louis T. Wigfall Papers, Library of Congress; Toombs to Julia Toombs, May 13, 1862, Toombs Papers, University of Georgia.

13. Toombs to Stephens, May 17, 1862, in Phillips, ed., *Correspondence*, pp. 594–95.

14. Cobb to Marion Cobb, May 13, 16, 1862, Cobb Papers, University of Georgia.

15. Stephen R. Mallory to Angela Mallory, May 27, 1862, Stephen R. Mallory Papers, University of Florida, Gainesville; Stovall, *Toombs*, pp. 246, 249.

16. Adam Alexander to Edward Porter Alexander, May 23, 1862, Edward Porter Alexander Papers, Southern Historical Collection.

17. J. Howard De Votie to his parents, June 4, 1862, James H. De Votie Papers, Duke University.

18. Cobb to Marion Cobb, June 13, 1861, Cobb Papers, University of Georgia.

19. Toombs to Julia Toombs, May 19, 1862, Toombs Papers, University of Georgia.

20. Thompson, *Toombs*, p. 187 n.

21. Toombs to George Hill and Others, June 11, 1862, in Phillips, ed., *Correspondence*, p. 595.

22. Thompson, *Toombs*, pp. 186–87.

23. Cobb to Marion Cobb, June 13, 1862, Cobb Papers, University of Georgia.

24. Daniel H. Hill to My Dear Genl, May 5, 1876, *Profiles in History* catalog (Beverly Hills, CA, n.p., n.d.), copy in Robert Toombs File, Fredericksburg National Military Park, Fredericksburg, VA.

25. Peter W. Hairston to Frances Hairston, July 27, 1862, Peter W. Hairston Papers, Southern Historical Collection.

26. James Longstreet, *From Manassas to Appomattox* (Philadelphia, 1896), p. 113.

27. A. L. Long, *Memoirs of Robert E. Lee* (New York, 1887), p. 166.

28. Cobb to Marion Cobb, June 13, 1862, Cobb Papers, University of Georgia.

29. Hill to My Dear Genl, May 5, 1876, *Profiles in History* catalog.

30. *OR*, ser. 1, vol. 11, pt. 2, p. 689; Toombs to Stephens, July 14, 1862, in Phillips, ed., *Correspondence*, pp. 599–600.

31. John H. McIntosh, *History of Elbert County, Georgia* (Atlanta: n.p., 1968), p. 115.

32. Toombs to Stephens, July 14, 1862, in Phillips, ed., *Correspondence*, p. 600.

33. Ibid.

34. *Atlanta Southern Confederacy*, September 4, 1862.

35. Lafayette McLaws to Dear General, November 30, 1885, James Longstreet Papers, Emory University.

36. Stovall, *Toombs*, p. 257.

37. Hairston to Frances Hairston, July 27, 1862, Hairston Papers, Southern Historical Collection; *Atlanta Southern Confederacy*, September 4, 1862.

38. Toombs to Stephens, July 14, 1862, in Phillips, ed., *Correspondence*, pp. 600–601; *Atlanta Southern Confederacy*, September 4, 1862.

39. Sallie McCullom to a friend, July 14, 1862, HCA auction catalog (Burlington, NC, n.p., n.d.), item 167.

40. Jeremy F. Gilmer to Loulie Gilmer, August 17, 1862, Jeremy F. Gilmer Papers, Southern Historical Collection.

41. The correspondence between Toombs and Hill to this stage is in Stovall, *Toombs*, pp. 254–56. Hill's own copies of the correspondence are in the Daniel H. Hill Papers, Virginia State Library, Richmond.

42. *Atlanta Southern Confederacy*, September 4, 1862.

43. Toombs to Stephens, July 14, 1862, in Phillips, ed., *Correspondence*, p. 601.

44. Woodward, ed., *Chesnut*, p. 352.

45. *Atlanta Southern Confederacy*, September 4, 1862.

46. Cobb to Marion Cobb, July 16, 1862, Cobb Papers, University of Georgia.

47. *OR*, ser. 1, vol. 17, pt. 2, p. 770.

48. Stovall, *Toombs*, pp. 249–50.

49. Cobb to Marion Cobb, July 23, 1862, Cobb Papers, University of Georgia.

50. Ibid., August 10, 1862.

51. Henry Kyd Douglas, *I Rode with Stonewall* (Chapel Hill: University of North Carolina Press, 1940), p. 114.

52. Gilmer to Loulie Gilmer, August 17, 1862, Gilmer Papers, Southern Historical Collection.

53. This is a somewhat confused episode, mainly because Toombs's and Longstreet's accounts differ widely, and neither should be completely trusted, Longstreet's because it was written more than thirty years later

when his memory was failing badly, and Toombs's because, even though written only three days later, it is characteristically self-serving and ex-culpatory. See Longstreet, *Manassas to Appomattox*, p. 161, and Toombs to Stephens, August 22, 1862, in Phillips, ed., *Correspondence*, pp. 603–4; Raphael J. Moses Autobiography, p. 55, Southern Historical Collection. The unsigned account in the *Augusta (GA) Daily Constitutionalist*, September 24, 1862, is clearly well informed and supports some of both versions, and being contemporary, and perhaps less biased, agrees in the main with the version presented here.

54. Toombs to Stephens, August 22, 1862, in Phillips, ed., *Correspondence*, p. 604. The unsigned account in the *Savannah (GA) Daily Constitutionalist*, September 24, 1862, quotes this "usurpation of authority" charge exactly, suggesting that the writer's informant may have been Toombs himself.

55. Moses Autobiography, p. 54, Southern Historical Collection. Stovall, *Toombs*, p. 106, repeats essentially Moses's recollection of Longstreet saying that Toombs "needed only discipline" to make him a good commander.

56. Sorrel, *Recollections*, pp. 100–101; Stovall, *Toombs*, p. 259.

57. *Augusta (GA) Daily Constitutionalist*, September 24, 1862; Stovall, *Toombs*, p. 259; Toombs to Stephens, August 22, 1862, in Phillips, ed., *Correspondence*, p. 604.

58. Toombs to Stephens, August 22, 1862, in Phillips, ed., *Correspondence*, p. 604.

59. Longstreet, *Manassas to Appomattox*, p. 166.

60. *Savannah Daily Constitutionalist*, September 24, 1862, says that Toombs got the order either August 28 or 29, but given his last minute arrival on the battlefield, the later date is the more likely.

61. Longstreet, *Manassas to Appomattox*, p. 189.

62. *Savannah Daily Constitutionalist*, September 24, 1862.

63. *OR*, ser. 1, vol. 12, pt. 2, pp. 591, 600.

64. Stovall, *Toombs*, pp. 261–62.

65. Ben LaBree, ed., *Camp Fires of the Confederacy* (Louisville, KY, 1898), pp. 342–44.

66. Moses Autobiography, p. 55, Southern Historical Collection.

67. Unless otherwise cited, most of the account of Toombs at Antietam that follows is drawn from Phillip Thomas Tucker's excellent *Burnside's Bridge: The Climactic Struggle of the Second and Twentieth Georgia at Antietam Creek* (Mechanicsburg, PA: Stackpole Books, 2000).

68. Longstreet, *Manassas to Appomattox*, pp. 257–61; Stovall, *Toombs*, pp. 263–64.

69. Charles W. Squires, "The 'Boy Officer' of the Washington Artillery, Part I," *Civil War Times Illustrated* 14 (May 1975): 20.

70. Accounts of Toombs's wounding, varying in some details, appear in

Gilmer to Loulie Gilmer, October 4, 1862, Gilmer Papers, Southern Historical Collection; Stovall, *Toombs*, p. 268; Thomas Munford to Ezra A. Carman, December 10, 1894, Ezra A. Carman Papers, National Archives; Stephen M. Weld, *War Diary and Letters of Stephen Minot Weld, 1861–1865* (Boston: Massachusetts Historical Society, 1979), p. 83.

71. Gilmer to Dear Sir, September 28, 1862, and Gilmer to Loulie Gilmer, October 4, 1862, Gilmer Papers, Southern Historical Collection.

72. Stovall, *Toombs*, p. 270.

73. Toombs to Linton Stephens, December 2, 1862, in Phillips, ed., *Correspondence*, p. 608.

74. Percy Scott Flippin, *Herschel V. Johnson of Georgia* (Richmond, VA: Dietz Printing Company, 1931), p. 221 and note.

75. Toombs to Stephens, March 2, 1863, in Phillips, ed., *Correspondence*, p. 611.

76. Gilmer to Loulie Gilmer, December 25, 1862, Gilmer Papers, Southern Historical Collection.

77. The *Official Records* are completely devoid of references to Toombs during the period December 1862 to March 1863, and when the brigade is mentioned, Benning is listed as being in command.

78. Toombs to Stephens, March 2, 1863, in Phillips, ed., *Correspondence*, p. 611.

79. Stovall, *Toombs*, p. 272.

80. Toombs to His Brigade, March 5, 1863, in Phillips, ed., *Correspondence*, pp. 612–13.

81. Jones, *Diary*, 1: 273.

82. *Richmond Enquirer*, March 7, 1863.

83. Robert E. Lee to Samuel Cooper, March 3, 1863, Toombs Compiled Service Record, National Archives.

84. Davis to Lewis, September 21, 1863, in Rowland, comp., *Davis*, 6: 44.

8. UNCIVIL WAR

1. Schott, *Stephens*, p. 350.

2. Brown to Stephens, July 2, 1862, in Phillips, ed., *Correspondence*, pp. 597–98.

3. Johnston and Browne, *Stephens*, pp. 413–14.

4. Ibid., p. 415.

5. Ibid., p. 417; Schott, *Stephens*, p. 352.

6. Johnston and Browne, *Stephens*, pp. 417–20.

7. Brown to Stephens, September 1, 1862, in Phillips, ed., *Correspondence*, pp. 605–6; Stephens to James Calhoun, September 8, 1862, Cleveland, *Stephens*, pp. 747–49.

8. Cleveland, *Stephens,* pp. 749–60.

9. Johnston and Browne, *Stephens,* p. 426.

10. Ibid., pp. 426–27.

11. Brown to Stephens, January 30, February 16, 1863, in Phillips, ed., *Correspondence,* pp. 610–11.

12. Johnston and Browne, *Stephens,* p. 437; Brown to Stephens, March 16, 1863, in Phillips, ed., *Correspondence,* p. 614, and Toombs to Stephens, April 21, 1863, p. 615, Toombs to W. W. Burwell, June 10, 1863, p. 619.

13. Johnston and Browne, *Stephens,* p. 441.

14. Stephens to Davis, June 12, 1863, in Rowland, comp., *Davis,* 5: 513–15.

15. Johnston and Browne, *Stephens,* p. 443.

16. Ibid., pp. 444–45.

17. *The American Annual Cyclopaedia and Register of Important Events of the Year 1863* (New York, 1864), p. 218.

18. Toombs to Burwell, June 10, 1863, in Phillips, ed., *Correspondence,* p. 619.

19. Thompson, *Toombs,* pp. 206–7.

20. Toombs to Linton Stephens, July 19, 1863, Stephens Papers, Emory University.

21. Toombs to Stephens, July 14, 1863, in Phillips, ed., *Correspondence,* p. 621.

22. Toombs to Howell Cobb, August 29, 1863, Howell Cobb Papers, Duke University.

23. Toombs to the editor of the *Augusta (GA) Constitutionalist,* August 12, 1863, in Phillips, ed., *Correspondence,* pp. 622–27.

24. Ibid., Toombs to Burwell, August 29, 1863, pp. 628–29.

25. George W. Lamar to Davis, August 16, 1863, in Crist and Dix, eds., *Papers,* 9: 346, and S. Wyatt to Davis, August 31, 1863, p. 362, David W. Lewis to Davis, September 9, 1863, p. 380.

26. Toombs to Stephens, November 2, 1863, in Phillips, ed., *Correspondence,* p. 630.

27. Thompson, *Toombs,* p. 209 n; Flippin, *Johnson of Georgia,* p. 221 and note.

28. Schott, *Stephens,* p. 385.

29. Johnston and Browne, *Stephens,* pp. 447–49.

30. Schott, *Stephens,* p. 391.

31. Ibid., pp. 395–97.

32. Cleveland, "Toombs," pp. 456–57.

33. Thompson, *Toombs,* pp. 209–10.

34. Toombs to Beauregard, February 13, 1864, and Toombs to Thomas Jordan, February 26, 1864, Toombs Combined Service Record, National Archives; Toombs to anonymous, February 14, 1864, *Literary and Historical Manuscripts & Americana from the Collection of the Late Phillip G. Straus,* Parke-Burnet auction catalog (New York, 1962), item 52.

35. Cleveland, "Toombs," p. 457.

36. Cleveland, *Stephens*, pp. 761–86; Schott, *Stephens*, pp. 403–9.

37. Edward Younger, ed., *Inside the Confederate Government: The Diary of Robert Garlick Hill Kean* (New York: Oxford University Press, 1957), p. 140.

38. *OR*, ser. 4, vol. 3, pp. 278–81.

39. Johnston and Browne, *Stephens*, pp. 463–64.

40. Schott, *Stephens*, pp. 421–22.

41. Toombs to Stephens, April 1, 1864, in Phillips, ed., *Correspondence*, pp. 638–39.

42. Sarah Lawton to her father, April 6, 1864, Alexander-Hillhouse Papers, Southern Historical Collection.

43. Stovall, *Toombs*, pp. 276–78.

44. Toombs to Stephens, August 30, 1864, in Phillips, ed., *Correspondence*, p. 651.

45. Ibid., September 23, 1864, p. 652.

46. Cleveland, *Stephens*, pp. 191–97.

47. Ibid.

48. Schott, *Stephens*, p. 429.

49. Stephens to the Public, November 10, 1864, in Phillips, ed., *Correspondence*, pp. 654–55; Cleveland, *Stephens*, pp. 796–804.

50. Younger, ed., *Inside the Confederate Government*, pp. 188–89.

51. Johnston and Browne, *Stephens*, pp. 475–80.

52. Ibid., pp. 480–84.

53. Ibid., pp. 484–85; Schott, *Stephens*, pp. 440–48.

54. Stephens to Wigfall, February 13, 1865, *Profiles in History*, catalog no. 17 (Beverly Hills, CA, 1992), p. 40.

55. Johnston and Browne, *Stephens*, p. 486.

56. Schott, *Stephens*, p. 449.

57. Richard Taylor, *Destruction and Reconstruction: Personal Experiences of the Late War* (New York, 1879), pp. 213–14.

58. Cleveland, "Toombs," pp. 457–58; Thompson, *Toombs*, p. 217.

59. Stephens, *Constitutional View*, 2: 588.

60. Toombs to Stephens, March 16, 30, 1865, in Phillips, ed., *Correspondence*, pp. 660–61.

61. Woodward, ed., *Chesnut*, p. 635.

9. EXULTATIONS, AGONIES, AND LOVE

1. Avary, ed., *Recollections*, pp. 140–41; Stovall, Toombs, p. 281.

2. John H. Reagan, *Memoirs, with Special Reference to Secession and the Civil War* (New York: Neale Publishing Company, 1906), pp. 214–16; Thompson, *Toombs*, pp. 217–18.

3. Burton Harrison, Extracts from a Narrative, in Rowland, comp., *Davis*,

7: 8; William C. Davis, *Breckinridge, Statesman, Soldier, Symbol* (Baton Rouge: Louisiana State University Press, 1974), p. 522.

4. Undated clipping, Sutton S. Scott notebook, Alabama Department of Archives and History, Montgomery.

5. Toombs to Rhett Jr., December 20, 1882, Rhett Papers, South Caroliniana Library.

6. *OR,* ser. 1, vol. 49, pt. 2, p. 955.

7. *New York Tribune,* June 28, 1865; *Washington Daily National Intelligencer,* June 20, 1865.

8. *OR,* ser. 2, vol. 8, pp. 714, 716.

9. This account of Toombs's flight, except where otherwise noted, is from Stovall, *Toombs,* pp. 286–307.

10. Avary, ed., *Recollections,* pp. 99–124 passim.

11. Ibid., pp. 129–530 passim.

12. Brown to Stephens, November 9, 1865, in Phillips, ed., *Correspondence,* p. 670; Schott, *Stephens,* pp. 454–58.

13. Toombs to Stephens, December 15, 1865, in Phillips, ed., *Correspondence,* pp. 673–76.

14. Thompson, *Toombs,* p. 222.

15. Harrison, Extracts, in Rowland, comp., *Davis,* 7: 8.

16. Toombs to Henry Cleveland, October 5, 1866, Cleveland, "Toombs," p. 458; Toombs to Stephens, September 28, 1866, Stephens Papers, Library of Congress.

17. Stovall, *Toombs,* pp. 311–12.

18. Ibid., pp. 312–13.

19. Toombs to John C. Breckinridge, April 30, 1867, in possession of the author. Stovall, *Toombs,* p. 313, suggests that Toombs went first to Canada and remained there for some time before going to Georgia, but Toombs's letter to Breckinridge specifically says that he landed in New Orleans and went straight to Washington. In the letter he also says that he will go to Canada in July, however, so Stovall is essentially correct but simply has the chronology wrong.

20. Toombs to Breckinridge, April 30, 1867, in possession of the author.

21. Stovall, *Toombs,* p. 313.

22. Thompson, *Toombs,* pp. 226–27; Toombs to George W. Crawford, June 29, 1868, Robert Toombs Papers, University of Georgia, Athens; Statement on Robert Toombs, August 17, 1872, Georgia, 36, Wilkes County, p. 173, R. G. Dun & Company Papers, Harvard University Graduate School of Business Administration, Boston.

23. Toombs to Stephens, November 14, 1867, in Phillips, ed., *Correspondence,* p. 689.

24. Ibid., Toombs to Stephens, August 9, 1868, p. 703.

25. Stovall, *Toombs,* pp. 322–27.

26. Toombs to Stephens, January 24, 1870, in Phillips, ed., *Correspondence,* p. 707, and February 8, 1870, p. 708.

27. Toombs to Stephens, September 4, 1870, Stephens Papers, Library of Congress.

28. Thompson, *Toombs,* pp. 231–32.

29. Stovall, *Toombs,* pp. 335–36.

30. Gaines M. Foster, *Ghosts of the Confederacy: Defeat, the Lost Cause, and the Emergence of the New South* (New York: Oxford University Press, 1987), p. 111; Charles D. Saggus, *Agrarian Arcadia: Anglo-Virginia Planters of Wilkes County, Ga. in the 1850s* (Washington, GA: n.p., 1996), p. 161.

31. Toombs to Alfred Colquitt, October 29, 1877, Toombs File, Georgia Department of Archives and History; Thompson, *Toombs,* pp. 236–48; Stovall, *Toombs,* pp. 337–52.

32. Alexander H. Stephens, *The Reviewers Reviewed: A Supplement to the "War Between the States," etc.* (New York, 1872).

33. M. J. Kenan to Stephens, October 10, 1870, Stephens Papers, Library of Congress.

34. Schott, *Stephens,* pp. 487–88.

35. E. Ramsay Richardson, *Little Aleck: A Life of Alexander H. Stephens* (Indianapolis: Bobbs-Merrill, 1932), p. 312.

36. Toombs to Stephens, July 15, 1872, Stephens Papers, Library of Congress.

37. Schott, *Stephens,* p. 491.

38. Toombs to Stephens, March 14, 1874, in Phillips, ed., *Correspondence,* pp. 718–21.

39. Ibid., March 10, 1875, p. 721, October 30, 1876, pp. 722–23, December 17, 1876, pp. 723–25, and December 28, 1876, pp. 725–26.

40. Ibid., November 2, 1877, p. 732.

41. Toombs to unknown, May 13, 1858, Alexander Autographs sale catalog, November 3, 1998, p. 52, item 433.

42. Stovall, *Toombs,* p. 366.

43. Toombs to Stephens, January 30, 1879, in Phillips, ed., *Correspondence,* p. 736.

44. Toombs to Stephens, February 14, 1870, Stephens Papers, Library of Congress.

45. Cleveland, "Toombs," p. 459, is one of the earliest sources for Toombs's famous remark about pardon, which exists in several versions. Cleveland himself speculated that it may be apocryphal, though Toombs used the expression himself in at least one letter; still, that does not mean that it originated with him.

46. Thompson, *Toombs,* p. 251.

47. Davis, *Rise and Fall,* vol. 1, opposite p. 242.
48. Speech at unveiling of the statue of Benjamin H. Hill, May 1, 1886, Benjamin H. Hill File, Georgia Department of Archives and History.
49. Toombs to Rhett Jr., December 20, 1882, Rhett Papers, South Caroliniana Library.
50. *Philadelphia Times,* July 12, 1879.
51. Toombs to Stephens, March 10, 1879, in Phillips, ed., *Correspondence,* p. 737, and April 25, 1880, p. 742.
52. Avary, ed., *Recollections,* pp. 427–28.
53. Receipt, January 23, 1883, Governors' Papers, Alexander H. Stephens, Georgia Department of Archives and History, Atlanta; Schott, *Stephens,* pp. 511 ff.
54. Johnston and Browne, *Stephens,* p. 554.
55. Stovall, *Toombs,* pp. 371–72; Cleveland, "Toombs," p. 459.
56. Toombs to unknown, December 3, 1884, Signature House auction catalog (Monckton, MD, November 30, 1996), p. 26, item 184.
57. Stovall, *Toombs,* pp. 372–73.
58. Reed, *Brothers' War,* pp. 279–80.
59. The novel *Bethany, A Story of the Old South* (Washington, DC: D. Appleton, 1929), by Thomas E. Watson, has a good example of the common depiction of Toombs as a drinker even in Southern fiction (pp. 178–83).
60. Stovall, *Toombs,* pp. 369–70.
61. Ibid., pp. 374–75.

INDEX